THE WHITE HOUSE AND CAPITOL HILL

The White House and Capitol Hill

THE POLITICS OF PRESIDENTIAL PERSUASION

NIGEL BOWLES

CLARENDON PRESS · OXFORD
1987

Oxford University Press, Walton Street, Oxford OX2 6DP
Oxford New York Toronto
Delhi Bombay Calcutta Madras Karachi
Petaling Jaya Singapore Hong Kong Tokyo
Nairobi Dar es Salaam Cape Town
Melbourne Auckland
and associated companies in
Beirut Berlin Ibadan Nicosia

Oxford is a trade mark of Oxford University Press

Published in the United States
by Oxford University Press, New York

British Library Cataloguing in Publication Data
Bowles, Nigel
The White House and Capitol Hill : the
politics of presidential persuasion.
1. United States, Congress 2. Presidents
United States
I. Title
353.03'72 JK585
ISBN 0-19-827478-5

Library of Congress Cataloging in Publication Data
Bowles, Nigel.
The White House and Capitol Hill.
Includes index.
1. Presidents—United States. 2.United States.
Congress. 3. United States. Executive Office of the
President. Office of Congressional Relations. 4. United
States—Politics and government—1945- . I. Title.
JK585.B68 1987 353.03'72 86-23754
ISBN 0-19-827478-5

Processed by the Oxford Text System
Printed in Great Britain
at the University Printing House, Oxford
by David Stanford
Printer to the University

This book is dedicated to my parents
for their love and their patience

ACKNOWLEDGEMENTS

Thanking those who helped with research is always a pleasure, made more so here because the guidance I have received with this book was without exception generously given.

In the early stages of preparation, Joel Goldstein, David Mayhew, Nelson Polsby, and Herbert Nicholas were encouraging, and kindly responded to enquiries with wise advice. Later, Tom Cronin, Eric Davis, Larry Dodd, Louis Fisher, Joe Frantz, Tom Hammond, Hugh Heclo, Joe Hogan, John Manley, Tom Mann, Richard Neustadt, Norman Ornstein, Austin Ranney, Russ Renka, and Steven Wayne gave freely of their time, and assisted greatly.

At Oxford, where an earlier version of part of this book began life as a D.Phil. thesis, I benefited considerably from comments on several chapters by Michael Brock, Max Hartwell, Jim Sharpe, Barry Supple, and Lawrence Whitehead. Vincent Wright was a supportive and perceptive critic; the late, grievously missed, Philip Williams taught me much about American politics, and showed great patience in his suggested reconstructions of early drafts, whilst David Goldey was a superb university supervisor whose wise advice was both penetrating and constructive.

At Edinburgh, Malcolm Anderson, Mary Buckley, Henry Drucker, and Desmond King have all read parts of the book; for their most helpful observations, and their friendship, I am indebted to them. Vivien Hart, of the School of English and American Studies at the University of Sussex, read an entire draft; her advice was of vital assistance. In London, Edgar Jones kindly read part of an early version. Lindsey Charles was definitively professional in her general guidance and suggested amendments, and warmly supportive; I shall always be deeply grateful to her.

I benefited from two years work for the Rt. Hon. James Callaghan, MP. As Harry McPherson remarked of his service with Lyndon Johnson, it was a political education; I am grateful to Mr Callaghan for it.

Many former members of the White House staff serving under the six most recent presidents were interviewed for this study. Five were interviewed twice, and six three times. More than thirty members of Congress and Congressional staff also agreed to be interviewed. I owe a special vote of thanks to Harry McPherson, Larry O'Brien, Barefoot Sanders, George Christian, and Larry Temple; they did much to improve my understanding of White House politics. In addition, Larry and Louann Temple have been wonderfully kind in several visits to Austin; I am indebted to them both.

The archivists of the John F. Kennedy Library and Lyndon Baines Johnson Library gave invaluable assistance. I owe the Director of the Johnson Library, Harry Middleton, and his staff a special vote of thanks. In particular, I must thank Claudia Anderson, Linda Hansen, Tina Lawson, and Nancy Smith—all superbly skilled archivists. The Lyndon Baines Johnson Foundation made three grants available to study at the Library; I am most grateful to the Trustees for their generosity.

Without the warm encouragement of Barbara Herzberg in Washington, and her late husband Donald, this book would not have been started, much less finished. My debt to them is immense.

Much of the secondary work for this book was done at Rhodes House and Nuffield College Libraries, Oxford; Sussex University Library; the Graduate Library of the University of Texas at Austin; and the British Library of Political and Economic Science. I should like to thank the staff of these libraries for their assistance.

My sincere thanks are due to the students in my US Government seminar at the University of Edinburgh. Their observations and thoughts have helped me considerably in thinking through some of the questions raised in this book.

Mona Bennett, Jenny MacDonald, and Hilary Johnston kindly typed a draft of the book on to computer disk with great efficiency and good humour; I am grateful to them all.

My editor at OUP, Henry Hardy, and his most able assistant, Nina Curtis, were thoroughly supportive throughout, and forgiving of my tardiness.

My debt to these and many other friends and colleagues is great. They take much of the credit for any merit this book may have, but no responsibility for errors of fact or interpretation. That is mine alone.

Edinburgh   NIGEL BOWLES
June 1986.

CONTENTS

I

THE WHITE HOUSE AND CAPITOL HILL

INTRODUCTION

This book is a study of the White House Office of Congressional
Relations and concentrates on its operation during Lyndon
Johnson's administration. A detailed analysis of one unit in
one branch of American government, it explores the means
by which Lyndon Johnson and two of his successors have
attempted to co-ordinate the relations of the executive branch
with Congress to their own legislative ends. It raises additional
general questions about the institution of the presidency, the
nature of presidential power, and the range and limits of
presidential influence over Congressmen and senators.

Since the 1930s, the institutionalised presidency has become
the focus of American government, and its legislative role has
assumed particular importance. Whatever the views and
purposes of individual presidents, liberal or populist, moderate
or conservative, the legislative function is one which cannot
be disregarded. Liberal presidents such as Lyndon Johnson
may have substantial, explicit, legislative designs; populists
such as Jimmy Carter may look to reorganise government,
betraying the old progressive obsession with procedures and
animus against party. New Right politicians such as Ronald
Reagan may endeavour to reduce or eliminate liberal
programmes and their associated bureaucracies. All these
purposes require a strong and prominent presidential office
whose occupant assumes rather than eschews the role of
legislative leader. Liberals have no hope of enacting legislative
proposals without it; populists depend upon it for the successful
transformation of government's role; conservatives, however
enthusiastic their rejection of 'big government' during election
campaigns, have since the establishment of the Great Society
social programmes in the 1960s also depended upon a strong
presidency to effect the policy changes they seek. Even with

Republican control of the Senate since 1981, it was through
the presidency that the conservatives' main hopes of change
lay. In the wake of the weak Ford and Carter presidencies,
preservation of the status quo was not, for Reagan or his
supporters, an attractive course: a radical recasting of the role
of the federal government paradoxically obliged Reagan to
expand, rather than contract, the presidency's prestige and
reach in pursuit of his economic legislative objectives during
his first year in the White House. It is also likely to be the
repository of future conservative hopes.

The pressing need that presidents of all ideological com-
plexions and designs have for a strong presidency is paralleled
by the fact that their objects require continuous dealings with
Congress. The Congressional role is crucial. These objects in
turn oblige modern chief executives to devote much of their
own time and an important part of their White House staff
resources to legislative liaison, to engagement and brokering
with legislators. The task of directing, managing, and
organising relations between executive and legislature is far
too large for one individual, whether his executive abilities
are great or small, his political judgement fine or uncertain.
Staff support is essential.

The strategic problem for presidents is that their power is
inherently limited. It is always limited because the fragmentation of the institutions of government severely cir-
cumscribes their ability to determine the passage of legislation
and the implementation of policies; the 'genetic code' of the
constitution cannot be escaped.[1] It is usually limited because
of the political weaknesses of individual presidents and
ideological or party hostility in Congress. Presidents therefore
have to persuade both the public and politicians. Successive
presidents have found specialised staff to be necessary for this
enterprise: OCR staff were for Johnson (as they have been
for all presidents since Eisenhower) a means of overcoming
the division between the executive and legislative branches,
of bridging the institutional gap, to his advantage. But
although a liaison staff in the White House is an indispensable
part of the institutionalised presidency, whatever the president's objectives, it is not a substitute for presidential skill,

[1] Nelson, M., *The Presidency and the Political System*, Washington, DC, 1984.

interest, or comprehension. Congress will not be bludgeoned into submission, as Nixon learned to his cost; it must be courted into partnership, as Carter learned to his.

For Johnson the problem was especially great; his substantial legislative purposes required that the institutional separation of executive and Congress be bridged with unusual speed and clarity. His staff therefore acted (as John Kennedy's did but in the absence of Congressional advantage) as both intermediary and representative. They relayed Congressional views and party opinion to the president and other members of the administration, and impressed the president's upon legislators. They acted as messengers and ambassadors, but also reassured supporters, persuaded the undecided and crosspressured, and wooed the reluctant. The demands that Johnson made of Congress could not have been co-ordinated within the administration, nor lobbied through Congress, without the constant political and administrative support provided by specialist staff in the Office of Congressional Relations (OCR). The OCR thus became for Kennedy and Johnson, as comparable units did for Carter and Reagan, the privileged vantage point for observing executive–legislative relations at the time and so of great importance for analysing them subsequently.

POLITICS, POLITICAL SCIENCE, AND THE PRESIDENCY

The presidency has in recent years attracted the attention of many scholars; it is no longer disregarded to the extent which justly drew Heclo's criticism in his report to the Ford Foundation in 1977.[2] To classic works by Corwin, Neustadt, and Rossiter have been added books by Nelson, Heclo, Hodgson, Lowi, Pious, and others.[3] Detailed historical studies

[2] Heclo, H., *Studying the Presidency*, New York, 1977.

[3] Cronin, E. S., *The President: Office and Powers*, 4th edn., New York, 1957; Neustadt, R. E., *Presidential Power*, 3rd edn., New York, 1980; Rossiter, C., *The American Presidency*, 2nd edn., London, 1960; Nelson, *The Presidency and the Political System*; Heclo, H., and Salamon, L. M.,(eds.), *The Illusion of Presidential Government*, Boulder, 1981; Hodgson, G., *All Things to All Men*, 2nd edn., Harmondsworth, 1984; Lowi, T., *The Personal President*, Ithaca, 1985; Pious, R., *The American Presidency*, New York, 1979.

of individual presidencies drawing on primary sources, (previously, to Heclo's justified disappointment, often ignored by American political scientists) have provided a welcome new dimension to scholarly understanding of the possibilities and limits of the office of chief executive. Greenstein's *The Hidden-Hand Presidency*, a perceptive (if not entirely persuasive) revisionist history of Eisenhower's political practice, is the best of this genre.[4]

The intensity of the engagement between presidency and Congress in the post-war era, peaking in the Johnson and Nixon presidencies, has prompted considerable discussion of the nature of the balance of power between them. There has been much less systematic consideration of the means by which presidents secure the passage of their legislative proposals, the approval of nominees to judicial or executive office, and the ratification of treaties. In the early 1960s, a number of scholars expressed concern that the president's capacity to govern was seriously inhibited by the vagaries of the party system and the institutionalised obstructions presented by a fragmented Congress dominated by powerful committee chairmen.[5] These were swept away by Lyndon Johnson's legislative successes; almost all of his civil rights and Great Society bills were passed by the three Congresses with which he served as president.[6] Yet liberal celebrations of the strong presidency, briefly sustained by the thrill of legislative productivity, turned sour with the aggrandisement and then the gross abuse of presidential war-making powers under Johnson and Nixon, together with the general corruption of presidential politics during the latter's incumbency. Arthur Schlesinger was only one of several historians to rejoice in the strong presidency when the office was in Kennedy's hands at the beginning of the 1960s. When it was in the control of Kennedy's rivals at the end of the decade and in the early years of the next, Schlesinger considered that the effectively unchecked powers of the office imperilled constitutional government, as they certainly did.[7]

[4] Greenstein, F., *The Hidden-Hand Presidency*, New York, 1982.
[5] Burns, J. M., *The Deadlock of Democracy*, Englewood Cliffs, 1967.
[6] See chapter two.
[7] Schlesinger, A. M., *A Thousand Days*, Boston, 1965; Burns, J. M., *Presidential Government*, Boston, 1965; Schlesinger, A. M., *The Imperial Presidency*, New York, 1974.

Later, after the governing frustrations and electoral defeats of Presidents Ford and Carter, scholarly attention focused on the inabilities of presidents to do in office what they promised on the hustings. To this extent, the problem resembled that of the early 1960s, but the nature of the difficulties had altered. Party reform had prised apart the electoral and governing coalitions while Congressional reform and heightened interest-group activity made the assembly of legislative coalitions ever more difficult. The building blocks of Congressional coalitions had, according to Anthony King, disintegrated into sand.[8] Legislative stasis and presidential failure were probable and, as Godfrey Hodgson argued, made almost certain by inflated public expectations of what presidents could do in office.[9] Richard Pious took the view that since presidents now conspicuously lacked the means to lead party, Congress, or people, and their consequent chances of governing as Roosevelt and Johnson had done in the past were so slim, they should rely on such political opportunities as their constitutional prerogatives afforded them.[10]

In his important contribution, *The Personal President*, Theodore Lowi bemoaned the presidency's accretion of responsibilities, arguing that the office's salvation lay in addressing the problem of overextended government and not in futile attempts to cope with the products of its excesses.[11] As Lowi had written in *The End of Liberalism* sixteen years before, so he now reiterated that government was the problem. Lowi regarded Reagan's apparent success in revitalising the presidency and (briefly) realising again its transforming legislative energy as illusory for Reagan had, he argued, failed to make the power of the office-holder commensurate with his responsibilities.[12] Undoubtedly, the growth of the federal government's role, and the enhanced prominence of the presidency within the political system, had together thrust new responsibilities and great public expectations on the office-holder. Nonetheless, Reagan demonstrated in his first

[8] King, A., 'The American Polity in the Late 1970s', in King, A.,(ed.), *The New American Political System*, Washington, DC, 1978.
[9] Hodgson, *All Things to All Men*.
[10] Pious, *The American Presidency*.
[11] Lowi, *The Personal President*.
[12] Lowi, T., *The End of Liberalism*, New York, 1969.

year, and to an extent thereafter, that the presidency remains
the only political office from which it is possible to move the
country and to galvanise the lethargic American body politic.
To that extent, the scholarly response to the Carter presidency
was ill-judged. If opportunities are not created and exploited
by the president, there is no alternative source of national
political action. In a fragmented system, a president has many
competitors, but no peer.

This book is a study of how presidents and their legislative
liaison staff mobilise and deploy presidential resources, to
promote presidents' legislative and political fortunes, thereby
examining the political process of presidential persuasion of
members of Congress and senators in circumstances of varying
opportunity and difficulty. The detailed politics of presidential
management of relations between *Both Ends of the Avenue* (itself
the title of a useful collection of essays edited by Anthony
King) have recently attracted sustained attention from a
number of scholars.[13] Brauer, Davis, Edwards, Hogan, Jones,
Kellerman, Polsby, and, in a fine case-study, Garrow, have
published work which has in important respects altered, and
in others refined, academic understanding of the problems
posed by presidential management of the executive branch's
relations with Congress. The most recent of these publications,
The Political Presidency, by Barbara Kellerman, is an especially
lucid and perceptive analysis which examines the importance
of presidents' political skill in making good their legislative
intent.[14] Developing Neustadt's thesis that presidential power
consists of the power to persuade others, she argues that:[15]

. . . the ability to persuade depends on effective bargaining. The
skilled bargainer convinces others that it is in their own best interests

[13] King, A.,(ed.), *Both Ends of the Avenue*, Washington, 1983.

[14] Brauer, C., *John F. Kennedy and the Second Reconstruction*, New York, 1977; Davis,
E. L., 'Building Legislative Coalitions in Congress', Ph.D. dissertation, Stanford
University, 1977; Davis, E. L., 'Legislative Liaison in the Carter Administration',
Political Science Quarterly, vol. 95, no. 2, Summer 1979; Edwards, G. C., *Presidential
Influence in Congress*, San Francisco, 1980; Hogan, J. J., 'Analysing Recent US
Presidential–Congressional Relationships', *Political Studies*, vol. 33, no. 1, Mar. 1985;
Jones, C. O., 'Carter and Congress', *British Journal of Political Science*, vol. 15, no. 3,
1985; Kellerman, B., *The Political Presidency*, New York, 1984; Polsby, N. W., *Congress
and the Presidency*, 3rd edn., Englewood Cliffs, 1976; Garrow, D. J., *Protest at Selma*,
New Haven, 1978.

[15] Kellerman, *The Political Presidency*, pp. 15 and 21.

to go along, to allow themselves to be persuaded. . . . the president's success as a directive leader—the degree to which he accomplishes what he set out to accomplish—seems to depend to a considerable degree on his own personal capacities. And whether we like it or not, this boils down to his skill at leadership depending on his skill as a political operator.

In this book, I adopt a similar stance to Kellerman: presidential skill matters. In this respect, too, I share fully her reservations of the approach adopted and conclusions reached by George Edwards in his book *Presidential Influence in Congress* and, by implication, the passing affirmation of his conclusions by Hargrove and Nelson in *Presidents, Politics and Policy*.[16] Edwards's study is welcome in several respects—not least in subjecting a vexed question to systematic quantitative analysis. But in claiming that presidential legislative skills have no bearing upon legislative outcomes, it is unpersuasive. His employment of aggregate data is, as Kellerman rightly observes, (and Edwards himself at one point concedes), an unsatisfactory measure of presidential influence.[17] His unweighted aggregate measures are suggestive, not conclusive. They do not cope with the inherent complexities of the political interactions of president and Congress. In particular, the approach fails to discriminate between important and minor legislative initiatives, takes account neither of the individual political pressures acting upon legislators (for Congress is not an homogeneous whole, but an incipiently fissiparous assembly of coalitions and groupings) nor of the awkward fact that many Congressmen privately acknowledge that finely judged presidential interventions sometimes alter their own calculations of political interest.[18] Moreover, the time, effort, and resources which hard-pressed chief executives have in recent years devoted to the orchestration of their administration's relations with Congress suggests that Edwards's view is faulty.

[16] Hargrove, E. C., and Nelson, M., *Presidents, Politics and Policy*, Baltimore, 1984, p. 229.
[17] Kellerman, *The Political Presidency*, pp. 49–50; Edwards, *Presidential Influence in Congress*, p. 190.
[18] Interviews with Congressmen J. Jones (D-OK), J. Pickle (D-TX), and J. Brademas (D-IN).

Presidents' decisions to make legislative initiatives are affected by public circumstances and calculations of opportunity and interest; outcomes are shaped by the interaction in Congress of partisan balance and ideological complexion, and by external pressures upon the judgements of individual legislators.[19] Where calculations of victory and defeat by the president and contending Congressional factions suggest a close outcome, presidential pressure, privately and publicly deployed, is often decisive: legislation is amended, bargains of explicit kinds are arrived at, and (more usually) implicit understandings are reached. A president's hints of future assistance to helpful Congressmen and senators, and Congressmen's affirmations of loyalty to a president whom they feel bound temporarily to oppose, are the stuff of the political exchange between them. The importance of presidential skill and judgement in this process can be neither affirmed nor denied by broad quantitative measures.

The approach adopted here does not suffer from this difficulty. It comprises an examination in three chapters of the means by which President Johnson attempted to influence legislators, followed by two detailed case studies. There follow two further case studies which compare the political circumstances and techniques evident in the Johnson presidency with those of Carter and Reagan. The analysis implies a different relationship between presidents' political judgement and Congressional responses from that which Edwards discovered. It shows that the quality of such judgement, as revealed in the effectiveness of the means by which presidents bring their influence to bear, affects their chances of legislative success.

SOURCES AND RESEARCH PROBLEMS

Lyndon Johnson's administration offers an especially good combination of circumstances for studying presidential influence as exercised through the agency of the OCR. For the first three years of his presidency Johnson was legislatively

---

[19] Cobb, R. W., and Elder, C. D., *Participation in American Politics*, Baltimore, 1975.

successful to a wholly unusual degree; for the last two, he was busily engaged in the defence of his domestic and foreign policies set in train during that time. The OCR was always active, as much in the latter period as the earlier. The shifts of party support, changes in the authority and competence of the OCR staff, and the changing nature of the public agenda provide an era of unusual richness for the scholar of Congressional relations, reflected in the remarkably high quality of presidential papers which it produced.

The chapters on Carter and Reagan apart, the book draws extensively on papers from the John F. Kennedy and Lyndon Baines Johnson presidential libraries, supplemented by interviews with members of the White House staff from the two Democratic administrations of the 1960s; the chapter on the Carter presidency also relies heavily upon interview data. Analysis based upon the reinforcing combination of these two approaches provides a powerful means of evaluating the behaviour of those involved in the politics of relations between president and Congress. The benefits provided by documentary sources are great: they indicate the lines of thought of political actors at the time and so afford the opportunity of a more complete and subtle historical explanation than would otherwise be possible. They are, of course, partial sources in the sense both of their incompleteness (whether because of prior selection or closure by archivists) and in a few cases of their having been written more to persuade historians than to inform correspondents. The extent of the latter difficulty for this study is unclear, but is obvious in only a few papers. This does not, of course, dispose of the problem, for the issue is one of deliberate deception. In practice, however, busy White House staff have little enough time for matters of the moment without concerning themselves with detailed scholarly assessment. The first difficulty is rather greater. Some politicians and their staff have weeded their papers before donating them to presidential libraries, and others are doing so, as two interviews showed.[20] But the problem presented by those papers still closed for reasons of national security or under the terms of the copyright holder's deed of gift is small.

[20] Two confidential interviews with former members of Kennedy's and Johnson's staff.

Within the field of Congressional relations few are closed for the first of these reasons, while of those many more in the second which were once closed and are now open, most reveal little of particular surprise; they are not of a qualitatively different kind from those opened long before.

As indicated above, interviews and oral histories of participants allow scholars to check their sources, examine the plausibility of alternative perspectives on particular events, and compare competing judgements of the actions of those whom they observed. Interviews make easier the resolution of discrepancies with evidence gleaned from elsewhere, and the clarification of ambiguities; checked and cross-checked, they provide the means to verify or cast doubt upon hypotheses generated by the author's research. The value of interviews as suggestive of lines of enquiry, or to test and re-test what documentary sources affirm or hint at, is great. Early interviews for this book also produced numerous observations which, though they appeared unimportant at the time, took on new importance in the light of views and evidence which emerged later.[21] There are, of course, methodological limitations: interviewees' memories fade and are sometimes inaccurate, almost always incomplete, and occasionally simply wrong. Some interviewees persuade themselves and the interviewer of the accuracy of their recollections which only later prove to be at fault. Whilst most interviewees are glad to assist, helpfulness is not necessarily correlated with the accuracy of an interviewee's memory. Sometimes, too, interviewees attempt to deceive—though only rarely, for conflicting evidence is usually too readily available to make such an effort worthwhile. In other instances, time's colouring of past events is unwitting.

The use of case-studies, too, offers striking advantages in addition to posing general methodological difficulties, as Lowi and Eckstein (among many others) have discussed.[22] Both of the studies employed here are drawn from Johnson's last year

[21] Williams, P. M., 'Interviewing Politicians: The Life of Hugh Gaitskell', *Political Quarterly*, vol. 51, no. 3, 1980.

[22] Lowi, T., 'American Business, Public Policy, Case-Studies and Political Theory', *World Politics*, vol. 16, no. 4, 1964; Eckstein, H., 'Case Study and Theory in Political Science', in Greenstein, F. I., and Polsby, N. W., *Handbook of Political Science*: vol. 7: *Strategies of Inquiry*, Reading, 1975.

in office: the income tax surcharge, and the nominations of Abe Fortas to the Chief Justiceship, and of Homer Thornberry to the Court. In each, the political weakness of the president and the White House lobbying organisation is emphasised. The income tax surcharge was won only at a high budgetary and political price; the Supreme Court nominations were not confirmed by the Senate. The first was therefore a qualified defeat for Johnson; the second, unmitigated. To that extent, they were untypical of his presidency which was built around the generation and passage of a large number of liberal domestic legislative programmes and reforms. However, the extraordinary legislative successes of 1964-6 made for such an exceptional historical period that examination of the OCR's operation then is less revealing than when a depleted office had to lobby for a diminished president facing a recalcitrant Congress—much the more common circumstance. The intensity of the lobbying campaigns in each case generated plentiful evidence of high quality. With the exception of the Civil Rights Act of 1964, and the Elementary and Secondary Education Act of 1965, (both of which have been extensively studied elsewhere), the two case studies in this book drawn from 1968 illustrate better than any individual campaigns in the 88th or 89th Congresses the techniques employed by the president and his legislative staff.

Similarly, Carter's and Reagan's presidencies offer greater scope for drawing conclusions about presidential lobbying of Congress than Nixon's or Ford's. Nixon began his first term by appointing an able and well-respected former liaison aide to Eisenhower, Bryce Harlow, to the task of managing his relations with Congress, and kept in close touch with Republican and Democratic leaders during the transition. Thereafter, he paid little personal attention to relations with Congress, isolated himself from all but a select few on Capitol Hill, and to a growing extent conceived of most Congressmen and senators as enemies to be confronted rather than politicians to be courted, and of the institution of Congress as one to be circumvented if at all possible.

The engagement between Ford, the first wholly unelected president, and Congress was intense, very much warmer than under Nixon, but limited in duration and achievement.

It consisted for the most part of an attempt by the president to constrain the assertive 'Watergate' Congress elected in November 1974 by means of vetoes (most of which were sustained) and, under the provisions of the 1974 Budget and Impoundment Control Act, by requests for deferrals and rescissions.[23]

ORGANISATION OF THE BOOK

The questions addressed in this study are examined from the perspective of the presidency. This does not, however, imply that it is considered the sole source of legislative initiative: as Orfield has shown, such a view was untenable even during Johnson's administration when the president's influence over the composition of the political agenda in Washington was greater than it has been in more recent times.[24] As formulated here it does, I believe, provide a detailed account of the means by which presidential resources are arranged and directed to give effect to presidential wishes. That is important in helping to establish the nature and limits of presidential power. In determining the sources of presidential success, it is insufficient to consider presidential constitutional prerogatives alone; Franklin Roosevelt, Lyndon Johnson, and Ronald Reagan achieved such legislative successes as they did because of the way they maximised and deployed the resources of the office, not because of their reliance upon the formal constitutional grant of authority.[25]

The book is organised in ten chapters. Following this introduction, the second briefly sets out the political context of relations between executive and legislature under Presidents Kennedy and Johnson, discussing the rare conjunction in 1965–6 of a reformist president, with a liberal-dominated Congress and a highly competent presidential OCR staff ready to shepherd a large number of Great Society and civil rights bills through Capitol Hill. The effects of the loss of the liberal majority in the 1966 mid-term elections upon the

[23] Edwards, *Presidential Influence in Congress*, p. 21.
[24] Orfield, G., *Congressional Power and Social Change*, New York, 1975.
[25] Light, P., *The President's Agenda*, Baltimore, 1982, p. 14.

president's legislative record are briefly considered before its effects are explored more fully in chapter seven. In addition to the relative conservatism of the 90th Congress, the OCR itself was weaker than before, and the president's domestic reform programmes increasingly beset by public hostility, programme failures and difficulties, and the budgetary pressures caused by the enveloping political disaster of the Vietnam war.

Chapters three to seven examine the organisation and operation of the OCR on domestic policy during the Johnson presidency. The first three chapters are analytical, followed by two case studies. This design was chosen to illustrate the organisation and staffing of the OCR and the ways in which it altered between 1963 and 1969; to consider the importance of external political circumstances such as the ideological composition and party balances in Congress to the passage of types of legislation; and to examine how White House lobbying worked in two important instances.

Chapter three shows how the OCR was organised to maximise the president's political strength. It sets out the arrangements made by Larry O'Brien as head of the OCR under Kennedy and Johnson until 1965. The paradox of White House Congressional relations emerges here: as the forces of Congressional conservatism gained strength from 1966 onwards, the OCR became weaker; its staff had reached their period of greatest efficiency and dispatch in the second phase of Johnson's presidency during the 89th Congress when the Congressional balance was favourable.

Chapters four and five consider the essence of the problem: White House reward and punishment. Congressional support or opposition, and the role of the OCR in indicating presidential approval or disapproval of senators' or Congressmen's actions. It is argued that persuasion is the key: the OCR's remit was to add an extra string to the presidential bow. This, as the book emphasises, was as true of small presidential favours organised by the OCR as it was of the strategic means of political persuasion including federally funded projects and buildings and federal patronage. The importance which the president and his OCR staff attached to careful liaison with members of Congress as a prelude to successful lobbying is stressed and their general approach to managing the executive's relations with Congress, by preparing the political and psychological context within which members made their voting decisions, is explored. Unprepared Congressional ground bore little legislative fruit.

Chapters eight and nine explore firstly the causes of Jimmy Carter's legislative failures, and secondly Ronald Reagan's remarkable early legislative success. Carter, like most presidential candidates since Eisenhower and Stevenson in 1952, had run for office without party; unlike most of them, he campaigned against party and then found himself unable to govern for the lack of party coalitional support. Especially at the beginning of his administration, he misunderstood the nature of the relationship between the executive and legislative branches and the implied need for his systematic, directed engagement with those who held his presidency's fate in their hands. But he also failed to organise at the outset an able, experienced group of liaison aides who understood the imperatives of building coalitions on Capitol Hill. The dispersal of power in Congress among many new subcommittees, strengthened by vastly increased staff resources, made the legislature a different and more difficult animal with which to deal in 1977 than in 1965. But the hostile approach of president and liaison staff to their task made unpropitious circumstances worse, and the reserves of goodwill for a newly elected Head of State were speedily dissipated.

President Reagan well understood the need to prepare his presidential programme, his dependence upon partisan and ideological support in Congress, and the need to forge Congressional majorities for decisive legislation by a combination of intensive lobbying and public appeals; he maintained remarkable Republican voting unity on the key economic measures during his first year in office. Although he too had a separately organised campaign from Congressional colleagues, Reagan presented a united public front with most of them and, unlike Carter, was clear about his aims and carried his campaign themes into government with efficiency and despatch. Nominal Democratic control of the chamber obliged him to add to Republican strength by seeking

conservative Democratic support. Later failures notwithstanding, Reagan's strategy (the obverse of Johnson's) met
with decisive early success using a range of tactics (many of
them similar to Johnson's) designed to build upon unusual
Congressional and ideological advantage. The successes of
Reagan's first year, like the failures of Carter's term, sprang
in large part from the differences between the two presidents'
marshalling of their political resources. Thereafter, presidential–congressional relations assumed their customary
conflictual pattern—if not quite the metaphorical 'war in the
trenches' which Lowi colourfully identifies in *The Personal
President*.[26]

The final chapter draws conclusions about the importance
and effectiveness of the OCR under Johnson and his successors.
It sets the OCR near the centre of recent presidencies. At
least in the early years of Johnson's administration, and in
Reagan's first year too, the specialist legislative staff's marriage
of organisational coherence in Congressional liaison and
lobbying made them central parts of the White House Office
and a valuable source of specialist staff support to the president
in the bridging of the separation between the executive and
legislative branches.

[26] Lowi, T., *The Personal President*, p. 189.

2

THE OFFICE OF CONGRESSIONAL RELATIONS (OCR)

CONGRESSIONAL RELATIONS UNDER PRESIDENT EISENHOWER

The OCR was established in the White House not by Franklin Roosevelt or Harry Truman, under whom the presidency became the political centre of an expanded federal government, but by Dwight Eisenhower. He established it in 1953 primarily to shield himself from the patronage and project requests of majority Republican party members in Congress, made more insistent by their having been out of power at both ends of Pennsylvania Avenue for a generation. Initially, he had little need to promote his legislative programme: indeed, in 1953 he broke with the modern tradition and did not present one to Congress.[1]

Eisenhower had little aptitude for or interest in Congressional relations, and did not involve himself in detailed consideration of them. He wrote in his memoirs of the 'frustrations' of dealing with 531 separate opinions on Capitol Hill and of 'tiresome' legislative meetings.[2] The skill and experience of his OCR staff was therefore all the more important to his presidency, especially given the clumsy disregard for Congressional sensibilities shown by some of the lesser lights in his cabinet.[3]

The new OCR was directed by General Wilton B. Persons, whom Eisenhower had long known, worked with in NATO, and who had headed the Army's fledgeling Congressional

[1] Not a single Republican senator in 1953 had ever served with a Republican in the White House and only 15 of the 211 Republicans in the House had done so (Eisenhower, D. D., *Mandate for Change*, New York, 1963, p. 192).

[2] Eisenhower, *Mandate for Change*, p. 300.

[3] Charles Wilson, Eisenhower's Defense Secretary, openly insulted senators during his confirmation hearings in 1953. Fenno, R. F., *The President's Cabinet*, New York, 1959, p. 209.

liaison office during the Second World War. Of the six OCR aides who served Eisenhower in his two terms, one had himself been a Congressman, and three had closer ties to the Democratic Party than to the Republicans, a useful attribute when control of Congress lay in Democratic hands from 1955 onwards.[4] Bryce Harlow, who led the Office towards the end of Eisenhower's presidency, having been a member of it from 1953, had acquired useful Congressional experience as staff director of the House Armed Services Committee.[5] Harlow ranked low in the White House staff hierarchy, however, and was an inconspicuous lobbyist. His visits to Capitol Hill were mostly confined to lunches with the House Minority Leader, Charles Halleck, and meetings with the Republican leadership in the Senate.[6] Eisenhower himself followed Truman's practice of holding weekly legislative meetings with leaders of his own party, irrespective of whether they formed the majority in Congress or not, and strove to unite Congressional Republicans on the few key legislative demands he made of them.[7]

None the less, Eisenhower's management of his relationships with the Democrats was still more important in the establishment of productive relations with Congress; in this respect, the president was fortunate that the Democrats in the House and Senate were led by Sam Rayburn and Lyndon Johnson, both of whom gave him steady support on a range of policies. In 1953, Rayburn supported the president on 74 per cent of the roll-call votes; although the Republicans controlled both chambers, only eight Congressmen supported Eisenhower more frequently. Further, Democratic votes, garnered by Rayburn, enabled the president to win on fifty-eight votes he would otherwise have lost—some on important issues such as drought aid, foreign aid, and reciprocal trade legislation.[8] With the active lobbying assistance of OCR staff, Rayburn and Johnson made the crucial tactical decisions and moves necessary for the passage of

[4] The former Congressman was the Californian Republican Jack Anderson.
[5] Hess, S., *Organizing the Presidency*, Washington, DC, 1976, p. 70.
[6] MacNeil, N., *Forge of Democracy*, New York, 1961, p. 254.
[7] Eisenhower, *Mandate for Change*, p. 195.
[8] Hardeman, D. B., 'Sam Rayburn and the House of Representatives', in Livingston, W. S., Dodd, L. C., and Schott, R. L., (eds.), *The Presidency and the Congress*, Austin, 1979, pp. 236–7.

Eisenhower's 1957 Civil Rights Act and the later, less significant, Act of 1960.[9] The president and his staff had ample cause to be grateful for the Democratic support which Rayburn and Johnson frequently delivered, as Harlow acknowledged shortly before Eisenhower's final term ended. He wrote to the Speaker thanking him for his help, and added a postscript: 'Without you and Lyndon these past eight years, I shudder to think what might have happened.'[10]

A DEMOCRATIC OCR

The organisation of the OCR under President Kennedy was substantially the same as for the first year of Johnson's administration, and is discussed in the following chapter; just two aspects of Kennedy's relations with Congress, the preparation of Congressional liaison during the transition, and the early difficulties which he and his staff faced, need to be considered here to place that analysis in context.

The president-elect and his senior advisers considered the process of Congressional liaison highly important. Accordingly, Kennedy's transition team carefully planned the shape, size, and purpose of the new OCR. Even before the election in 1960 Richard Neustadt advised Kennedy on the preparation of his Congressional business after the election. He observed that consultations with the legislative leadership were a prerequisite for success, while the committee chairmen, too, would expect to be fêted.

They would, said Neustadt, 'be touchily awaiting signs of recognition from the President-elect . . . Congressional leaders will have to be consulted on, or at least informed of, the President-elect's immediate legislative plans. Their help will be needed in considering—and above all in sustaining—priorities.'[11]

After Kennedy's narrow victory, the hectic task of preparing the transition moved into full swing. No previous Democratic

[9] Evans, R., and Novak, R., *Lyndon B. Johnson: The Exercise of Power*, New York, 1968, p. 237; Eisenhower, D. D., *Waging Peace*, New York, 1965, p. 160.
[10] Hardeman, 'Sam Rayburn and the House of Representatives', p. 239.
[11] Neustadt to JFK, 30/10/60, President's Office Files, Box 31, 'Neustadt, Richard E., 15/9/60 11/10/63' (John F. Kennedy Library).

president had given such high priority to courting members of Congress and senators, or considered a formal legislative liaison office necessary. But Kennedy was elected, albeit by a tiny majority, on a platform of presidential activism in foreign and domestic affairs, as his campaign rhetoric and inaugural address indicated. His domestic policies were cautiously liberal. The president-elect, the vice-president-elect, the Speaker of the House, and Senator Mansfield (who was to be Majority Leader) agreed five legislative priorities at Palm Beach on 20 December: an increase in the minimum wage, federal aid to schools and colleges, area redevelopment, housing, and medical care for the elderly.[12] These were opposed (particularly in the House) by the conservative coalition in Congress composed of Republicans and Southern Democrats, buttressed by southern Democratic control of the most important committee chairmanships. These two factors eliminated the nominal party advantage of 263 : 174 which the Democrats held in the House.

Kennedy employed his OCR staff not merely as co-ordinators of his legislative initiatives, but as symbolic expressions of his legislative intent. Thus Larry O'Brien, the director of his presidential campaign, was appointed as his most highly paid adviser with the title 'Special Assistant to the President for Congressional Relations and Personnel'. Kennedy had pondered the matter for some time before Neustadt pressed him in early December to retrieve O'Brien from the Democratic National Committee and bring him into the transition team to prepare for government. Kennedy approved the proposal and stressed to Congressional colleagues that, as his emissary to Congress, O'Brien had full authority to speak for him.[13]

O'Brien was meticulous in his attention to political detail during the transition, and took considerable care to ensure that his colleagues in the OCR would maximise the president's prospects in Congress. He began interviewing candidates for OCR staff positions just six days before the inauguration, and

[12] Wicker, T., *JFK and LBJ*, New York, 1968, p. 61.
[13] O'Brien, L. F., *No Final Victories*, New York, 1974, p. 110; Neustadt to JFK, President's Office Files: Staff Memoranda, Box 64, 'Neustadt, R. E., 1960', Dec. 7, 1960 (John F. Kennedy Library).

selected them with an eye not only to their political experience and judgement, but also to their regional knowledge and connections. The strength of Democratic conservatives obliged him to choose an assistant for House liaison whose background was similar to those Congressmen with whom he would have to deal. Henry Hall Wilson's background in North Carolina (a state whose Democratic delegation were inconstant in their support of both Kennedy and Johnson, and hence often heavily lobbied by OCR staff) helped secure the post for him.[14]

New to their posts, with no OCR colleagues from former Democratic administrations to whom to turn for advice, O'Brien and his staff avoided the gross political errors which so quickly lost President Carter and his staff support sixteen years later. Mistakes were inevitably made, but soon corrected. Indeed, as late as 15 May 1961, John Brademas, a rising Democratic representative from Indiana, complained that he had 'seen no evidence of the Congressional liaison people', but thereafter he was regularly courted.[15] Others were irritated that the press sometimes knew of major federal grants before they did, and by the occasional failure of overworked staff in the section of the OCR dealing with Congressional correspondence to return their telephone calls or acknowledge their letters sufficiently quickly.[16]

Together with minor irritants of this kind, some OCR staff felt frustrated by winning little advantage from the president's patronage policy. O'Brien soon appreciated that the prospects for leverage were poor, not least because by 1961 just four out of every eight thousand non-merit jobs were presidential appointments.[17] O'Brien, heeding Bryce Harlow's advice, distanced himself from patronage and arranged for John Bailey, the chairman of the Democratic National Committee, to assume the responsibility. O'Brien none the less took the political credit on behalf of the president when a patronage

[14] O'Brien, *No Final Victories*, p. 101.

[15] Maguire to O'Brien, 15/5/61, 'O'Brien: House: Maguire Files' (John F. Kennedy Library).

[16] Manatos, Box 1, 'Memoranda: 13/2/61–28/2/61'; Wilson to O'Brien, 27/2/61, Wilson, Box 1,'Memoranda: 25/2/61–28/2/61' (John F. Kennedy Library).

[17] Interview with O'Brien, Nov. 1978; Sorensen, T., *Kennedy*, New York, 1965, p. 349.

request was granted. Mike Manatos explained the principle underlying OCR announcements of patronage and projects in an early memo to his secretary: 'We are', he observed, 'the good news department.'[18]

However, OCR staff sometimes bore the brunt when senior politicians were offended or major posts involved. Speaker McCormack's chosen candidate for head of the Civil Aeronautics Board was not nominated, a rough parallel with the Carter White House's failure to consult Speaker O'Neill before appointing Massachusetts Republicans to senior positions. Much later, Senator Nelson, a Wisconsin Democrat in his first term, was in 1963 only informed of the appointment of John Gronouski (a political opponent from his home state) as Postmaster-General, and not consulted about it. Nelson's anger was quelled only when the president hurriedly agreed to meet him. Although Kennedy declined to withdraw the nomination, he prudently offered to visit Wisconsin during a forthcoming tour to speak on Nelson's behalf. The senator gratefully accepted.[19]

The White House gained more from Kennedy's shrewd sense of political courtship. Concentrating on weakening the conservative coalition, Kennedy attended to the requirements and foibles of senior southerners, such as Carl Vinson, the Georgian Democratic chairman of the House Armed Services Committee, who could occasionally be persuaded to support him.[20] He even extended the hand of presidential favour to implacable conservative opponents such as Harry Byrd, the chairman of the Senate Finance Committee, to whose birthday party the president once made a surprise visit by helicopter, though the gesture did Kennedy little good—Byrd ungraciously declared that public funds should not have been used for the visit.[21] Small favours—tickets to White House dinners, boat trips on the president's yachts—were appreciated by Democratic colleagues, especially since most had not served with a Democratic president and were unused to such attention, particularly where they could exploit it for their

[18] Manatos, Box 1, Memo to Dorothy Davies, 17/2/61, 'Memoranda: 12/2/61–9/3/62' (John F. Kennedy Library).

[19] Paper, L. J., *John F. Kennedy*, New York, 1975, pp. 174-5.

[20] Sorensen, *Kennedy*, pp. 347-8.

[21] Paper, *John F. Kennedy*, p. 333.

own purposes. The White House assisted helpful Democrats in the 1962 mid-term elections by arranging for a cabinet member, the vice-president, or, as a special mark of approval, the president himself, to speak on behalf of incumbents.[22] As O'Brien observed before the 1962 mid-term elections, 'The White House certainly remembers who its friends are'.[23] Equally careful records were kept of opponents: those Congressmen and senators who opposed the president when their district's politics did not oblige them to do so were denied campaign help. Carefully maintained records of every district, its economic and social circumstances, and the political pressures these placed on representatives enabled OCR staff to judge what might be done to persuade each of them to follow a presidential lead on different matters.[24]

Consistent with O'Brien's determination to ensure that the administration's liaison with Congress was devolved to departments whenever possible, the organisation of departmental liaison was moved from the Offices of the Departmental General Counsels to separate, specialised offices at Assistant Secretary level, thereby making the function symbolically and substantively more prominent.[25] The Post Office continued to be a special centre in government for monitoring the behaviour of members of Congress, as it had been since Woodrow Wilson's presidency. Mike Monroney, the Assistant Postmaster-General in charge of Congressional affairs, recorded every favour performed by the Post Office for members and sent the updated records to O'Brien for his own use.[26] Further, cabinet secretaries were themselves required to lobby actively for the president's measures in their contacts with legislators. Since this was in their own interests, it was easy to elicit a response: Treasury Secretary Douglas Dillon was regularly in contact with Wilbur Mills, the influential chairman of the House Ways and Means Committee, and Agriculture Secretary Orville Freeman worked

[22] O'Brien to JFK, 9/2/62, O'Brien, Box 31, 'White House Staff Files: Legislative Background Material: Congressional Elections' (John F. Kennedy Library).

[23] MacNeil, *Forge of Democracy*, p. 260.

[24] O'Brien, Box 31,(John F. Kennedy Library).

[25] The Commerce Department was the last to change in 1963 (Holtzman, *Legislative Liaison*, Chicago, 1970, p. 11).

[26] MacNeil, *Forge of Democracy*, p. 262.

assiduously to explain the president's farm legislation to House members.[27] Only when Kennedy and Johnson requested cabinet members to assist cabinet colleagues with special legislation of their own (as they often did to relieve pressure on overworked staff) did they meet with resistance.

POLITICAL AND INSTITUTIONAL BARRIERS

Chaired by Howard Smith, an able, shrewd, deeply conservative Virginian, the House Rules Committee was in matters 'of civil rights the single most important institutional asset of the conservative forces in Congress. With the support of William Colmer, a Mississippi Democrat, and the aid of the committee's four Republicans, Smith was able to delay, or obstruct completely, legislation of which he and his colleagues disapproved. The president and his OCR staff well remembered the open opposition of Colmer and John Bell Williams, a fellow Mississippian, to the Kennedy–Johnson ticket in November 1960.[28] Accordingly, he decided shortly after the election to undermine this conservative faction's strength by increasing the committee's membership. For a month, Kennedy entrusted the matter to the Speaker. But at the president's breakfast with the Congressional leadership on 24 January, Rayburn acknowledged that he did not have the votes necessary to secure House approval for the change. At the president's direction, O'Brien and his staff then lobbied for further support. The president's commitment to the expansion was complete for his legislative prospects depended upon it. The White House press corps were amused, but not deceived, when, in commenting on the matter in a press conference later that day, Kennedy declared that he gave his view 'merely as an interested citizen'.[29]

Cabinet members were asked to assist. Stewart Udall, the new Secretary of the Interior, telephoned certain members from western states, asking them to support Rayburn. None did, despite Udall's thinly veiled threat that if they failed to

---

[27] MacNeil, *Forge of Democracy*, p. 261.
[28] O'Brien to JFK, 9/2/62, (John F. Kennedy Library).
[29] Wicker, *JFK and LBJ*, p. 76.

do so, their project requests might encounter opposition. Udall was careful to distance the president from the threat by suggesting that Rayburn, and not Kennedy, would punish them. But the clumsy attempt to extract a quid pro quo did the administration's cause no good at all. Not only did all four Congressmen vote against expansion, but Dirksen, the Senate Republican leader, exploited the error by observing that Udall's intervention 'was in the nature of serving notice on all new Frontiersmen—check your guns and your voting record at the door, the project line forms on your right'.[30] O'Brien, in a foretaste of lobbying tactics on future occasions, co-ordinated his tactics with Andrew Biemiller, the chief lobbyist of the AFL-CIO, who approached a number of legislators with whom he had special influence.[31] Kennedy made several telephone calls himself, keeping in close touch with Congressional supporters such as Richard Bolling (D-MO), Bob Jones (D-AL), and Carl Vinson, concentrating on winning over wavering southerners; to that end, he also spoke to Harold Cooley,(D-NC), Dean of the North Carolina delegation.[32]

Kennedy won by just five votes, with 217 in favour of expansion, despite the efforts which he and his OCR staff made to present the matter as a demonstration of loyalty to a new president. Sixty-four Democrats opposed him and just seventeen Republicans were persuaded to defect from their party leadership. It was, as Kennedy commented afterwards, a salutary reminder of the problem of bargaining with Congressmen unsympathetic to his proposals, over whom he had few sanctions: 'with Rayburn's own reputation at stake, with all of the pressures and appeals a new President could make, we won by five votes. That shows you what we're up against.'[33]

Without Congressional support, Kennedy could do little to advance his programme. As the OCR staff gradually gained in experience and, in the thirty-two months that followed, became accepted as the president's personal emissaries to the

[30] Wicker, *JFK and LBJ*, p. 77.
[31] O'Brien, *No Final Victories*, p. 106.
[32] O'Brien, *No Final Victories*, p. 107.
[33] Sorensen, *Kennedy*, p. 341.

Hill, the unfavourable ideological composition of Congress remained the key factor in limiting Kennedy's legislative progress. His OCR staff were charged with the task of maximising presidential resources and deploying them to greatest effect on the president's behalf. In the lengthy process of legislating, where Congressional structures and politics favoured delay and obstruction in domestic policy, it none the less proved exceedingly difficult to create and sustain a majority liberal–moderate coalition through subcommittee, committee, and floor stages. This lay at the heart of the failure of Medicare, Aid to Education, civil rights, and explains why the final condition of the 1961 Minimum Wage Bill was not more to the president's liking. As Neil MacNeil wrote, the president had 'become the chief advocate, the chief lobbyist, and the chief legislator of the United States'.[34] Kennedy's creation of a prominent, powerful OCR directed by a senior staff member having his full trust and support had indeed thrust to the forefront of American politics the legislative role of the president. Yet the distinction between Kennedy's formal assumption of the role and his giving it political effect was great; adverse partisan and ideological balances combined to defeat the bulk of his programme.

THE JOHNSON PRESIDENCY

The legislative fortunes of John Kennedy's successor were equally affected by the Congressional, and wider public, contexts, within which his presidency developed and his OCR staff liaised with and lobbied Congressmen and senators. Three distinct phases of Lyndon Johnson's tenure can be discerned: the first covered the period from Kennedy's assassination until the 1964 presidential election, the second that of the 89th Congress, and the third, that of the 90th.

In the first of these, Johnson benefited politically from the shocking circumstances of Kennedy's death. He invoked his predecessor's name in his first address to the Joint Session of Congress, pleading for Congressional and public support to prosecute Kennedy's legislative programme. The theme of

---

[34] MacNeil, *Forge of Democracy*, p. 269.

continuity had obvious political advantages for the new
president: it resonated with a horrified public, and broadly
fitted Johnson's calculations of his own and his party's
interests. Staff and departmental officials appointed by
Kennedy remained in their posts: in the OCR, Wilson stayed
until 1967 and Manatos (head of Senate liaison) to the end
of Johnson's term in 1969. Elsewhere, notably in the State
and Defense Departments, departmental heads continued in
office, linking the Kennedy and Johnson administrations more
tightly, and for longer, than Roosevelt's and Truman's. Such
continuity was both symbolically and substantively important.
Thus Johnson inherited his predecessor's programmes, and
pressed them ardently upon the same Congress (where
conservative coalitions of Republicans and southern Democrats
in both Houses had obstructed Kennedy's legislative progress),
exploiting the inchoate mixture of fear and yearning for
leadership which together temporarily weakened political
resistance.

Johnson's rhetorical emphasis upon 'continuity', and his
similarly couched private persuasion of Congressional politicians, veiled his modification of Kennedy's legislative
priorities. In this sense, the first phase of Johnson's presidency
set the tone for the rest: he involved Congress in the promotion
of economic growth, the enactment of civil rights, initiation
of the Great Society, and the beginnings of America's full
engagement in Vietnam. The income tax cut, Kennedy's first
priority, was soon passed, stimulating the economic growth
upon which the later expansion of domestic liberal spending
programmes depended. The non-white unemployment rate
fell from 8.2 per cent in 1964 to 5.8 per cent by the last
quarter of 1965 while the overall rate of unemployment fell
from between 5.5 per cent and 6 per cent in 1962–3 to 4.7
per cent in the spring of 1965. The tax cut added $24 billion
(annualised) to GNP by the second quarter of the same
year.[35]

However, as Richard Bolling and others had anticipated,
the new president made the passage of a comprehensive Civil
Rights Act before the 1964 elections his major objective.[36]

[35] Okun, A., *The Political Economy of Prosperity*, Washington, DC, 1970, pp. 47–8.
[36] Richard Bolling, Oral History, Johnson Library, Tape no. 1, p. 18.

The political circumstances were wholly different from those in which Johnson had crafted cautious compromise from his Senate colleagues in the 1957 and 1960 Civil Rights Acts. In 1964, he insisted, against the advice of many around him (including Abe Fortas), that the measure was to be passed intact, complete with a public accommodations title.[37] The House passed the bill (HR 7152) by a vote of 290 : 130, and under Hubert Humphrey's floor leadership, a Senate filibuster was broken by a cloture vote of 71 : 29 before final passage in a vote of 73 : 27 in June. Johnson had shrewdly argued before a special Joint Session of Congress for the bill's adoption, citing it as a 'memorial to our beloved president'. But it sprang more directly from Johnson's own frustration with what he judged the Kennedy administration's passionless advocacy of civil rights, his desire to secure overwhelming northern black support in the 1964 election, and his determination to allay liberal doubts about his reforming purpose.[38]

The second and third of these motives partly informed his submitting anti-poverty legislation to Congress in the shape of the Economic Opportunity Act, thereby heralding the start of what Johnson later characterised as his 'Great Society' programmes, and were reinforced by his own exposure in early adulthood to poverty among Mexican–Americans in south-west Texas. Whilst the effectiveness of the legislation is disputed, there is strong evidence that the redistributive programmes initiated by Johnson (of which this is but one) were in large part responsible for lifting large numbers out of poverty by the end of his administration; economic growth alone does not account for the change.[39]

The opening for the rapid escalation of America's military involvement in Vietnam was provided by the passage of the Gulf of Tonkin resolution in August 1964, a craven ceding by Congress of its proper constitutional role, with profound implications for both the conduct of Johnson's presidency and

---

[37] Johnson, L. B., *The Vantage Point*, New York, 1971, p. 38.

[38] Transcript of telephone call between Vice-President Johnson and Theodore Sorensen, 3 June 1963, Johnson Library.

[39] Plotnick, R. D., and Skidmore, F., *Progress against Poverty*, New York, 1975, p. 171.

the office itself.[40] The incident which brought about the resolution's passage was adroitly managed by Johnson: the precise circumstances of the alleged attack on two American destroyers in the Gulf on 4 August remain unclear, but were sufficiently well arranged and presented to result in the resolution's passage with no dissenting votes in the House, and just two in the Senate. Johnson temporarily avoided being tarred a warmonger by liberal sceptics, but protected himself against criticism from his Republican opponent, Barry Goldwater. The incident caused a rapid rise in his opinion poll rating, and gave him an unparalleled grant of authority to work his will in Vietnam after the elections.[41]

Even before the 1964 elections provided Johnson with a personal mandate and the Congressional means to govern, he had therefore set the course for the rest of his administration in fiscal affairs, civil rights, Great Society programmes, and policy towards Vietnam. The results of the election opened up the unusual possibility in American government of powerful legislative leadership from the White House. If presidents had as recently as 1963 been said, plausibly enough, to be institutionally hampered in exercising leadership, the second phase of Johnson's presidency illustrated how quickly changing circumstances can alter judgements about the nature of American government.[42] Johnson's own election victory over the hapless Goldwater gave him 61 per cent of the vote—the largest since Roosevelt's defeat of Alf Landon in 1936. Goldwater won only six states: his home state of Arizona and, as a portent of crumbling Democratic strength there, five in the Deep South. In thirty-two states outside the south, Goldwater carried not a single Congressional district.

The Democrats gained two seats in the Senate and thirty-eight in the House, giving them partisan advantages of 68 : 32 and 295 : 140 respectively.[43] More importantly, Johnson's ability to govern was decisively enhanced by ideological advantage: northern Democrats (most of them liberals) increased their numbers by thirty-seven, and conservative Republicans suffered badly—forty with ratings of

[40] Lowi, T., *The Personal President*, Ithaca, 1985, p. 178.
[41] Berman, L., *Planning a Tragedy*, New York, 1982, pp. 34–5.
[42] Burns, J. M., *The Deadlock of Democracy*, Englewood Cliffs, 1963.
[43] *Congressional Quarterly Almanac, 1964*, p. 1010.

less than 20 from the liberal Americans for Democratic Action organisation (ADA) lost.[44] Membership of the liberal Democratic Study Group in Congress grew from 127 in 1964 to 165 in 1965, including almost all Democrats from outside the south. Of the sixty-nine freshmen Democrats in the 89th Congress, about two-thirds had benefited from DSG campaign contributions. Unsurprisingly, most of them joined the Group after their election and lent nearly unanimous floor support to Johnson's Great Society measures, reinforced by their substantially increased representation on key committees.[45] The support of organised labour for most of Johnson's policies, so valuable to the president and his OCR staff, gained a further point in the 89th Congress when the AFL-CIO's Committee on Political Education (COPE) estimated that it had as many as 60 'friends' in the Senate, and 248 in the House.[46]

With the exceptions of the failure of the bill to grant the District of Columbia home rule, and the three unsuccessful attempts to impose cloture on the repeal of clause 14(b) of the Taft–Hartley Act, all of Johnson's major domestic objectives were enacted, constituting an extraordinary period of domestic reform. The combination of a reforming president and a liberal majority in Congress in broad agreement with the president's priorities was decisive. The first session of the 89th Congress alone saw the passage of Medicare, the Elementary and Secondary Education Act (ESEA), the establishment of a Department of Housing and Urban Development (HUD), and, most significantly, the Voting Rights Act which gave federal guarantees of the right to vote to southern blacks. The constitutionality of the latter was upheld by the Supreme Court under the fifteenth amendment, and reinforced by the Court's prohibition of the payment of poll taxes in state elections.

Much of the Great Society legislation, especially ESEA, the rent supplements programme, and the 1966 Model Cities Act, were products of task forces of professional and

---

[44] *Congressional Quarterly Almanac, 1964*, pp. 1014–15.
[45] Eidenberg, E., and Morey, R. D., *An Act of Congress*, New York, 1969, p. 38; Duke, P., and Sawsilak, A. B., 'The "Group" that Runs the House', *The Reporter*, 20/5/65, pp. 29–31.
[46] Vale, V., *Labour in American Politics*, London, 1971, p. 118.

interest-group representatives, drawn from outside government, whose contributions were intended to widen the coalition of support for the measures outside Congress, refined by executive task forces, of which O'Brien or a senior OCR colleague was always a member and active participant. These groups' recommendations were then discussed with key Congressmen and senators before legislative proposals were sent to Capitol Hill; shrewd disarming of likely opponents before the submission of bills to Congress made the bill more acceptable, and the OCR's task of lobbying easier, as Johnson fully appreciated.[47]

The 1966 mid-term Congressional elections resulted in an unusually sharp rebuff to Johnson's party in Congress: the president's partisan advantage was diminished, and his ideological advantage eliminated. In the aggregate, the GOP gained three seats in the Senate and forty-seven in the House, resulting in new party balances of 64 : 36 and 248 : 187 respectively. Of the forty-seven Democrats who had won in traditionally Republican districts in 1964, twenty-four lost, or retired only for their party colleagues to lose. As conservative Republicans had polled especially poorly in 1964, so liberal Democrats suffered most now, particularly in the south where Johnson's strongest supporters in Arkansas, Georgia, North Carolina, and Virginia were all defeated.[48]

This 90th Congress, encompassing the third and final phase of Johnson's presidency, cut short Johnson's prospects of significantly expanding the range of Great Society programmes. Even where liberal reforms passed into law, appropriations were sometimes cut or denied altogether, as happened with the Urban Development Act of 1968. Significantly, the greatest progress occurred in civil rights, where the budgetary implications were minimal: the Civil Rights Act of 1968 was passed after a cloture vote in the Senate which, with vigorous lobbying from the OCR and the president's personal intervention, won the support of the

[47] Kearns, D., *Lyndon Johnson and the American Dream*, New York, 1976, p. 224; Leuchtenburg, W. E., 'The Genesis of the Great Society', *The Reporter*, 21/4/66; Thomas, N. C., and Wolman, H. L., 'The Presidency and Policy Formation: The Task Force Device', *Public Administration Review*, vol. 29, no. 5, Sept.–Oct. 1969, p. 460.
[48] *Congressional Quarterly Almanac, 1966*, p. 1398.

Republican leadership there. Even so, the bill would have failed had Martin Luther King's assassination not temporarily disarmed some of its opponents; it passed the House just six days after his death.[49]

Pressures to constrain the growth of federal spending on domestic projects did not arise simply from conservatives in Congress seizing their political opportunity. The growth of the federal deficit between 1966 and 1968 was caused almost entirely by the rapid increase in spending on the Vietnam War; by 1968, the war had cost $75 billion in total, and accounted for $25 billion in 1968 alone. As such, it was almost wholly responsible for the federal budget deficit, the consequent squeeze on domestic expenditure, and the inflationary pressures.[50]

The political implications of fiscal restraint, encapsulated in the president's protracted and unsuccessful attempts in 1967 and 1968 to persuade a divided Congress to enact a tax surcharge without expenditure limitations on social welfare and urban programmes, were many. Johnson's standing among liberals in Congress and elsewhere was significantly weakened. Critics to the left of him were more sensitive than he to the need (identified by the authors of the Kerner Commission's report on urban unrest) for increases rather than reductions in urban spending to alleviate the economic entrenchment of black disadvantage. Temporarily obscured by the fast non-inflationary growth of two years before, the economic vulnerability of urban blacks was underlined anew by the threat of Johnson's deflationary proposals to deal with an overheating economy and weak dollar, the consequences of his attempt to finance the Vietnam War without increasing taxes.[51]

Domestic economies made to sustain a foreign war were especially unwelcome—as much with articulate white middle-class college students (who often benefited from qualified draft exemptions) as with working-class whites and blacks (who did not). But draft exemptions did less to still student discontent than political opposition and moral outrage,

[49] Miller, M., *Lyndon*, New York, 1980, p. 515.
[50] Schick, A., *Congress and Money*, Washington, DC, 1980, pp. 24–7.
[51] Wills, G., *Nixon Agonistes*, New York, 1977, p. 472.

leavened with the threat of the draft, did to fuel it. For such students, and urban ghetto dwellers, the burgeoning American commitment in south-east Asia served as the locus of protest, and radicalised them on domestic questions too, just as the issues of poverty and race at home fed the militancy of anti-war protest.

President Johnson was thus faced with the dilemma of a war he could neither win nor end. Either course might have been preferable to pursuing the conflict, caught as he was in the approach to a presidential election between conservative critics led by Nixon and Wallace, and dissenting liberal pretenders to the Democratic nomination who quickly exposed his weakness within the party and precipitated his withdrawal from the race. The Tet offensive was a military disaster for the Vietcong, but their decisive political success; it made a nonsense of repeated American claims of imminent victory, and intensified liberal and conservative criticism which duly split the Democratic Party, mortally wounding Johnson's presidency. The hedging of political and tactical bets, arguably a pragmatically safe middle course in 1964, was now a policy without prospect of military success abroad or popular appeal at home.[52]

Johnson's coalition quickly fell apart. Many blacks, liberals, and blue-collar workers left the ranks, albeit for different reasons, and often in different directions. Richard Scammon told a number of Johnson's senior staff in August 1967 that 'Vietnam and riots' would continue to be the most important political issues before the country; the successful candidate, he said, would capture the frustrations of the 'unyoung, unblack and unpoor. . . the people who bowl regularly'.[53] For these, the shift demanded by many blacks, from the *de jure* equality of the 1964 Civil Rights Act and 1965 Voting Rights Act to a *de facto* equality of opportunity was unacceptable. The failure of Johnson's Vietnam policy was evident to many within and without government, yet went unacknowledged. The Tet offensive brought neither quick

[52] Gelb, L. H., and Betts, R. K., *The Irony of Vietnam*, Washington, DC, 1979, p. 109.

[53] Cater, Wattenberg, and Duggan to the president, 19/8/67, Cabinet Papers, Box 10, 'Cabinet Meeting, 20/9/67 (4 of 4)'.

financial relief nor a systematic reassessment of the link between military means and foreign policy objectives, while urban and campus unrest kept the questions of poverty, race, and crime on television screens throughout the election year. The events were symbolised by the assassinations of King and Kennedy, the violence surrounding both party conventions at Chicago and Miami, and amplified in intense executive-congressional conflict over the Civil Rights and Crime Control Acts, the Supreme Court nominations of Fortas and Thornberry, and the tax surcharge.[54]

The centre of American politics held firm in the 1968 elections, despite widespread direct political action, and a third party electoral challenge from George Wallace. Humphrey lost the election to Nixon very narrowly, while the Republicans gained five seats in the Senate, but only four in the House. The electoral resolution none the less heralded the end of the Democratic domestic reforms which had themselves accelerated the changes in the Democrats' electoral coalition and Congressional composition, and made yet more difficult the Democrats' chances of winning the presidency. Important elements of the electoral support which confirmed Johnson in office four years earlier had split, scattering to McCarthy and Robert Kennedy in Democratic primaries, and to Nixon and Wallace in the general election. The failed prosecution of an unpopular foreign war and, with it, withered hopes prompted by Great Society legislation followed by domestic rebellion and economic discontent, broke Johnson and weakened the party he led.

[54] See chapters six and seven.

3

THE ORGANISATION OF THE OFFICE OF CONGRESSIONAL RELATIONS

PRESIDENTIAL INVOLVEMENT IN CONGRESSIONAL LIAISON

The creation of the OCR did nothing to increase the rare opportunities for presidential legislative leadership in American government; it merely enabled presidents to mobilise the resources of their office more effectively. The conjunction of an efficient OCR, a powerful president, public support, and a favourable Congressional balance did not occur until after the 1964 elections. Then, Johnson's personal political knowledge and skills were strengthened by OCR staff who, when he inherited them, had refined their political skills through three years of valuable experience. Their decision to stay lent a measure of continuity to Congressional relations which additionally benefited from the president's intimate concern with the details of the legislation which his staff managed.

Shortly after Johnson's election defeat of Goldwater in 1964, Larry O'Brien reviewed the purposes and operation of White House Congressional relations for the president, stressing that President Kennedy had vested in his OCR staff powers of legislative management and direction. He had demanded the fullest support for them, as his representatives: 'The emphasis throughout has been that the Program is the President's program and every element of the Executive Branch must be vitally concerned and totally involved. In other words, the White House expects full participation by the Executive Branch in all legislative struggles.'[1]

Johnson immersed himself in the OCR's work more completely than his predecessor had done; his long experience,

---

[1] O'Brien to Johnson, Ex FG 300/A, Box 321, 'FG 400: The Legislative Branch: 15/6/64–24/12/64'.

confidence, and skill made delegation to unelected assistants difficult for him. He craved information on Congress—not only on members' voting intentions, but also on their politics— their interests, and the political pressures upon them. Events which touched, even indirectly, on the politics of relations with Capitol Hill were his constant concern. He insisted that his OCR staff tell him of all contacts between the executive and members of Congress.[2] His supervision of the administration's relations with Congress was the better informed (though by no means necessarily better organised) because of it, and strikingly energetic. In other areas of presidential responsibility, such as foreign policy, his understanding did not match that of specialist advisers; in judgements about Congressional politics, Johnson had no peer. Claude Desautels, a member of his OCR staff, observed:[3]

. . . Lyndon Johnson was a kind of generator of interest, and he was thorough in his knowledge of legislation, and so interested in even the smallest piece of legislation. As long as it was on that 'must' [priority] list, he wanted you to go out and win it. He'd go over the list with you and say, 'Well, what are we doing about this? Where are we here, and where are we there? What are we doing?' As a consequence, you'd sometimes get sixty, seventy, eighty bills on that list, and he knew exactly where they were . . . knew them all, and he'd follow them.

Johnson had direct lines to his senior OCR staff whom he could contact immediately by pressing a button with the individual assistant's name on his desk or coffee-table telephone bank; staff could also reach him on a direct line (marked POTUS—President of the United States).[4] Usually, however, they telephoned him through his personal or appointments secretary.[5] When news of Congressional votes on important items of legislation was expected, OCR staff members sometimes arranged a line in advance with the White House switchboard, wishing to be the first to brief the president for congratulatory telephone calls to Congressional and floor

[2] 'Priority' Legislation referred to the entire list of the administration's legislative proposals, and included virtually all major legislation passed by Congress.
[3] Interview with Claude Desautels, 21/11/78.
[4] Interview with Henry Hall Wilson, 20/12/78.
[5] Wilson, H. H., 'How it worked when it worked', unpublished manuscript, 1979, p. 12.

leaders.[6] OCR staff—especially O'Brien, Wilson, Manatos, and Sanders--had free personal access to the president, too. This enabled them to raise important Congressional problems with him directly, and showed other members of the White House staff the special status which Johnson accorded them, and the importance he attached to their work.[7]

Johnson read large numbers of minutes to him from OCR staff on Congressional matters, on general political issues, and on the tactical details of the progress of legislation. Reaching him quickly by paper was simple: urgent memos from OCR staff members were marked out for the president's immediate attention by a red tag stapled to the top left-hand corner; routine papers from liaison staff were normally reserved for his bedtime reading. Additionally, an annotated copy of the *Congressional Record* was prepared every morning by 7.30 a.m. for the president to read during breakfast: a White House car delivered a copy of the *Record* to the home of a staff member (Jake Jacobsen until he was replaced by Bill Blackburn) who read it on his way to the White House. He then drafted a report based on it, with key speeches and voting records highlighted; the report and the *Record* itself were then delivered to the president in the main bedroom.[8]

Priority legislation was a prominent agenda item for most cabinet meetings. Towards the end of the administration, when the Congressional balance was less favourable, the task of passing legislation very much more difficult, and as his energies were drawn into the problem of Vietnam, Johnson cajoled cabinet secretaries to acquaint themselves fully with their department's legislation, ensure that their own legislative liaison teams were able and efficient, and, when the White House requested it, assist with other departments' legislation. But his cabinet secretaries were, as all cabinet secretaries are, preoccupied with their own concerns; senior OCR staff were sometimes frustrated by the reluctance of individual cabinet members to help the White House lobby for other departments'

[6] Wilson, 'How It Worked', p. 27.

[7] Wilson, 'How It Worked', p. 29; interview with Mike Manatos, 21/11/78.

[8] Blackburn, W., Oral History, Johnson Library, Tape no. 1, pp. 5-6; Wilson, 'How It Worked'.

appropriations bills.[9] By contrast, Johnson, without the responsibility of administering a large bureaucracy, had the capacity and the will to engage in battle on a wider front. Craig Raupe, the Director of Congressional Liaison at the Agency for International Development (AID), wrote to an OCR staff member in June 1964 thanking him and his colleagues for their lobbying help. Whilst there were many factors working in AID's favour on the recently passed foreign aid bill, the president's backing had been decisive:[10]

The one overwhelming reason. . . is the President's own personal involvement on our behalf. Not only were our critics apparently satisfied that all the 'water' had been squeezed out already, but they were impressed by the almost daily evidence of the President's determination to fight for his whole bill. We in AID are keenly aware of this fact and are deeply grateful.

The president's immersion in the details of liaison and lobbying had its dangers, too, for his enthusiasm sometimes got the better of him. Before he established a rapport with O'Brien and his staff, Johnson sometimes attempted to bargain with senators directly before being asked to do so by his OCR staff. On one especially important occasion, he told O'Brien of his delight at having secured the agreement of Senator Harry Byrd, chairman of the Senate Finance Committee, to begin hearings on the administration's tax bill in return for which Johnson had agreed to limit the federal budget for Fiscal Year 1964 to below $100 million. Unfortunately, O'Brien had already secured Byrd's agreement to begin hearings without conceding a budget limit. Henry Hall Wilson, recalling the incident, noted that this 'made in the future for a lot more base-touching before deals were made'.[11]

Even so, Johnson was constantly tempted to involve himself directly, and particularly with senior legislators—organisational procedures had little significance for him. Later in his presidency, this inattention had damaging implications

[9] Cabinet Papers, Box 4, 'Cabinet Meeting, 24/3/66'; Cabinet Papers, Box 9; 'Cabinet Meeting, 17/5/67 (2 of 2)'; Cabinet Papers, Box 10, 'Cabinet Meeting, 6/9/67 (2 of 2)'; Cabinet Papers, Box 10, 'Cabinet Meeting, 20/9/67 (4 of 4)'; Cabinet Papers, Box 12, 'Cabinet Meeting, 14/2/68 (2 of 2)'.
[10] Raupe to Desautels, 15/6/64, Reports on Legislation, Box 6.
[11] Wilson, H. H., Oral History, Johnson Library, p. 16.

for the management of relations with Congress. But for so long as he was able to ride the waves of political advantage, the completeness of Johnson's involvement in Congressional matters was more an advantage than a hindrance. To some others in government, even to an aide in the vice-president's office, the OCR, institutionally prominent under Kennedy, now seemed almost to merge with Lyndon Johnson's personality and political style:[12]

. . . to a large extent, Johnson ran his own office with regard to Congressional liaison. In fact, I had never thought of a distinct *Office* of Congressional Relations as such before you mentioned it. The Office was important, but it was ministerial, and the people running it were just assistants, and very much subordinate to a dominating president who saw himself as the OCR—and by God, he was.

That was, perhaps, a reflection as much of the position of the vice-president and his staff as a spare wheel, as of the status of the OCR. Congressional liaison had to be presidential to be effective—and the president's staff were unwilling to share their limited power with the vice-president or his aides; both Humphrey and his staff were marginalised.

THE VICE-PRESIDENT

Even at the outset of the Kennedy presidency, when staff lacked legislative experience and expertise, Vice-President Johnson had a limited role in liaison with the Senate. When seventeen Democratic senators opposed his taking the chair of the Senate Democratic Conferences, Johnson declined to pursue the matter; he quickly appreciated that the responsibilities of the vice-presidency were likely to be even fewer than he had supposed.[13] He maintained his interest in the voting of the Texas Democratic delegation (as he did when president) but was only occasionally asked to lobby them on the president's behalf.[14] Even at Congressional

---

[12] Confidential interview with a member of Vice-President Humphrey's staff.
[13] Kearns, D., *Lyndon Johnson and the American Dream*, New York, 1976, pp. 164–5; Humphrey, H. H., Oral History, Johnson Library, pp. 40–1.
[14] Interview with Desautels.

leadership breakfasts when vice-president, Johnson rarely contributed to discussion.[15] Although always invited to the strategy meetings between O'Brien, Manatos, and Mansfield in the private room of the Majority Leader's Senate office, he was an infrequent attender.[16] The rebuff which Johnson had received at the hands of Senate Democrats in 1961 had offended him; he also knew that Kennedy's staff were determined to restrict his role and political influence.[17]

In his own presidency, Johnson's knowledge and skill reduced the need for the vice-president to liaise with the Senate. Between Kennedy's death and the November 1964 election, Humphrey acted as an unofficial channel between the Senate and the OCR, but his legislative role was almost as limited as Johnson's had been under Kennedy.[18] Any involvement by Humphrey in liaison with the House was resented by many Congressmen, including the leadership.[19] Whereas the vice-president had a clear constitutional bond to the Senate as the body's president, he had none to the House, as Speaker McCormack once forcefully reminded him.[20]

As the clear organisational patterns of Congressional liaison became confused late in the administration, Johnson contemplated asking Humphrey to assume a more prominent legislative liaison role. *The New York Times* of 24 April 1967 reported a White House decision that Humphrey should direct executive liaison with Congress; the realisation had dawned that the task required a full-time director, and that O'Brien could not effectively perform the dual roles of Postmaster-General and OCR head.[21] The leaking of the plan caused Johnson to abandon it.[22]

[15] Evans, R., and Novak, R., *Lyndon B. Johnson: The Exercise of Power*, New York, 1968, p. 331.

[16] Interview with Desautels.

[17] Interview with H. C. McPherson, Jnr., 9/11/78; interview with W. Cennell, Chief-of-Staff to Vice-President Humphrey, 13/11/78; interview with W. Welsh, Administrative Assistant to Vice-President Humphrey, 8/11/78; interview with J. G. Stewart, Legislative Assistant to Vice-President Humphrey, 9/11/78.

[18] Interview with Cennell, 13/11/78.

[19] Interview with Wilson.

[20] Interview with Wilson.

[21] 'President Picks Humphrey to Push Bills in Congress', *The New York Times*, 24/4/67; confidential interview with a member of Vice-President Humphrey's staff; interview with McPherson.

[22] Confidential interview with member of Vice-President Humphrey's staff.

THE OCR STAFF

Larry O'Brien was the architect of the Congressional relations system under President Kennedy and conducted the OCR's work. He wished to leave the White House after the 1964 election to enter private business, but, after Johnson's plea that he stay, agreed to continue for a further year.[23] By 1965, the president arranged for O'Brien to become Postmaster-General in succession to John Gronouski but told O'Brien that he still wished him to lead the Congressional staff. On one occasion, noticing that O'Brien was frequently at the Post Office's headquarters and no longer available to him in the White House six days a week, Johnson impatiently pressed him to recruit more departmental assistants so that he could again concentrate on Congressional liaison.[24] O'Brien worked part time in the White House which, in combination with Johnson's decision not to appoint a full time successor in the OCR, seriously confused administrative arrangements established by Kennedy and initially continued by Johnson. (Henry Wilson, O'Brien's deputy since 1961, was nominated by O'Brien to succeed him, but did formally not do so.[25]) In other White House staff work, an absence of clear responsibilities could be a creative advantage, if imaginatively exploited by the president. But the OCR depended for its effectiveness upon recognised procedures to an extent which Johnson seemed not to appreciate. Constantly demanding energetic action from those around him and in the departments, he declined to implement appropriate organisational arrangements which would have promoted it.

O'Brien's assistant, Claude Desautels, also gained his political experience in western Massachusetts and (unlike O'Brien and Wilson) had had extensive prior Congressional experience. His main responsibility was to co-ordinate the work of the Congressional correspondence section with that of other OCR staff; letters from the Hill were directed to his

[23] Interview with Lawrence O'Brien, 29/11/78. O'Brien was closer in age to President Kennedy than the other senior staff, and felt rather less dependent upon him.
[24] Interview with O'Brien.
[25] Interviews with Wilson and O'Brien.

office. Desautels followed O'Brien to the Post Office in 1965 and took no further active part in Congressional liaison.[26] Jean Lewis took on much of his work. From the beginning of Kennedy's term, she had been responsible for the administration of Congressional correspondence, ensuring that White House colleagues met the deadlines for acknowledgement of, and action on, such mail.[27]

CONGRESSIONAL CORRESPONDENCE

Johnson directed that all Congressional mail—whether to him personally, or to other staff in the White House—should be answered on the day of receipt. Shortly after Johnson became president, O'Brien issued instructions for the administration of Congressional mail, and outlined his own role in it:[28]

1. I will acknowledge all mail the day it is received to insure immediate contact with the member.
2. If it is the President's decision to reply personally, please be sure that the Presidential letter is processed through the Congressional Correspondence office—Mrs Jean Lewis—to complete our records.
3. If the letter requires attention by a member of the White House staff, it will be sent to him by route slip for a draft of a further reply. The draft should be returned to Mrs Lewis.

This procedure altered only slightly during the first three years of Johnson's presidency, but it had to be periodically restated when White House staff outside the OCR failed to comply. The importance of this arrangement was clear enough: Congressmen knew well the political damage which needless administrative delay could cause them. Yet the White House's task was demanding for few enquiries were simple; many required OCR staff to request answers on complicated matters of policy from departmental officials. Lewis's job required sound general political judgement, and an ability to anticipate

---

[26] Interviews with Wilson and Desautels.
[27] Interview with Jean Lewis, 8/12/78.
[28] O'Brien to the White House staff, 5/2/64, Ex FG 300/A, Box 321, 'FG 400: The Legislative Branch: 22/11/63–14/6/64'.

sources of possible embarrassment and difficulty, as Henry Wilson observed:[29]

Much of this mail had to be referred to departments for technical answers, and Jean had the responsibility of jabbing up the departments to produce. But some of it was politically inspired, and letters written for this purpose had to be handled warily. If we bobbled them, a hostile Congressman could make points against us, at least in his local papers, by alleging that the president had ignored a plea for mercy about some subject or other. We could get into trouble if these sleepers weren't expeditiously spotted and squelched. Also, games were constantly being played in parliamentary manœuvre. These, too, could cause problems if not perceived and addressed. Our confidence in Jean's fund of common sense and information was richly rewarded. Not once did she get us into trouble.

Other OCR staff were organised in two sections, one dealing with the Senate and the other with the House; differences of size, character, organisation, and tradition between the two chambers made it a wise division. Mike Manatos was the only member of staff assigned solely to the Senate, and served Kennedy and Johnson throughout their presidencies; he had had lengthy Senate experience, having worked as a legislative and administrative assistant to three Wyoming senators during the 1950s. At the time when Majority Leader Mansfield suggested to Kennedy that Manatos would be well suited to liaison with the Senate, Manatos was chairman of the Senate Administrative Assistants' Association.[30] His contacts with Senate staff, and with some senators, were therefore excellent. The first of these attributes was often apparent: White House colleagues believed—sometimes unfairly—that Manatos relied too heavily on his contacts with staff for their assessment of senators' views.[31]

Some White House and Congressional colleagues thought him politically naïve.[32] OCR staff who worked with members of the House also took the view that his task was relatively

[29] Wilson, 'How It Worked', pp. 16–17.
[30] Manatos, Oral History; interview with Manatos.
[31] Interview with Wilson; confidential interviews with members of the Johnson White House staff.
[32] Confidential interview with a member of the Johnson White House staff.

simple in comparison with their own. There were only 100 politicians with whom to deal, and senators were usually inclined to 'arrogate to themselves the authority to talk to the top man'.[33] But Manatos was an able administrator, and in some measure handicapped by working for two presidents with extensive combined Senate experience. This was especially so during Johnson's incumbency for his political reputation rested fully upon his legislative skill. Manatos performed precisely the task which the president required—that of a messenger, a carrier of information, gossip, and intelligence. Johnson did not intend that Manatos should bargain with senators as Wilson occasionally did in the House, and O'Brien did in both chambers.[34] In any event, Manatos's previous Senate employment was widely known. The status of Senate aide coloured his White House employment, and, as some of his colleagues acknowledged, made any expansion of his role difficult even had he had the inclination to carry it out.[35]

The House, being larger, required a bigger White House specialist staff. Except for the first ten months of 1961, when Wilson took sole charge of House members, Congressmen were assigned to three OCR aides. Wilson, a North Carolinian, assumed responsibility for those from southern and border states, among whom were a disproportionately large number of important committee chairmen.[36] The second group comprised Democrats from the eastern and northern cities, many of them from city machines, and a large number of liberals—the two categories overlapped. Dick Donahue, a brilliant Kennedy campaign worker in 1960, took charge of them; Chuck Roche, a former journalist, succeeded Donahue in 1965 and stayed until the end of Johnson's term. The third group, the remainder of the Democratic House members, mainly from the West and mid-West, were initially Chuck Daly's responsibility. He left the White House in 1964 to assist Pierre Salinger, Kennedy's press secretary, in his unsuccessful race for the Senate in California. Daly was in turn succeeded by Dave Bunn, from Colorado, who stayed

[33] Interview with Wilson.
[34] Interview with Wilson.
[35] Confidential interviews with members of the Johnson White House staff.
[36] See chapter one.

in the OCR until securing a senior regional appointment in the Post Office two years later.[37] Bunn was himself replaced by Irv Sprague from California.[38] In addition to his specific regional responsibilities, Wilson supervised the entire House liaison system until he left to become president of the Chicago Board of Trade in 1967.[39] His successor was Harold Barefoot Sanders, a Texan lawyer, who had previously worked in the Justice Department's Civil Rights Division. After O'Brien finally left in the spring of 1968 to run Robert Kennedy's presidential campaign, Sanders took full charge of the OCR.[40]

The changes in the OCR's staff between 1963 and 1969 conceal a general decline in the quality of staff members in the last phase of Johnson's presidency, linked to a weakening of the OCR's own organisation and administrative practices stemming from the unsatisfactory compromise which Johnson insisted on to ensure that O'Brien continued to play an active part in Congressional liaison. There was no reasonable prospect that O'Brien would be able to devote the time and effort at the White House which the direction of Congressional relations for Lyndon Johnson required. Wilson was from 1965 to 1967 obliged to assume much of the responsibility without being accorded the formal authority by Johnson, or being placed on the appropriate pay-scale, both of which had damaging implications for the authority of the OCR within the White House Office and in its dealings with Congressmen and senators. (As noted above, Kennedy set O'Brien's pay just above that of the other senior White House staff in order to emphasise the primacy which the president placed upon Congressional relations within the White House, and O'Brien's importance as head of the OCR. In 1966, fully a year after O'Brien ceased to be full-time OCR head, Wilson earned $28,000 a year—the same as Manatos, and less than that of thirteen other White House staff members.[41])

Not only were the OCR's practices less ordered, its power diminished, and Wilson's position weaker, Congressional

[37] Interview with O'Brien.
[38] Interview with Irvine Sprague, 7/12/78.
[39] Interview with Wilson.
[40] Interview with Harold Barefoot Sanders, 24/4/79.
[41] Memo to Marvin Watson, 2/4/66, WHCF Gen FG 11-8-1 (27/5/65), Box 70, 'FG 11-8-1: 1/10/65-31/12/66'.

liaison had become more demanding. By the time Sanders arrived in May 1967, the Congressional balances were less favourable, the liberal edge had been blunted, and the president's advantage lost.[42] Great Society legislation faced more critical examination in a Congress increasingly pre-occupied with the politics of urban turmoil and an unpopular foreign war. Thus the shrinking of the OCR and its lack of a director (even after Sanders's arrival, O'Brien continued to involve himself in liaison, as the president required) hampered the efficiency of the White House's liaison work at a most inauspicious time. The problem was compounded by the poorer quality of OCR staff. Some, such as Chuck Roche and John Gonella, contributed little; the first was undisciplined, the second uninspired. Had Johnson not been so strongly averse to removing incompetent subordinates, neither would have been retained.

Roche was often a thorough hindrance. Having responsibility for liaison with northern urban Democrats, he drank regularly with groups of them, and invariably to excess. He was rarely seen on Capitol Hill; his preferred haunt was downtown, especially in Young's Bar. He was, as one senior White House colleague put it, 'worse than useless'.[43] Johnson had known of these difficulties from at least the spring of 1967 onwards when Wilson diplomatically asked for a White House car and driver to take Roche home in the evening: 'The nature of the members assigned to Chuck necessitates his spending evenings with them and I just do not think that he should be placed in a position of driving his own car back and forth under those circumstances.'[44]

By Roche's own admission, in March 1968 he had only one quarter of the work-load that he had had in 1965.[45] This was scarcely for want of work to do: his colleagues were desperately trying to persuade Congress to pass the tax surcharge but Roche and Gonella declined to adhere to

[42] In 1966, the balances were 68 : 32 in the Senate and 293 : 140 in the House. In 1967, they were 64 : 36 and 246 : 187 respectively.

[43] Confidential interview with a member of the Johnson White House staff.

[44] Wilson to Watson, 17/3/67, Ex FG 11-8-1, Box 110, 'Ex FG 11-8-1, Roche, Charles D., 18/1/66 . . .'.

[45] Roche to Johnson, 11/3/68, Ex FG 11-8-1, Box 110, 'Ex FG 11-8-1, Roche, Charles D., 18/1/66 . . .'.

agreed procedures. In the last phase of the administration, Sanders urged all OCR staff to submit a daily list of all their Congressional contacts to the president but, even after Johnson added his personal request that they do so, there was little response. Sprague was the only staff member to follow Sanders's instructions, providing the information necessary for the legislative programme and relations with Congress to be adroitly managed.[46]

By 1968, with a series of contentious measures facing strong opposition on Capitol Hill, Sanders resorted to inviting other White House staff to assist him temporarily. Bob Hardesty (a speech-writer), Harry McPherson, Larry Temple, de Vier Pierson, and others all contributed, in an attempt to compensate for deficiencies within the OCR.[47]

THE OCR AND THE DEPARTMENTAL LIAISON OFFICES

In the first days of the new 89th Congress, Johnson took the opportunity of a cabinet meeting to emphasise the importance of selecting only the best-qualified people for Congressional liaison work in the agencies, and insisted that the OCR was to be the main unit of direction and co-ordination:[48]

. . . I don't share any of the euphoria about the future. To get action on the program—and to obtain what the country needs and expects—all of us must work even more diligently than last year. I would remind you: (1) I want you to get the best legislative liaison you can; (2) I want you to devote overtime to the new members and your new committees; (3) and I want your people to work closely with each other through Larry O'Brien.

The legal restrictions placed on the lobbying activities of departments and agencies by Congress had little discernible effect upon departmental legislative liaison offices during the Kennedy and Johnson presidencies. In contrast to other periods, and despite the inclusion in appropriations acts of the continuing restrictions on lobbying by the executive, there were no Congressional charges that agencies violated federal

[46] Sanders, Oral History, Johnson Library, Tape no. 2, p. 34.
[47] See chapter eight.
[48] Cabinet Papers, Box 1, 'Cabinet Meeting, 11/1/65'.

law. (From 1949, and increasing in frequency thereafter, such clauses ostensibly prevented any such appropriated funds for the running of departments being used for publicity or propaganda purposes designed to influence the passage of legislation in Congress. Vague prohibitions on any Congressionally appropriated funds being used by a department or agency for the lobbying of Congress were first enacted in 1918, and are now contained in 18 USC 1913 [1970][49].) In fact, few OCR members gave a second thought to the constraints, as Henry Wilson impatiently observed: 'Hell, I never even read the damned bill! If I didn't break the law fifteen times a day, I felt I wasn't doing my duty!'[50]

White House OCR-departmental liaison offices relationships also developed freely. OCR staff instituted procedures designed to make agency liaison offices responsive to their demands and sensitive to their ordering of political priorities. Taking his cue from Johnson's early emphasis on the importance of agency liaison officials, O'Brien insisted that the OCR should have a dominant role in the hiring of liaison officers in departments and agencies. He recognised that most routine liaison work would fall on their shoulders since it was they who were most conversant with their own legislation and could devote to it the time it deserved.[51]

Departmental liaison officials were charged with the responsibility of shepherding their legislation through its detailed scrutiny by House and Senate committees. In so doing, they were accustomed to dealing with bureaucratic conflicts in the departments; this allowed White House Congressional staff to concentrate upon the broader strategies and tactics of liaison and lobbying and on matters of major import. With most legislation, there was no need to call on OCR staff for assistance. The White House none the less insisted that they be kept informed of legislative developments and difficulties, and required all agency liaison officials to submit weekly reports so that problems might be deflected.[52]

[49] Fisher, L., *White House-Congress Relationships: Information Exchange and Lobbying*, Washington, DC, 1978, pp. 51-2.
[50] Interview with Henry Wilson.
[51] O'Brien, L. F., *No Final Victories*, New York, 1974, p. 110; interview with O'Brien.
[52] Interview with Sanders.

These were due to be filed with Claude Desautels by 12 noon each Monday. With the full batch of reports available to him, Desautels prepared a summary for the president, drawing his attention to special difficulties on which his advice was needed. Desautels usually finished the report by the late afternoon, when he discussed it with O'Brien, before drawing items from it in the drafting of an agenda for the customary breakfast meeting with the Congressional Democratic leadership.[53]

These arrangements enabled OCR staff to use agency liaison officials to assist when necessary with floor action. Conversely, OCR members wishing to discuss a bill with a Congressman or senator took a departmental liaison official along to provide specialist advice. They were too busy to be thoroughly conversant with the details of the administration's entire high-priority legislative proposals and had no chance of quickly mastering less important bills for which departmental officials requested assistance, as they sometimes did.[54] After Claude Desautels left the White House in 1965, the procedures for dealing with these papers became less well ordered, although, with the aid of occasional reminders to agency heads, they were generally complied with, especially during Barefoot Sanders's tenure.

Despite Johnson's early and repeated pleas, liaison offices experienced a decline in the quality of their staff as his presidency aged. Some departmental officials were technically accomplished, politically shrewd, and responded readily to the White House's attempted orchestration of liaison across government. The Department of Housing and Urban Development, established in the latter phase of the administration, boasted an especially adept lobbying team, as Barefoot Sanders confirmed.[55] The staff at the Treasury were also competent, using the bridge of their common professional contacts with the tax-raising committees and committee staff to effect and, save in the last year, to the president's ends. Elsewhere, however, OCR staff had cause for concern. HEW liaison posed difficulties for them by charting their own, and not the

[53] Interview with Desautels.
[54] Interview with O'Brien.
[55] Interview with Sanders.

president's, course. As early as December 1964, the difficulties which O'Brien had had with them and liaison offices in certain other departments were sufficiently worrying to be brought to the president's attention. Accepting that the demands placed upon the agencies by the rapid generation of legislation were incessant, he committed to paper his reservations about the bureaucratic self-interest of much of the departments' work:[56]

I note you have already instructed the Cabinet to upgrade and strengthen Congressional Relations. It is woefully weak in the Departments and Agencies. . . there is still not a full realisation of the team effort required. To further encourage improvement in liaison activity in the Departments and Agencies, I would suggest automatic inclusion of legislative problems on the Agenda for all Cabinet meetings; and perhaps consideration of a Cabinet Member charged with the responsibility to coordinate relations with his fellow Cabinet Members and the Congress.

O'Brien's first suggestion for change was accepted. The second was not but the president's repeated insistence on the need for a unified approach to Congressional relations had an effect: liaison work in some departments improved in the middle phase of the administration. In one of the periodic meetings between the OCR and departmental liaison officials, chaired occasionally by the president or vice-president, Henry Wilson suggested that in his remarks to them Johnson should pay tribute to the high quality of their work.

Wilson's successor, Barefoot Sanders, met the departmental legislative liaison officers every Monday morning at 8.30 a.m. for 30–45 minutes. He normally chaired the meetings himself and discussed the legislative programme for the coming week, explaining the president's attitude to each bill.[57] Under Sanders's leadership, the OCR (prompted by the president) relied more heavily on certain departmental liaison offices than O'Brien had to do in the earlier years—the weaknesses in Sanders's own staff made reliance upon capable departmental

---

[56] O'Brien to Johnson, Ex FG 300/A, Box 321, 'FG 400: The Legislative Branch: 15/6/64–24/12/64'.

[57] Sanders to Johnson, 24/5/68, WHCF Ex LE/FI 11-4, 1/5/68, Box 54, 'LE/FI 11-4: 16/5/68–27/5/68'.

officials an attractive option.[58] But it also posed anew the old difficulty of ensuring that they marched to the beat of the White House drum and not to those of departments or agencies with political interests of their own. This proved a severe problem in 1968 when a skilled and politically strong Treasury were able to fend off OCR attempts to control them in the case of the income tax surcharge, a bill of the greatest political sensitivity in a split Democratic party.

NON-OCR WHITE HOUSE STAFF

Joseph Califano's establishment from 1965 as White House Chief of Staff in all but name allowed him to encroach upon legislative liaison questions—an enterprise made easier by O'Brien's appointment as Postmaster-General which left a partial vacuum at the OCR. Califano extended his responsibilities from the formulation of the legislative programme into a watching brief over Congressional matters and made some administrative changes. Procedures for dealing with Congressional mail were modified and, crucially, all papers prepared by White House staff members dealing with Congressional matters were copied to him. Califano also decreed that he should receive copies of all daily and weekly legislative reports prepared by Wilson and Manatos for the president's reading and assumed responsibility for all bill-signing ceremony recommendations, presidential statements accompanying the signing of bills, and veto messages.[59]

Ensuring that non-OCR White House staff complied with the pleas of OCR staff to be informed of all contacts between the White House and individual members was difficult. Throughout Johnson's presidency, OCR staff repeatedly reminded their White House colleagues that the OCR was the president's main channel of communication with Capitol Hill. If non-OCR staff were contacted by senators or representatives, then their specialist colleagues had to be told; if they were not, their assessments were the poorer for it. The

[58] Interview with Sanders.
[59] Califano and O'Brien to the White House staff, 23/7/66, Califano Files, WHCF 1764, 'Legislative Program 1966-67'.

paper from Califano and O'Brien in July 1966 cited above was reissued in identical form within nine months, an indication of how agreed procedures quickly dissolve under the unremitting pressure of work in the White House— especially one such as Johnson's where staff assignments were more fluid than in some other administrations and where, especially in the latter part of his presidency, the president cared little for sound administrative practice.

Organisational lapses were not solely to blame: on at least two occasions, Califano himself deliberately circumvented the OCR and bargained with senators alone. In June 1966, two weeks after agreeing with O'Brien and the president that Congressional contacts should be notified to Wilson or Manatos, Califano arrranged for the Model Cities Bill to be floor-managed by Senator Paul Douglas. In doing so, he damaged the bargaining strategies of the OCR staff. Further, Manatos discovered Califano's '*sub rosa* operation' only by accident, as he told O'Brien:[60] 'I registered a vigorous protest with Joe and Larry Levinson [Califano's deputy] that in my estimation they were leading the President to defeat and that they were acting for themselves and not for me. I also told these two eager-beavers that I believed I could speak for you.'[61]

In the course of the 90th Congress, Califano again caused OCR staff difficulties. Liaising with both Wisconsin senators on the financial crisis at the American Motors Company, Manatos discovered that Califano had once more outflanked the OCR by discussing the matter with Gaylord Nelson directly and by arranging for the Economic Development Administration, a bureau in the Department of Commerce, to help. Manatos sent a sharp minute to Califano, copying it to O'Brien and senior White House staff, setting out once again the proper procedure for the co-ordination of administration efforts:[62]

It is my understanding that all presidential assistants would make known to the Congressional Relations office all contacts with

[60] Manatos to O'Brien, 9/6/66, Manatos, Box 15 (1295), 'Douglas, Paul H. (D-Ill)'.
[61] Manatos to O'Brien, 9/6/66.
[62] Manatos to Califano, 6/2/67, Manatos, Box 14 (1295), 'Nelson, Gaylord (D-WI)'.

members of the Senate. Apparently some offices are not following
that procedure. I felt foolish to learn from Gaylord that he had
been talking to 'Joe Califano who arranged for someone from EDA
to go to Kenosha for an on-the-spot survey.' . . . a little bit of
inter-office cooperation would prevent such embarrassing situations.

Just as departmental legislative liaison officers were sometimes
invited to help, so non-OCR White House staff were often
asked to assist with lobbying on particular bills where their
skills or contacts were valuable, or the specialist White House
staff simply overworked. Usually, assignments of such staff to
members were made because of prior personal acquaintance,
shared ethnic background, interests, or politics. At Johnson's
own suggestion, lists were compiled early in 1965 of legislators
with whom individual staff members 'would become clearly
identified, thus providing backup for the Congressional
relations operation as the occasions arise'. The assignments
resulted in Marvin Watson being given a large group of
Texan Congressmen to keep in touch with.[63] Sometimes, too,
the staff were asked to help with general liaison initiatives.
At the beginning of the second session of the 89th Congress,
Johnson approved Wilson's suggestion that staff should
telephone Democratic House members, many of them ex-
hausted by the pace and scale of the legislative programme
in the first session as they arrived back in Washington for the
second. Wilson explained the idea to staff outside the OCR:[64]

Purpose of the conversations:
  1. To make members know we are thinking about them.
  2. To give them the chance to air griefs, and
  3. To acquire basic information about the mood of the districts,
     to be set forth by you in a report for the President's information.

There was nothing here by way of seeking a vote; persuasion
was not the point of the exercise. Wilson's concern in this
instance was to re-establish the foundations for a fruitful,
long-term, political relationship, a principle which equally
applied to the general liaison work of his OCR colleagues.

[63] O'Brien to senior White House staff, 2/4/65, Henry Wilson Files, Box 10,
'White House Staff'.
[64] Wilson to Douglass Cater, WHCF Gen FG 405, Box 332, 'FG 410 House of
Representatives: 22/11/63 17/3/66'.

LIAISON WITH THE CONGRESSIONAL LEADERSHIP

The OCR's links with the Congressional leadership were close. From the beginning of Kennedy's administration, it was well understood in the White House that the leadership's co-operation was essential if the president's programme was to have any chance of enactment. After the successful struggle of OCR staff to expand the membership of the House Rules Committee in January 1961, Speaker Sam Rayburn's relationship with O'Brien quickly matured. In the first weeks, O'Brien visited Rayburn regularly, but met him only in the outer office. As he gained the Speaker's trust, however, he began, 'to Sam's utter amazement. . . to be doing headcounts'.[65]

On Rayburn's death, McCormack succeeded to the office of Speaker, and used it as a pulpit from which to preach traditional liberal politics. Unlike Mansfield in the Senate, McCormack gladly made personal appeals to crosspressured colleagues on important votes.[66] The Speaker accepted both the idea and the practice of legislative leadership from a president of his own party, and strove to make congruent the political priorities of the presidential and Congressional parties. To that end, the scheduling needs of the OCR figured prominently in his calculations. At working lunches with committee chairmen, arranged with the knowledge and co-operation of senior OCR staff, he urged them to ensure that priority legislation was reported out of the committees quickly. Johnson appreciated McCormack's loyalty, while recognising his political and administrative weaknesses caused, in part, by his advanced age.[67]

In succeeding Lyndon Johnson as Senate Majority Leader, Mike Mansfield (whom Johnson had chosen as Majority Whip in 1957) had a most difficult task. The contrast between the two (and the politics of the times in which they served) could scarcely have been greater: Johnson led from the front as Majority Leader; Mansfield allowed a consensus to develop before adopting a public view. Johnson dominated the Senate

[65] Interview with O'Brien.
[66] Interview with Sanders.
[67] Sanders, Oral History, Tape no. 2, p. 13.

and made the office of floor leader more powerful than it had previously been; Mansfield retired to outer rooms.[68] Mansfield made some office space available to senior OCR staff from the beginning of Kennedy's presidency; it was he who proposed (unsuccessfully) that then Vice-President Johnson should preside over Senate Democratic caucuses.[69]

Mansfield was not a vigorous partisan on behalf of either Kennedy's or Johnson's policies. Whereas Johnson had accumulated power in the Majority Leader's office, Mansfield was content for it to disperse.[70] Johnson became frustrated as a result, and for collaborative support looked more to the Majority Whip Hubert Humphrey than he might otherwise have done.[71] But the OCR exerted some indirect influence over Mansfield through Manatos's friendly relationship with Stanley Kimmit, Secretary of the Majority, and hence a senior adviser to the Majority Leader. Manatos spent much of his working day in and around Mansfield's office. A natural focal point for Democratic senators, he was among his legislative charges there rather than removed from them; he was also freer to see Mansfield when he needed to, and to work with his staff. The arrangement was not without its difficulties: some senators resented what they interpreted as conspicuous executive intrusion into Congressional affairs. (Aware of senatorial propriety, Manatos was careful not to be seen near the Senate floor during roll-calls.)

Kimmit and Manatos worked closely together on a range of matters—especially in the perennial attempts to ensure the efficient scheduling and reporting of bills so as to permit an early adjournment *sine die* to act on the legislation before their committees—this was particularly true with appropriation bills, where delays in the Senate were common.[72]

Johnson had a closer political relationship with Everett Dirksen, the Republican Senate leader, than with Mansfield, his party colleague. Dirksen's vote and leadership were essential to the success of the cloture vote on the 1964 Civil Rights Act, as was his support for the 1968 Civil Rights Act

[68] Peabody, R., *Leadership in Congress*, Boston, 1976, p. 340.
[69] Evans and Novak, *Lyndon B. Johnson*, p. 326.
[70] Interview with McPherson, Apr. 1981.
[71] Interview with W. Welsh.
[72] Confidential interview with a senior Senate staff member.

with its open-housing title. Johnson cultivated Dirksen assiduously throughout his presidency, a wooing assisted by his OCR lieutenants; much business was done in personal discussion over drinks—a forum in which Johnson excelled. Senior OCR staff properly regarded Dirksen as a key figure, and either they or the president himself consulted him prior to legislative proposals being submitted to Congress in order to gain his support. To do so was, as one member of the OCR explained, a matter of recognising Dirksen's importance: 'In the Senate, you just deal with the powers that be— Dirksen'.[73]

On one occasion, after Dirksen had originally promised a 'Yes' vote to Manatos, Mansfield warned the OCR that his opponent's resolve was weakening. Indeed, he finally voted 'No', although the White House won the roll-call. Dirksen explained to Manatos that political pressures had obliged him to change his mind and vote against the president. His change of heart was not intended to to defeat the measure (for he knew that it would pass) but to protect himself from criticism by Republican colleagues more conservative than he.[74]

This exchange was not untypical of the relationship between Dirksen and Johnson's OCR staff. Its strength was an important factor in the president's favour—and especially so on civil rights legislation where Dirksen had more freedom of manœuvre with his Republican colleagues than on other Great Society matters. It had no parallel in the House. For four years, O'Brien tried to encourage the Republican leader, Charlie Halleck, and win his confidence, but the effort came to nothing, as O'Brien observed: 'When we have on the record meetings, it's all on top of the table. [But] I can't really get confidential [with the Minority Leadership] and open the books, or it will be in the press and out in the party [Congressional Republican] immediately.'[75]

In the case of the Democratic Congressional leadership, informal relations rested on the foundation provided by the regular weekly meetings. They met at the White House with the president and senior OCR staff for a working breakfast

---

[73] Interview with Wilson.
[74] Interview with Manatos.
[75] Interview with Desautels.

on most Tuesdays when Congress was in session. As discussed above, this meeting was the major organisational event of the OCR's working week, a fixed point towards which the Office's administrative procedures were directed. Drawing on its occasional use during the Kennedy presidency, Johnson indulged his fondness of gadgets, and assisted his guests' concentration, by the use of detailed charts showing the stage reached by each bill on his priority list.[76] The meeting was carefully prepared with a briefing from O'Brien for Johnson drawing on the agenda and papers prepared by Desautels which Johnson had digested as part of his bedtime reading. With all the papers available to them, the president then discussed with O'Brien what he wanted from the meeting and how to get it:[77]

I would go up to the president's living quarters as he was about to get up, and review the agenda for the meeting at 8.30 a.m. The meeting was a free exchange of view—I interjected quite often, when I could make a contribution. I wouldn't expect the president to have as much knowledge on headcounts, for instance, as I had.

During his period in the White House, Wilson wrote a further background paper, finalised immediately before the meeting was due to begin, to acquaint the president with last-minute information and assessments. Johnson had an understanding with Wilson that he would not quote any material from the background paper: 'Without this arrangement I wouldn't have felt free to tell him what I thought. President Johnson a couple of times forgot this stricture and feathers were unnecessarily ruffled. . .'[78]

Discussion concentrated on the status of 'priority' legislation, and on obstacles to its being reported out of committee. Towards the end of a Congressional session, the setting of priorities for reporting bills from committee and their scheduling for floor discussion became difficult—hence the importance which the president and his OCR staff attached to chairmen dealing promptly with 'priority' legislation in their committees.

[76] Interview with O'Brien.
[77] Interview with O'Brien.
[78] Wilson, 'How It Worked', p. 41.

The main items on the agenda having been disposed of, a discussion followed on an agreed line that the Congressional guests should adopt with the reporters awaiting them at the main door of the White House's west wing. Johnson's staff took great care with this, remembering well the difficulties which similar briefings had caused President Kennedy when journalists inferred much from differences in tone between the views of the president and those of the leadership. As O'Brien acknowledged in a submission to Johnson in 1964, the arrangements made for it had during Kennedy's presidency been inadequate, 'the weakest aspect of these weekly affairs'.[79] The informal conference was important: comments made and answers given there were carefully scrutinised by Congressional colleagues, their staff, and bureaucrats. They also provided a welcome opportunity for the leadership to advertise their access to the president, and the importance of their involvement in national affairs to a public increasingly fed on a diet of television news which focused upon the Oval Office.[80]

CONGRESSIONAL COMMITTEE POLITICS
AND ASSIGNMENTS

Committee chairmen sometimes found themselves in need of the assistance of the president's staff to prompt an important committee vote. Senators and Congressmen lacked the White House's presidential resources to persuade the uncommitted to attend a committee meeting—this often consisted simply of impressing upon loyal, but busily distracted, Democratic members the importance of a bill. In September 1966, for example, Senator Lister Hill (D-AL) who, as chairman of the Senate Labor Committee, was closely involved with the OCR's planning on many Great Society bills, asked Manatos to effect committee action on the Vocational Rehabilitation Bill. Manatos responded by contacting the Democrats, asking them to assist their chairman in quickly reporting a bill as close as possible to the version Johnson and Hill preferred. He felt sufficiently confident to approach two senior members

---

[79] O'Brien to Johnson, 2/12/64.
[80] Wilson, 'How it Worked', p. 42.

of the committee's staff, requesting them to 'give me a hand in getting Senator Hill to announce an executive session of his Subcommittee and of the full Labor Committee'.[81] His intervention was successful: both the subcommittee and the full committee soon met, and the bill was reported out just ten days later.

OCR colleagues were obliged to keep in close touch with important opponents as well as allies. Chairman of Ways and Means, and so of the Democratic Committee on Committees as well, Wilbur Mills was unsympathetic to Lyndon Johnson's programme of domestic reform and what he judged to be its damaging fiscal implications. He was perhaps the single most powerful Congressman of the decade: his co-operation was vital for the enactment of the president's economic policies.[82] Power-brokers in Congress—in Johnson's phrase, the Congressional 'whales'—commanded attention whether they were implacably opposed to Johnson's legislative programme or, as in the cases of Mills and Dirksen, willing to bargain and negotiate, and adjust to prevailing political winds.

CONGRESSIONAL COMMITTEE ASSIGNMENTS

The power of committees in the pre-reform Congress encouraged OCR staff to influence their composition when the opportunity arose. Traditionally thought the exclusive prerogative of Congress, the allocation of newly elected members of Congress to committees, and the modification of party ratios on them, were matters in which both Kennedy's and Johnson's Congressional relations staff involved themselves—as did their predecessors and successors. The reasoning was quite straightforward: the composition of committees could determine the chances of enactment of the president's programme; it was therefore desirable to place supporters rather than opponents on them. The process was none the less risky. In a system of separated powers, Congressional prerogatives were jealously guarded and attempts by the

[81] Manatos to O'Brien, 20/9/65, Ex LE 5, Box 169, 'LE 5, Box 169, LE 5: 7/5/65–17/1/66'.

[82] O'Brien to Wilson, 27/5/65, O'Brien, Box 17, 'Mills, Rep. Wilbur, D. (D)'.

executive to interfere in its internal procedures were, if discovered, certain to arouse the wrath of political opponents, and might well be resented by allies: indeed, a prime justification of the seniority system was that it ensured Congressmen's immunity from presidential pressure.[83] Senators were especially jealous of their chamber's prerogatives and dignity. Reflecting their views, Mansfield guarded the chamber from executive presssure and White House aides had few opportunities to influence committee assignments there. The death of Estes Kefauver allowed Manatos to tell Mansfield of Kennedy's preferred successor on the Appropriations Committee, but White House pressure was normally confined to the House of Representatives.

O'Brien speculated in 1963 that the presence of Gerald Ford and Silvio Conte—two internationalist Republicans— on the Foreign Operations Subcommittee of the House Appropriations Committee reflected the interest which Eisenhower had taken in the fate of his foreign aid bills.[84] In the previous year, after the mid-term elections had given the Republicans only small gains in the House, Wilson took a close and effective interest in discussing with the leadership committee appointments which would give Kennedy the greatest possible advantage:[85]

. . . I would say that cooperation from the Leadership was about total. I can't think of a single appointment made in the House at the onset of the 88th I would have made differently. For example, they ran completely roughshod over Cannon on the Appropriations appointments. Furthermore, word was all over the Hill that appointments had to clear with us, and I was totally involved.

OCR interest in committee appointments assumed a more important character after the landslide Democratic victories in the 1964 elections. O'Brien and Wilson were intensely interested in exploiting the political advantage from the new (and certainly temporary) Congressional party balance. Wilson urged upon O'Brien the need to reduce southern

[83] Hinckley, B., *The Seniority System in Congress*, Bloomington, Ind., 1971.

[84] O'Brien to Johnson, 10/12/63, Wilson, Box 18, 'Wilson (1963–1964 Congressional File) F.'

[85] Wilson to O'Brien, 10/1/64, Wilson, Box 5 'Presidential'; Fenno, R. F., *The Power of the Purse*, Boston, 1966, p. 53.

conservative power on important committees; it was, he argued, essential to impress upon the House leadership the need to keep southerners out of Democratic vacancies on such committees as Ways and Means—a task made easier by the party's increased majority in the House having come from northern liberals.[86] Wilson provided a detailed analysis of individuals' claims to seats on committees by region and state, doing so purely with the administration's parliamentary advantage in mind. His efforts were supported in late December 1964 by a long paper from William Gibbons, Deputy Director of the Congressional Liaison Service in the Agency for International Development (AID), in which he assessed the several possible permutations of assignments to the Foreign Affairs and Appropriations Committees. Gibbons naturally paid close attention to the Foreign Operations Subcommittee of the Appropriations Committee where he was anxious to see an acceptable candidate receive a place in the event of the party ratio on the subcommittee being altered in the light of the Democrats' increased majority.[87]

As senior chairmen occasionally asked the OCR for assistance in ensuring support for legislation before their committees, so their freshmen colleagues asked the White House to lend their support to their requests for particular committee assignments. After the 1964 elections, for example, John Conyers, a Michigan freshman Democrat, asked Chuck Daly to do what he could to back his claim for a place on the Judiciary Committee. Daly asked Henry Wilson to help and to see if William Ford, a colleague from the Michigan delegation, could be given membership of the Education and Labor Committee in order to make way for Conyers. Wilson succeeded in doing both.[88]

Such OCR discussions with the Congressional leadership were reasonably successful at this period; the White House's preferred candidates were even elected to Ways and Means, membership of which was determined at the time by the Democratic caucus. Mills, far too shrewd to engage in disputes

---

[86] Wilson to O'Brien, 7/12/64, WHCF FG 411 House Committees, Box 333, 'FG 411 House Committees'.

[87] Gibbons to the Administrator of AID, Dec. 1964, Wilson, Box 7, 'Committee Assignments'.

[88] *Congressional Quarterly Almanac, 1965*, pp. 51 and 55.

from which he could not gain, did not demur. OCR staff also successfully persuaded the Speaker to alter party ratios on House committees to approximately 2 : 1 as a reflection of the overall party balance of 295 : 140. Senate committees changed to the same ratio, except for Finance where the Majority Leader was defeated by the chairman, Senator Long (D-LA), who, as the new Majority Whip, was determined to assert his authority over the committee and enhance his reputation in the Senate by resisting interference from without.[89]

The OCR was also instrumental in brokering an agreement with Speaker McCormack and Wilbur Mills on appropriate disciplinary action against two southern Democrats, John Bell Williams (D-MS) and Albert Watson (D-SC), who had supported Barry Goldwater for president in 1964. Despite heavy pressure on the Democratic leadership to expel them from the party, O'Brien, McCormack, and Mills agreed instead that both men should lose all seniority on their committees—seemingly a less drastic move, it had much the same effect in Congress. O'Brien told his White House colleagues on New Year's Eve 1964 that this solution was to be preferred, for it left the next move up to Williams and Watson: 'it is probably the best possibility available to us. Both Mills and McCormack re-emphasised their disturbance with these two members and felt that they would be faring well with this amount of punishment. Also, it is apparent that if something along this line isn't worked out, the consensus would be to purge them.'[90]

On 2 January, the Democratic caucus followed their lead and stripped Watson and Williams of their seniority. Williams remained within the Democratic fold (and eventually became Governor of Mississippi) but Watson left within days, joining the Republican Party on 12 January. He resigned from the House on 1 February in order to run as a Republican candidate in a summer special election, and was returned by a large majority as the first Republican representative from South Carolina since reconstruction.[91]

[89] *Congressional Quarterly Almanac, 1965*, p. 26.

[90] Note of a telephone call from O'Brien to Johnson, 31/12/64, WHCF FG 411 House Committees, Box 333, 'FG 411 House Committees'.

[91] *Congressional Quarterly Almanac, 1965*, p. 27.

The extraordinary results of the 1964 elections enabled the White House to exert unusual pressure on the leadership. But much presidential political capital was spent in the following two years, and the heavy mid-term losses of 1966 presented Johnson and his advisers with quite different problems. The Democratic advantage on the committees was diminished. Greatly concerned, Henry Wilson submitted a long paper to the president in January 1967, describing the difficulties he had with the House Appropriations Committee. Its chairman, George Mahon (D-TX), had exclusive authority over subcommittee chairmanships, appointments to subcommittees, and party ratios on them and would not discuss the subject, especially with OCR staff. Wilson told the president that McCormack was unwilling to take a stand against such a powerful colleague: 'The Speaker quite definitely does not feel that he has the authority to make suggestions to Mahon. I have discussed this in some depth with the Speaker and though he is eager to be cooperative, I am convinced that we must discard him as an effective instrument.'[92]

Johnson talked privately to Mahon, a fellow Texan, and with success. The one new Democrat placed on the Committee was the freshman David Pryor (D-AK), whom Wilson approved of—despite his having been enthusiastically sponsored by Wilbur Mills. The composition of the Foreign Aid Subcommittee, which had particularly concerned the White House, was also resolved in their favour. John J. McFall (D-CA), one of Wilson's preferred candidates, was appointed.[93]

HEAD-COUNTING

Assessing the strength of Congressional support was therefore a crucially important part of the work of Johnson's liaison staff, especially because they were unable to rely upon the accuracy of the counts provided by the Majority Whip, Hale Boggs (D-LA). When Sanders came to the White House in 1967 to direct liaison, Johnson advised him to be wary of

[92] Wilson to Johnson, 13/1/67, WHCF FG 411 House Committees, Box 333, 'FG 411 House Committees'.

[93] *Congressional Quarterly Almanac, 1967*, pp. 50–8.

Boggs's estimates of support. Sanders found it 'damned good advice'.[94] The Senate leadership were reluctant to share their own whip counts with the OCR. Occasionally, Mansfield's senior staff indicated to O'Brien and Manatos possible weaknesses in the OCR's assessments, but they were disinclined to collaborate as a matter of course.

As in other aspects of the OCR's activities, Johnson closely supervised the process of head-counting. His experience in assessing intention, motive, and the strength of individual pledges had been finely honed during his Senate leadership. It was a precondition for successful legislative leadership, as he reminded Hubert Humphrey, a more optimistic judge of political friend and foe alike: 'The most important thing around here is to know how to count. If you don't know how to count, you can't be a leader.'[95]

This ability was not shared by all liaison staff, either in the agencies or, especially in the latter days, in the OCR itself. Some departmental officials provided poorly substantiated vote counts to their OCR superiors; for the inexperienced and the hard pressed, it was tempting to accept casual indications of support as pledges. Similarly, Congressmen or senators who wished to end enquiries from the president's Congressional envoys often told them that their minds were set; early shows of apparent support might convince the more gullible lobbyists. Henry Wilson, aware of the problem, frequently cross-checked agency officials' reports, both to verify the reports themselves, and to establish the reliability of individual lobbyists' political judgements.

Johnson's emphasis upon the importance of selecting departmental liaison staff of high ability had special significance here. Inaccuracies in vote counts were damaging if undiscovered, and time-consuming if revealed only through checks made by senior OCR staff. When success or failure turned on slim majorities, small errors assumed potentially decisive importance. Wilson occasionally vented his frustration with careless reports from agency lobbyists by complaining to O'Brien, as he did after receiving an unhelpful assessment by colleagues in the Department of Commerce about an

[94] Sanders, Oral History, Tape no. 3, p. 12.
[95] Humphrey, Oral History, Tape no. 2, p. 28.

Accelerated Public Works appropriations bill in the 88th Congress:[96]

. . . [John Barriere] started going down the list about how somebody's assistant had said something to such and such a field man, etc. I asked him if he was certain we had not dropped votes we had before. He said he had not checked them but he was confident they would all stick. I told him the question was what votes Patman, Blatnick and Rains were willing, personally, to assure to the president.

Frank Dooley (another Commerce Department lobbyist) talked to me and to Walter Jenkins yesterday . . . He hasn't talked to anyone either—except Barriere. He's using the same count. I am sure you will agree it does not look too trustworthy.

Sanders, too, checked the reliability of estimates from departmental offices. When satisfied, he concentrated on the remaining 'undecided' members. On most Great Society and civil rights legislation, such 'undecideds' tended to come from similar areas: the border Democrats, moderate southerners (although they were usually much less dependable on civil rights), and liberal Republicans. The Texas delegation was accorded special attention. Strikingly diverse, it included liberals, populists, and conservatives; many often opposed the White House on important matters. Some were naturally susceptible to appeals from a Texan president who, anxious to secure as much support as possible from his home state, showed special interest in them. Furthermore, the many Texans on his staff had sound personal contacts with the delegation which were exploited by the assignment of non-OCR staff (some, such as Marvin Watson, themselves conservative) to keep in touch with them, and to lobby actively when their OCR colleagues thought it helpful.

Careful attention had to be paid to ensure that known and probable supporters would attend and vote with the administration. By contrast, those inclined to oppose the president's position were encouraged to stay away—in OCR parlance, to 'take a walk' on the day of the vote—finding a plausible reason to be out of Washington. Members were able to announce their position afterwards, at little cost to

[96] Wilson to O'Brien, 9/9/64, Manatos, Box 1 (967), 'Manatos: Legislation 1964—General Information: Mr O'Brien'.

themselves and to the White House's advantage. Alternatively, as often happened, the OCR agreed to call for a member's support only if it was absolutely needed. If it was not, the Congressman or senator could safely oppose it, pleasing supporters important to him without injuring the legislation's prospects. In any event, Johnson was always anxious to know of the marginal members' changing views and calculations, and so scrutinised headcounts from his staff, frequently offering observations (as vulgar as they were perceptive) on the fickleness of former colleagues.

For the OCR, there were two essential rules for head-counting which applied more generally to the OCR's liaison with Congress: firstly, that opposition was to be expected and even welcomed, and secondly, that the White House could not expect members to support measures which might harm them politically. There was nothing to be gained by bringing about the defeat of moderate Democrats through requiring too much of them. In any case, strength of opposition was often welcome: weak opposition might indicate that the the bill was insufficiently ambitious, as an OCR staff member noted:[97]

In the context of Washington politics, there are 535 elected fellows on the Hill, and 1 in the Oval Office—they deserve respect . . . and in the final analysis, you've got to have the member weigh his political position. It's just not a good idea to tell people to jump out the window on behalf of your bill.

And don't get bitter about the opposition. If you don't have the hot breath of the opposition on your neck when you're working to get a bill passed, there's something wrong with the system.

[97] Interview with O'Brien.

4

PROJECTS AND PATRONAGE

Congressional liaison in the Johnson presidency was a subtle and complicated political process. Popular wisdom has it that Lyndon Johnson personally exerted unremitting pressure on senators and Congressmen to conform to his political will. Yet most lobbying of Congress typically consisted neither in impassioned presidential appeals, nor in the exchange of federal largess for votes. Johnson did sometimes personally seek the support of members of Congress, but he was usually at one remove from bargaining and lobbying. When they judged it appropriate, OCR staff offered favours for a vote, but such simple exchanges were not typical. Most importantly, lobbying formed only a relatively small proportion of the OCR's activities; the less direct processes of routine liaison formed the core of its work.

These rested on the White House's determination to bridge the gap between the executive and legislative branches. Presidential government was impossible without the active support of powerful legislators, many of them politically independent of the president. Working in a system of government based on adversarial politics, where executive and legislative interests differed, Johnson's liaison staff were charged with the task of promoting this co-operation, of engaging Congressmen and senators in the president's political purposes, of making the president's interests and those of Congressmen and senators congruent. They had the task of making the political price of co-operation less than that of opposition—hence the need to bolster natural supporters, to court potential allies, and to woo the unconvinced.

Just as the OCR required Congressional co-operation for its legislative strategies and tactics to succeed, so it recognised that Congressmen and senators needed them, too. Pennsylvania

Avenue is, as successive generations of hard-pressed Congressmen have sometimes had to remind forgetful presidents, a two-way street. The White House sought the political co-operation of legislators, who in varying degrees were concerned with their re-election, political advancement, and power. OCR staff could do much to help. Constituents' problems could be addressed by requiring action from agencies and departments. At one level, the Social Security Administration was often requested to make an overdue payment; at another, agencies were occasionally instructed to fund the construction of new federal buildings or facilities. Patronage, awards of federal projects, and the placing of contracts, the postponement of the closing of a military base until after an election, and small but politically significant favours and benefits, were all employed to foster the mature relationships between the OCR and members of Congress which lay at the heart of liaison and were the prerequisite of successful lobbying. Congress itself had greater power than the executive to affect projects—but modern presidents have to use such power as they have to maximise their leverage. This chapter examines the major levers of presidential influence, federal projects, and patronage, and assesses their contribution to the president's objectives.

THE ROLE OF PARTY

Considerations of party figured prominently in OCR calculations. Democrats were invariably favoured for the award of federal projects, contracts, and patronage, and benefited more than the Republicans from small presidential favours. In short, staff used the executive branch's resources to reward Democrats for their support in the past, to encourage them for the future, and to improve their political prospects. OCR members knew that on most welfare legislation, the administration's view would be opposed by most Republicans in both chambers. Although they welcomed liberal and moderate Republican support, it was difficult to recognise it with favours for fear of angering Democrats.[1] No election help could be given to Republicans.[2] Johnson could not even tacitly support a friendly liberal Republican against a hostile conservative Democratic challenger; at most, he could withhold public support.

In the last phase of Johnson's presidency, Barefoot Sanders and John Gonella realised that their failure to cultivate a systematic political relationship with liberal Republicans, especially those in the House, made winning their support difficult. An OCR directive required Democrats to be given priority on telephone calls announcing the award of federal contracts and projects irrespective of the extent of the member's record of voting support for, or opposition to, the president. 'Some flexibility in our policy is definitely required', Gonella told Sanders in 1968.[3] Sanders agreed, but it was too late in the presidency to make profitable alterations in procedure. As OCR head, Sanders had followed O'Brien's strategy of working hard to 'chip away at the southern Democrats to bring them over to the administration's side'.[4] Any Republican support was considered a useful bonus and not counted upon. Earlier in the administration, there was no great need to seek Republican support—especially during the 89th Congress when overwhelming Democratic strength based on a sizeable liberal bloc gave the president ideological majorities. Later, however, when Republican support was often essential, surprisingly little was done to encourage it.

Russell Renka has examined O'Brien's southern Democratic strategy and shown how sharply it contrasts with this neglect of the Republicans.[5] O'Brien's approach distinguished between those southerners from 'TVA-type districts' and those from the 'black belt'. The former, including Phil Landrum, (D-GA)

---

[1] In the first six months of the 90th Congress, for instance, eleven Republicans voted with the administration four or more times on nine selected key votes which the OCR regarded as particularly important (Sprague to Sanders, 6/9/67, Sprague, Box 7 (1568), 'Sanders, Barefoot: Memos For').

[2] However, the rumour persists that Johnson intervened to ensure that a weak Democratic candidate was put up against Dirksen in Illinois in 1968.

[3] Gonella to Sanders, 20/1/68, WHCF FG 400 Box 326, 'FG 400: 1/1/68–31/1/68'.

[4] Interview with L. F. O'Brien, 24/11/78.

[5] 'Legislative Leadership and Marginal Vote-gaining Strategies in the Kennedy and Johnson Presidencies', a paper delivered to the South-Western Political Science Association, Houston, 12–15 Apr. 1978.

and Fats Everett (D-TN), supported some Great Society measures; the latter, such as William Colmer (D-MS) and George Andrews (D-FL), were as strongly opposed to these as to civil rights. Intransigent southerners were protected from presidential pressure and the OCR's inducements by the peculiarities of southern party politics, as Henry Wilson reminded President Kennedy in 1962:[6]

. . . we must bear in mind that the members from these states, with very few exceptions:

1. Can look for little or no help in their districts either financially or organisationally either to organised labor or to the party structure;
2. Must encounter their critical tests not in the general election, but in the primaries, where they get no help from having the President at the head of the ticket;
3. Have established through the years entrenched habits of voting with the Republicans;
4. Must look for their financial and community support to local business leaders who are totally responsive to the national pressure groups which oppose all our programs, and
5. Can gain little from us but a kind smile and a pat on the head.

'Smiles and pats' offered little attraction to Congressmen, or to senators, whose political survival depended upon their adhering closely to the conservative politics and mores of their districts or states; association with a reforming president was usually unwelcome to them.

Loyal supporters of Johnson's programmes, nearly all of them northern Democrats, were usually asked for their vote on particular measures. Even though they formed the president's natural constituency, their support was normally sought rather than assumed. As well as those OCR staff specifically assigned to northern members, the Democratic Study Group (DSG) were employed as intermediaries. During the summer and autumn of 1966, Wilson held weekly meetings with the DSG to discuss priorities for the administration's legislation in the remainder of the session. The DSG's whip system and small staff were useful to the White House, while

[6] Wilson to O'Brien, 18/7/62, President's Office Files: Staff Memoranda, 'O'Brien, Lawrence F.: 2/61 8/62' (John F. Kennedy Library).

liaison between the OCR and the full DSG membership helped quieten occasional rumblings of discontent from loyal liberal Democrats who felt that they were too often taken for granted by a demanding president.[7] Some members of the group believed that their their loyalty to the president's domestic policies caused them to be rewarded less generously than those who could not be depended upon and could therefore drive a harder bargain.

OCR LIAISON WITH INDIVIDUAL MEMBERS

(i) *Laying the foundations*

OCR staff tried always to attend personally to any political problem which Democratic supporters of the administration had. Theirs was the responsibility for appreciating the political importance of the matter for a Congressman or senator, however trivial it may have appeared to bureaucrats then, or scholars later. In the spring of 1964, for example, Fats Everett, a member of the House Public Works Committee, wanted a game warden, who had angered some of Everett's constituents by his actions, moved from his post. The warden was employed by the Fish and Wildlife Service, an agency of the Department of the Interior, for whom the matter was the most minor of matters, inviting routine acknowledgement and inaction. The Congressman, however, was cross and, determined not to be rebuffed, sought Henry Wilson's assistance. Wilson duly sent a crisp note to Oren Beaty, an Assistant to the Secretary of the Interior:[8]

If you have a spare hour sometime, I will be glad to illustrate graphically the indispensability of Everett to this Administration in the Congress. In return, his requests of us have been extremely moderate. And during the three and a half years I have been here he has not earlier become sufficiently worked up over anything like this to make a trip to my office to discuss it. . . The message is that when Fats Everett and a game warden come to grips in an issue like this, the game warden has got to give.

---

[7] Wilson, H. H., 'How it Worked when it Worked', unpublished manuscript, 1979, p. 42.
[8] Wilson to Oren Beaty, 2/5/64, Wilson, Box 18, 'Congressional File: E'.

I want to stress that this is something for you to handle personally and not buck to the Fish and Wildlife Service. Also, you'd better make the Secretary aware of the situation because I have assured Everett I will bring it to his attention.

Wilson's insistence that a loyal Democrat be helped with such a difficulty rested on the authority which he and his White House OCR colleagues had over the departmental liaison offices. In this instance, Beaty dealt with the matter satisfactorily, for which Wilson was careful to thank him: 'the motion you're showing on the game warden matter is the most useful item that has happened for us on the Hill lately. I know this sort of thing ties you people in knots, but it certainly helps to pass legislation.'[9]

Everett was appreciative of the OCR's intervention, too, as Wilson told O'Brien: 'Fats has expressed his appreciation so often and so effusively, it's getting right embarrassing.'[10]

This subject was a peculiar one. But Wilson's appreciation of its importance to the Congressman was exemplary, his political judgement correct. It also emphasised the OCR's authority over a department, and benefited the president in two respects: the specific difficulty was solved to the political advantage of the Congressman in his home district, and relations between White House Congressional specialists and an important Democratic Congressman, already friendly, were strengthened. This could only improve the OCR's prospects for persuading Everett to help the administration on a future bill where he might otherwise not have done so. The terms of trade did not have to be explicit to be understood. 'Washington is not', as a member of Kennedy's Congressional liaison staff once remarked, 'a city where you have to ask people to return favours.'[11]

Some senior Congressmen lacked Everett's discrimination in asking for help and his appreciation of it. Adam Clayton Powell (D-NY), whose inconstant loyalty to the Democratic Party was shown in his support of Eisenhower in the 1956 presidential election, had a rougher understanding of the exchange relationship between party colleagues in Congress

[9] Wilson to Beaty, 1/6/64, Wilson, Box 18, 'Congressional File: E'.
[10] Wilson to O'Brien, 1/6/64, Wilson, Box 18, 'Congressional File: E'.
[11] Interview with M. Manatos, 21/11/78.

and the White House. Chairman of the House Committee on Education and Labor, Powell had great power over many Great Society bills; White House staff were consequently obliged to bend rules, and accede to his many requests. These were occasionally bizarre, and often outrageous. As Desautels told O'Brien in March 1965, Powell abused the influence which his chairmanship gave him, and readily withheld committee action on bills if 'information he seeks is not made available to him'.[12]

Charles Daly had primary responsibility for dealing with Powell in the first years of Johnson's presidency. On one occasion in 1964, Daly prudently sought the assistance of senior colleagues Mike Feldman and Jack Valenti with the several matters which Powell had recently raised:[13]

. . . there are some problems I have had trouble handling. . . :

   1. Helping with his libel problems.

   2. Settling his income tax case.

   3. Obtaining McMurray's approval for Park Central Savings & Loan Association of Maryland. McMurray says this would be criminal; Powell says McMurray is prejudiced. . .

Powell's determination to use his political positon to extract presidential approval for what Desautels once termed his 'odious projects' in a straightforward exchange for committee action on administration bills was quite exceptional, as was his attempt to have presidential influence used for personal (and sometimes unlawful) ends.[14] The White House sought long-term relationships of greater subtlety than that which Powell demanded. Equally, Johnson required that the status and political dignity of the 535 legislators on Capitol Hill be fully recognised in the staff's dealings with them and insisted that there was no room in his administration for anyone who was other than properly respectful towards elected legislators.

[12] Desautels to O'Brien, O'Brien, Box 30 (1534), 'Powell, Adam Clayton (D-NY)'.

[13] Daly to Feldman and Valenti, 11/5/64, O'Brien, Box 30 (1534), 'Powell, Adam Clayton (D-NY)'; Joseph McMurray was chairman of the Federal Home Loan Bank Board. The Board chartered and supervised federal savings and loan associations (akin to building societies).
[14] Desautels to O'Brien, 31/1/64, O'Brien, Box 30 (1534), 'Powell, Adam Clayton,(D-NY)'.

Only if the preconditions of respect, helpfulness, and accommodation were satisfied could the White House expect it in return and the OCR's supplementary efforts ease the path of contentious legislation.[15] Larry O'Brien reflected on this approach—the blending of respect with prudent consideration—so that presidential influence might be more tellingly exercised through the agency of this small specialist group of staff:[16]

If a member of congress has extended himself for you, you keep that door open for him. We could give help at election times, for instance, by scheduling a cabinet secretary to speak for a congressman or senator. . . You don't go up to a member when a vote is coming up and say 'Hello, congressman, we haven't met in three months, but we've got a problem on a bill now'. You keep in touch with him. . . It's tough, because you've got a lot of bodies up there. But it's important to a congressman or a senator to be able to say 'I know I can pick up that phone, and I know I'll get a response'. . . . In a tough headcount, the important marginal difference is made, 9 out of 10 times, by the element of human relations.

(*ii*) *Patronage*

OCR staff were able to influence federal appointments in several areas. In the early months of an administration, there were senior political appointments to be made in departments and agencies—the 'Schedule C' jobs. For the rest of the administration, replacements for those 'Schedule C' officials who left, together with judicial nominations from federal district level to the Supreme Court, came within the president's purview. OCR members were similarly able to influence such appointments as regional postmasters and regional political appointments in federal departments.

All this was well understood on the Hill. With the arrival of a new Democratic administration in the White House in 1961, Congressional Democrats expected President Kennedy to respond favourably to requests for the initial round of political appointments—expectations which were reinforced when the president named Larry O'Brien his 'Special Assistant for Congressional Relations and Personnel', deliberately

[15] Interviews with O'Brien and Manatos.
[16] Interview with O'Brien.

combining the functions of patronage chief and Congressional liaison director.[17] O'Brien recalled that he and his staff had supposed (as his title invited legislators to do) that on coming into office their hard-headed use of patronage would enable them to control the bureaucracy and put Congressmen and senators in debt to the new president:[18]

We came in with the idea of stamping the president's authority over the whole executive branch, but quickly learned that it's just an impossibility. . . recommendations for jobs became a total bore as time went on. I suppose we had three to five hundred 'Schedule C' jobs to fill—believe me, if you can produce quality people for those sorts of jobs, it's as far as you can get.

This initial patronage round, the obligatory appointments of senior political posts in government, won the president little credit. It was perfectly well understood that an incoming administration of a new party would have to choose among its supporters and benefactors for such posts. There was inevitably a price for inefficient administration and injudicious judgement, but there was not much to be gained: the most that could be hoped for was that inexperienced White House staff would not ruffle too many Congressional feathers in allocating the president's political jobs. The exercise was largely one of damage limitation.[19]

Patronage was naturally a more important consideration for OCR staff at the beginning of Kennedy's administration than at that of his successor's. Johnson had no comparable opportunity of 'house-cleaning' since he assumed office, in unusual circumstances, from a Democrat and deliberately chose to emphasise the need for continuity. That was symbolically as well as substantively important, as much for staff and officials as for policy. None the less, the issue of patronage was never far from the thoughts of OCR staff. Unlike the widespread allocation of jobs at the outset of an administration, there was occasionally something to be gained from shrewd handling of individual patronage requests

---

[17] O'Brien, L. F., *No Final Victories*, New York, 1974, p. 101. Previously, Postmasters-General and Attorneys-General had frequently had key roles in dispensing patronage (see chapter one).

[18] Interview with O'Brien.

[19] See chapter one.

at a later point.[20] Even so, many Democratic senators and
Congressmen felt it their right to have the decisive say in
regional federal appointments, the former with US marshals,
US attorneys, and judicial nominations, the latter in regional
Post Office appointments. Indeed, for judicial nominations,
some US Democratic senators from the same state often had
a private arrangement whereby each had the 'right' to suggest
District and Circuit Court appointments from a part of the
state; others alternated in proposing names to be president
for submission to the Senate Judiciary Committee for approval.
Thus, Senator Stennis recommended Federal District Judges
from the northern half of Mississippi, and Senator Eastland
from the southern. This caused problems, since nominees of
both were often anxious to reverse progress on civil rights, or
at least unenthusiastic about enforcing civil rights legislation.[21]

Liberal Republican senators sometimes influenced judicial
nominations. Senator Hugh Scott,(R-PA), whose record of
support for Great Society and Civil Rights legislation was
good, once requested the privilege of nominating a federal
judge, having first secured the agreement of the Congressman
in whose district the prospective nominee lived, and the
Democratic senator, Joseph Clark.[22] In the 89th Congress
especially, it could harm a loyal liberal Democratic Congressman from a marginal constituency if his state's Republican
senator announced that he had persuaded the Democratic
administration to propose a Republican judge. In this case,
therefore, although Scott secured the agreement of Clark and
George Rhodes (the local Democratic Congressman) Henry
Wilson delayed announcing the nomination until after the
mid-term elections.[23] This minimised the political disadvantage
to Rhodes, while giving Senator Scott (who was not himself

[20] MacKenzie, G. C., *The Politics of Presidential Appointments*, New York, 1981,
p. 7.
[21] Sanders to Marvin Watson, 18/1/68, WHCF Ex and Gen FG 530, Box 355,
'FG 530/ST20–ST24'.
[22] Valenti to Johnson, 14/1/65, WHCF Ex and Gen FG 530, Box 355, 'FG
530/ST33–ST39'. Senator Clark was actually unenthusiastic about the patronage
system for nominating judges, and might well therefore have been more disposed to
make some allowance to Scott (Abraham, H., *The Judicial Process*, 3rd edn., New
York, 1975, p. 28).
[23] Wilson to Watson, 28/9/66, WHCF Ex and Gen FG 530, Box 355, 'FG 530
/ST33–ST39'.

running for re-election in 1966) his patronage nomination. Equally, the political advantage to Scott and his Republican colleagues was lessened by the delay, and their gratitude correspondingly less. As a means of influence over wavering members of Congress, patronage was relatively ineffective; it could normally be employed to satisfy what Democrats believed only to be the White House's political obligations to them.

Most patronage questions were entirely routine. Every spring, requests arrived from the Hill for help to find government summer jobs for the children of important constituents. The willingness of OCR staff to press departments or other agencies for assistance in such cases was largely determined by the voting record of the member concerned. For loyal supporters, temporary jobs were frequently found; whether the requests were for temporary junior posts or senior appointments, normal bureaucratic channels could be circumvented if the White House wished. For the Congressional leadership and loyal supportive committee chairmen in particular, the OCR went to some lengths to ensure that patronage requests, whether large or small, were met in full. For example, in sending a list of four names to John Macy in 1964, O'Brien noted: 'I can tell you confidentially that the requests listed below have been urged upon me by Senator Mansfield, and I am sure you realise how much weight we give to suggestions from that source. I would appreciate very much your looking into requests listed and advising me of developments.'[24]

For others, the White House often simply allowed a request to be processed, without their assistance, in the normal way. In the case of implacable opponents, no help was given at all. Few Republicans bothered to ask, knowing that there was little hope, but some conservative Democrats did. In forwarding an appeal from Armistead Selden to John Macy, chairman of the Civil Service Commission, a deeply conservative Democrat from Alabama who had recommended a constituent as a Federal Communications Commissioner, Henry Wilson appended a covering note: 'I wouldn't pay it

<hr />

[24] O'Brien to Macy, 9/9/64, Manatos, Box 12 (1293), 'Mansfield, Mike, (D-MT)'.

much attention, but you might just stick it in the file in the event she is appointed.'[25]

Wilson's note illustrates a further important administrative rule. Whilst a favoured constituent of Selden's was unlikely to be helped, it was clearly essential that if she were appointed, OCR staff should know about the decision before it was published. Departmental intentions had to be known in advance so that the president won as much credit as possible. The principle was the same as in the early days of Kennedy's presidency when O'Brien released 'good' news, and the chairman of the Democratic National Committee 'bad'. Even when a member had not sought a particular appointment, staff tried to inform her or him before a significant political appointment affecting the district or state was made. For a member to discover it in the pages of a local newspaper was poor politics, and bad Congressional relations. Unannounced appointments could cause serious embarrassment for a member of Congress, and so staff strove to avoid them. Even with clear procedures, however, mistakes occasionally occurred. In 1964, Senator Ed Long (D-MO), a loyal supporter of the president, told Manatos that two constituents were reported by *The Washington Post* to be under consideration for government appointments. Long had not been told.[26]

We certainly have no desire to be disagreeable; but as pointed out to you, it is embarrassing to be asked about these appointments when we have had no prior information in regard to them. Would appreciate it if you would check and advise us who Mrs Poland [one of the two appointees] is and if such appointment has been definitely made. Am sure you agree with me that the Senators should at least be extended the courtesy of having these appointments discussed with them before announcement to the Press. Am sure that such would possibly save embarrassment in situations that might develop.

Few members reacted to White House lapses so mildly. Proper procedures for informing interested Congressmen and senators of impending appointments were absolutely necessary if patronage was to be of any help to the White House.

[25] Wilson to Macy, 6/3/65, Files of John Macy, Box 340, 'O'Brien, Lawrence'.
[26] Senator Edward Long to Manatos, 22/2/64, Manatos, Box 11, 'Long, Edward V.,(D-MO)'.

Patronage's greatest value was in fostering long-term relationships with members; they were all too easily damaged
by its misuse.[27]

(iii) Federal Projects and Contracts[28]

In January 1966, Sherwin Markman, a member of the
White House staff who occasionally assisted with general
Congressional matters, examined White House records of
project awards to members of Congress. The analysis showed
that for a five-week period in late 1965 the cost of the projects
varied from $1,500 to more than $47 million:[29]

The results showed that 25.5% of the projects and 22.3% of the
calls to members involved projects under $100,000, and that 54.4%
of the projects and 57% of the calls covered projects over $1 million.
Eleven agencies were involved during the period concerned, but by
far the largest portions were from HUD and Defense: each had
45.9% of the total, together constituting 91.8% of all projects
covered.

Simple projections based on these figures suggest a total of
12,870 telephone calls to Congressmen and senators in 1965
to tell them of project awards in their district or state. Not
all were made by OCR staff—the liaison officers in the
departments and agencies made most of the smaller announcements. None the less, Markman's figures understate
the total number of telephoned announcements made to
members of Congress for they refer only to those projects
funded by a department or one of several major agencies such
as the General Services Administration (GSA), the Office

[27] Ironically, while still vice-president, Johnson himself undermined established
patronage release procedures in a case involving Senator Ralph Yarborough, a
liberal Texan senator with whom Johnson was perpetually at odds. In a memo
which he would certainly not have wished the future president to see, Manatos
angrily wrote to O'Brien: 'I was under the impression the Vice-President's agreement
was to give Yarborough a new deal. It's most embarrassing to call a United States
Senator with what you feel is news he would welcome only to find out that out of
the bigness of the Vice-President's heart he has been denied the announcement.'
(Manatos to O'Brien, 11/3/63, Manatos, Box 15 (1293), 'Yarborough, Ralph W.')

[28] Items categorised under the all-embracing heading of 'Projects and Contracts'
were of several types. For purposes of this study, programmes falling under the Area
Redevelopment Act, NASA projects, HUD Home-Building grants, and the like are
all included, as are OCR interventions with the Department of Defense to expand
military bases, or to delay or reverse decisions to close them.

[29] Markman to Wilson, 29/1/66, Wilson, Box 15, 'Staff Contacts 1966'.

of Economic Opportunity (OEO), or the Small Business Administration (SBA). Furthermore, staff often corresponded with a member or senator before formally releasing news of a project, something which was itself time-consuming. The White House aide whose primary responsibility this was spent three hours every day telephoning Hill offices with the 'good news' of a project's approval, an administrative chore which sometimes required assistance from departmental officials— on these occasions, officials spoke on behalf of the president, and not their department; a White House secretary spent another three hours daily completing records of the announcements.[30] (Until 1965, Claude Desautels was reponsible for supervising their compilation and updating which, with records of small favours and patronage, fill forty-two boxes in the Johnson Library's archives.)

The politics of federal projects and contracts were little different from patronage. Loyalty was rewarded and encouraged, and disloyalty punished—but usually in the aggregate and the long run. Contrary to popular wisdom, Johnson's staff did not make a practice of swapping 'dams for votes'. The terms of trade were rarely so crude. To have bargained with a senator or Congressman using White House approval of a specific project as a specific reward ran the risk that others would insist on similar treatment; the price of co-operation would rise, as Wilson commented: 'I never swapped a vote for a project—that would have been extremely crude, and wouldn't have worked. Once word got around, everybody would have wanted to trade their votes for projects. Nonetheless, we did reward our friends and punish our enemies.'[31]

This was a finer distinction than liaison staff allowed. Both executive and legislative participants knew that political friendships were of a mostly instrumental kind, and that there were no pure gifts. Denying that vote-trading of a simple kind took place, most White House staff described the dynamics of exchange in terms of reward and punishment, a form of open trading, though rarely acknowledged as such. When an exchange took place White House staff were

[30] Markman to Wilson, 29/1/66.
[31] Interview with Wilson.

prudentially disinclined to commit the details to paper; both
sides had vested interests in discretion. Allocating projects or
patronage for a particular return was usually regarded as
tantamount to bribery, and hence not to be encouraged.
However, to reward a Congressman in the course of a
long-term relationship of mutual co-operation and advantage
was thought the essence of liaison politics; in the absence of
such a relationship (because of a legislator's hostility to the
president's policies), staff rarely offered inducements for votes.
They did, however, sometimes offer rewards, as an incident
in the latter part of Kennedy's presidency indicates. In June
1963, Manatos wrote to O'Brien, having heard some gossip
from Louisiana Democrats:[32]

Senator Russell Long called to say that he has been talking to
Congressman Waggoner about the next ARA vote in the House.
According to Long, Waggoner can be had the next time around if
we would be willing to let him have a few ARA projects. Long has
volunteered to be the go-between and if we will give him the signal,
he will resume negotiations with Waggoner which he started on his
own initiative.

Wilson sent a pointed reply to Manatos the next day: 'I'd
tell Long Waggoner has to vote with us first and then we'll
talk.'[33]

   Thus political opponents found it difficult suddenly to join
in the self-generating cycle of 'support and reward', not simply
because a sudden conversion on a single issue might seem
suspect, but because fruitful political exchange relationships
were necessarily incremental and long-term.

   OCR staff took as much care with the project requests of
the Democratic leadership as they did with their patronage;
the leadership had little difficulty in winning approval for
them. Congressional whales, such as key committee chairmen
and the Republican leader Senator Dirksen, able to influence
committee or party colleagues, were also well placed to win
favours. This was even true of certain respected senior
conservatives who showed themselves willing to bargain: Carl
Hayden (D-AZ) agreed to support cloture on the 1964 Civil

   [32] Manatos, Box 11 (1293), 'Sen. Long, Russell B. (D-LA)'.
   [33] Wilson to Manatos, 22/6/63, Manatos, Box 11 (1293), 'Sen. Long, Russell B.
(D-LA)'.

Rights Act provided, firstly, that his vote was required to ensure its passage, and secondly that the president and his staff secured an agreement between Senator Kuchel (R-CA) and himself on the details of the Central Arizona Project.[34] As a swing vote on civil rights, and a respected senior senator, Hayden was in a stronger position than most conservatives to negotiate.

For less important Congressional figures, the granting of projects was linked to general assessments of their support for the president's policies. But as with patronage and even with small favours, loyal Democrats did not necessarily do as well as their voting records might suggest nor as well as some of them thought they should. Liberal and moderate Republicans did worse; only occasionally were they given advance notice of small projects. This was easy to arrange in a large state such as New York (where Senator Javits was sometimes favoured with a project announcement) but difficult in smaller states where there were fewer projects to be divided among the Democratic delegation.[35] The party link in projects between enticement and voting, reward and support, was best seen in states with split party representation in the Senate. Utah in 1963-5 provided an example with Senator Ted Moss, a strong Democratic supporter of the Kennedy and Johnson legislative programmes, and Wallace Bennett, a conservative Republican. Mike Manatos remarked in 1965 to Fred Dutton, a White House staff colleague, that he had done all he could for Moss: 'We've done everything for Ted Moss but convert to Mormonism—and they lost any possibility of winning me over when they abandoned polygamy.'[36]

Bennett, however, gained almost nothing from Kennedy or Johnson. Whilst lobbying senators on the 1963 tax bill, Manatos wrote to Larry O'Brien in late October:[37]

I talked to Secretary Dillon and advised him that we plan to sit down with Ted Moss in accordance with long-arranged plans to give him the announcement of the IRS Center in Ogden, Utah. Knowing Bennett as I do, we could hand him the entire state of

[34] In the event, it was not. The cloture vote was 71:27.
[35] O'Brien to Daly, 30/1/65, O'Brien, Box 27, 'Javits, Sen. Jacob K.'.
[36] Manatos, Box 13 (1293), 24/6/65, 'Moss, Sen. Ted (D-UT)'.
[37] Manatos to O'Brien, 31/10/63, Manatos, Box 13 (1293), 'Moss, Ted (D-UT)'.

Utah on a silver platter and while taking advantage of any releases, he would never lift a finger to help us. I do not mean that he will not support the tax bill, but I doubt that he could be persuaded to be the deciding vote.

The need for the president's staff to spend a disproportionate amount of time with marginal supporters focused attention upon their demands; their marginality in turn tended to increase their bargaining power. Most of the president's Congressional supporters generally did at least as well, especially if they were as persistent in their demands as in their support. But Congressmen's estimations of their worth did not always match the White House's calculation; just as important, the president's resources were finite, and choices had to be made.

Carl D. Perkins (D-KY) was one who relentlessly pressed OCR staff for federal largess. The ranking Democrat on the House Education and Labor Committee, he enthusiastically promoted all Great Society measures. In the spring of 1964, as he assisted the passage of the Economic Opportunity Bill (the Anti-Poverty Bill) through the House, he presented the president with numerous requests for projects in his district, a depressed mining area. However, he had already received approval for $16 million worth of projects in Fiscal Year 1964—$6 million above the quota provisionally allotted him.[38] In June of the previous year, Perkins had written to Wilson with a list of eighteen separate requests, all of which White House staff approved. Most of them were water and sewerage schemes which, Perkins said, '. . . have already been approved by the Accelerated Public Works people, but are being held up by ARA on the grounds that Kentucky has already received its allotment.'[39]

Perkins's combination of persistence, energy, and dogged support of Great Society and civil rights legislation was sufficient to win substantial federal aid for the seventh district of Kentucky, but he was seemingly oblivious to the constraints on the president. For the White House to have acted without regard to the total funds available would have been irresponsible; to have given Perkins excessively preferential

[38] Wilson to O'Brien, 31/1/64, Wilson, Box 19, 'Perkins, Rep. Carl D. (D-KN)'.
[39] Perkins to Wilson, 3/6/64, Wilson, Box 19, 'Perkins, Rep. Carl D. (D-KN)'.

treatment would have publicly created too great a gap between his rewards and those to comparably loyal colleagues. Short-term relations with these Democrats would consequently have been made difficult, placing the long-term relationships upon which the president's success depended at risk.

Members of the OCR therefore sometimes felt obliged to draw the line. Having persuaded Henry Wilson to release funds for a water project and a courthouse in Hazard, Kentucky, Perkins asked for a new courthouse in Pikeville. In a lobbying campaign worthy of OCR staff, he arranged for prominent lawyers, businessmen, sheriffs, and bankers from Pikeville to send telegrams to Robert Weaver, Administrator of the Housing and Home Finance Agency (HHFA), urging him to approve construction of the courthouse under the APW programme. Perkins's remarkable achievements in securing federal aid encouraged him to try again—but to Wilson's exasperation, as he told O'Brien in late January 1964. The Congressman was 'going like a mad bull after Pikeville. Calls me every fifteen minutes.'[40] Nor did Perkins let Wilson rest, as he later told O'Brien:[41]

Your good friend and mine, Carl Perkins, cornered me in a helicopter over Eastern Kentucky Friday. There being no escape but down, I chose the less fatal (although at the time I would not swear it was) alternative of listening. As you know, he wants a courthouse for Pikeville. . . I told him I would 'look into the matter', which is the purpose of this memo. Next time I will choose the other alternative.

Perkins's failure to persuade the White House to approve the courthouse's construction affected neither his support for Johnson's domestic programme nor his relationship with OCR staff; he cared more for Great Society programmes than for projects, however desirable to his constituents and useful to him, as Wilson correctly calculated: 'We're on the best of terms and he says he'll continue to go the full route with the President's programme. . .'.[42]

[40] Wilson to O'Brien, 27/1/64, Wilson, Box 19, 'p'.
[41] Wilson to Bill Moyers, 27/4/64, O'Brien, Box 29 (1533 4), 'Perkins, Rep. Carl D. (D-KN)'.
[42] Wilson to O'Brien, 6/2/64, Wilson, Box 19, 'p'.

Precisely because their relationship was friendly and secure, Wilson's refusal to approve the request damaged neither party nor did it harm Perkins's prospects of securing projects later. Perkins's membership of the Education and Labor Committee was as important to Johnson and OCR staff after the rejection as before. For him and OCR staff, as for other Congressmen and senators with similar views, the co-operative relationship was continuous and seamless, and the terms of trade implicit rather than openly acknowledged.

To do their jobs effectively, OCR staff had to pay full regard to the pressures on Congresssmen. Members were not, as one aide phrased it, 'to be expected to jump out of the window on our behalf'.[43] Asking members for a politically courageous vote if OCR staff thought it necessary in a close headcount was common, but the politics of their districts had to be taken fully into account. There was no long-term advantage to an activist president in damaging the electoral chances of those upon whom he depended. Equally, staff were more appreciative of those who supported the president on difficult votes than of those who did so only on issues which carried no political risk. Political imagination and patience were necessary and retaliation was undesirable, as Sanders told his staff: '. . . don't try to get "even", for there will always be another day and another vote'.[44]

Whilst direct trading was usually discouraged, staff sometimes mischievously hinted that federal help was subject to political influence—especially at election time. Just before the 1964 elections, the Democratic National Committee suggested that federal funds for Florida's barge canal might be stopped if Goldwater won the state. The editor of a local Florida newspaper wrote to George Reedy, the president's press secretary, asking for his observations on this and similar rumours. Wilson advised him to deny the rumours by phone, but to commit nothing to paper:[45]

[43] Interview with O'Brien.
[44] Sanders, H. Barefoot, 'Congressional Executive Relations during the 1960s', in Livingston, W. S., Dodd, L. C., and Schott, R. L.,(eds.) *The Presidency and the Congress*, Austin, Tex., 1979, p. 296.
[45] Spear, W. R., to Reedy, G. E., 31/8/64, and Wilson to Reedy, 10/9/64, Wilson, Box 6, 'White House Staff'.

. . . whatever is said or written would have to be to the effect that the President would not play politics with Federal funds. . . The reason I say there would preferably be no quote from you is that apparently our people have a pretty good thing going there and I would hate to see us put into a position of blowing it up.

The president gave blanket authority for OCR staff to make these judgements; their knowledge and expertise enabled them to assess whether legislators could be induced to support the president's programme. Their customary caution about using federal contracts and projects as crude bargaining chips was not always shared by White House staff colleagues or departmental liaison officers. The further removed White House aides were from the complexities of liaison politics, the less inhibited they tended to be about striking quid pro quos. When OCR staff heard of such developments, they invariably tried to stop them—not least because no Congressman or senator took kindly to bullying from unelected departmental officials, as OCR members readily explained to erring agency liaison staff (though they found it more difficult to do so to senior White House staff outside the OCR once O'Brien left to become Postmaster-General). In 1964, Henry Wilson admonished an officer in the Commerce Department in a case involving David Henderson who, like some other southern Democrats, had (much to the OCR's relief) supported ARA:[46]

Word is circulating all over North Carolina that you have put the hold on ARA project no. 777—technical assistance study for Cartaret County, North Carolina—on the ground that you intend to use it to get Dave Henderson (D-NC) to vote for ARA. Dave was right last time and he'll be right again, unless this queers him. You'd better move this project along and fast.

The OCR's success depended in part upon the extent to which its staff were able to exert such political and administrative authority over the departments and agencies on the president's behalf. During Kennedy's presidency and the two phases of Johnson's, this relationship often worked to the advantage of the White House. If OCR members were

---

[46] Wilson to Dooley, O'Brien, Box 15, 'Henderson, Rep. David N.,(D-NC)'. The House did not act on ARA in 1964. (*Congressional Quarterly Almanac, 1964*, p. 294.)

determined to secure approval of a particular project, they rarely failed; their political judgement always took priority in theory, and usually in practice, as an incident involving Thaddeus Dulski, a Democratic–Liberal New York Congressman, illustrates well:[47]

For the record and for your information. . . we did a tremendous favor for Thad Dulski today and he is very grateful to you. He has a Bill providing for a national shrine status for a house in Buffalo where Teddy Roosevelt was sworn in. Aspinall, the chairman of the committee handling the Bill, had arranged to have it reported providing Dulski could get favorable reports and Leo O'Brien was authorized to bring it to the Floor. The problem was that the Interior Advisory Committee on Shrines had given an adverse report.

   A). We got Interior, notwithstanding the above, to give a favorable report.

   B). We got Budget to limit its comments to no opposition. . . in some innocuous sentence.

This morning Thad Dulski got very upset by the last line in the Interior report which briefly stated that the Congress was unfavorably disposed on a similar bill back in '63—Dulski said this would kill the Bill. We told Interior to delete the last line in their report—they did. Dulski thanks you and praises you.

OCR staff applied the same principles to routine project and contract announcements as they did to patronage: if the project was approved, they took the credit to the president's advantage. Although in special circumstances, staff might decide that the department or agency concerned deserved some of the credit and therefore allow it to make the announcement, they usually exploited the political benefits to the president's advantage by bearing the good tidings themselves, as Henry Wilson described:[48]

If a Congressional request proved not to be feasible, the Departmental people, rather than we, brought the bad news to the Congressman. As a general rule, we tried to bring only good news from the White House. Occasionally, a Congressman would be so involved with a project that I would feel it appropriate to tell him personally that he had lost, and why. This way, he could tell his people that though

[47] O'Brien, Box 14, 'Dulski, Rep. Thaddeus J.,(D-NY)'.
[48] Wilson, 'How it Worked'.

he had failed to perform, he had taken it to the White House, to the top, and I would give him a letter to prove it.

Wilson thereby appreciated that the Congressman was in the 'credit-taking business' just as much as the president. Even when a request was rejected, OCR staff could soften the blow for the Congressman or senator concerned. For established friends and those whom they wished to court, they did so; others were left to fend for themselves.

The closure or elimination of a military base or federal facilities also presented opportunities to staff seeking to increase the president's leverage over legislators. For communities which came to rely on the income such bases provided, the prospect of closure was alarming, and hence a matter of concern to their representatives, especially in the approach to elections. A matter of weeks before the 1968 election, the Pentagon concluded that three Naval laboratories in a southern Californian Congressional district represented by Democrat John Tunney would have to be shut. Together with three Californian colleagues, Tunney had been marked out for defeat by the Republicans, and so anxiously sought OCR assistance. Although the formal announcement of closure had been delayed, the news was already leaking out, as Sprague reported to Sanders:[49]

. . . John Tunney is hysterical. This is the largest federal installation in his district and he thinks the closing will beat him. The word has somehow leaked out and employees at Corona [the base] began deluging him with calls late last night.

Tunney has enlisted the help of the California delegation and Chairman Chet Hollifield is attempting to arrange a meeting with Secretary Clifford tonight. Tunney said 'I could understand the Democratic Administration doing this to H. R. Gross or Wilbur Mills, but my God, I just couldn't survive.'

The closures were administered entirely by the Defense Department and although Clark Clifford, the Secretary of Defense, contemplated delaying them until after the election,

---

[49] Sprague to Sanders, 18/9/68, Sprague, Box 7 (1568), 'Sanders, Barefoot'. H. R. Gross was a conservative Iowan Republican. His presidential support score in the 90th Congress was 30 per cent. Tunney's support score in the same Congress was 72 per cent.

the cost of $1.5 million per month was deemed too high to justify it. OCR staff were alerted to the potential electoral damage only at a late stage, but Clifford's determination to economise outweighed the qualms of OCR staff. They were in any case not minded to protest especially strongly on Tunney's behalf for they did not share his pessimistic assessment of the closure's electoral effect. (Tunney was re-elected with 63 per cent of the vote.) Despite the weakening of the OCR in the later years of Johnson's presidency, OCR staff could certainly have delayed the closure had they judged it necessary.

A similar situation had occurred in late 1963, soon after Johnson became president, when the Army Department decided to close a supply depot in Schenectady, New York. Leo O'Brien, the Democratic Congressman affected, proposed that it should be phased out over a longer period than the Army wished, and sensibly persuaded O'Brien of the benefits to the new president of agreeing to his proposal. The OCR director arranged for the Secretary of Defense, Robert McNamara, to discuss the problem with the Congressman. Reporting on the results of his discussion, Wilson said that Leo O'Brien was in 'an excellent mood—totally understanding'. His mood improved further when Wilson agreed to ask Cyrus Vance, then Deputy Secretary of Defense, to implement the revised plan: 'I called Cy Vance, discussed above with him, and told him he absolutely must work out the two-year attrition thing. He said he'd get right on it and be back with me this afternoon.' Vance agreed to a run-down of the base acceptable to Leo O'Brien; Wilson telephoned him personally to tell him the good news.[50]

The OCR's opportunities for assisting in this way varied to some extent by region and district. Some districts and states acquired many bases and depots over time—often because of a traditional representation on a particular Congressional committee; committees thus became sluices through which federal funds flowed. Southern domination of committees such as Armed Services in both chambers, and the traditional underdevelopment of the region, explains the concentration of military bases in southern states. The Defense Department's efficiency measures of the 1960s enabled OCR

[50] Wilson, Box 19, '1963-64 Congressional File: N'.

staff to defend federal bases in the districts of helpful southern members from closure, as a minute from Henry Wilson to a senior Pentagon official shows:[51]

Would you get with Rep. Gonzales (D-TX), and tell him I sent you. . . and ask him if there any problems in the Defense area you can help him with. You'll get plenty. His district has always been represented by a member of the Armed Services Committee. Through the years they have totally loaded it up with installations, and he thus is compelled to fight a constant rearguard action to hold what he has. But he's totally our guy and we need to help him heavily at least to hold his *status quo*.

The OCR did not have a free hand. Even in cases such as Gonzalez's, it was not always possible to help; as budgetary constraints tightened in the later years of Johnson's presidency, so staff had to be more discriminating in their approach. Nevertheless, there were numerous opportunities to accumulate political capital on which to draw later.

Decisions to prevent closures brought little reward if OCR staff intervened before the closure was announced. Shortly after the 1964 elections, the Post Office Department proposed to shut a local post office in Fairfield, a town of 16,000 people in Alabama, despite its having been one of the few areas in metropolitan Birmingham to have supported the Democratic presidential and Congressional tickets. Wilson sensibly requested Dave Bunn to prevent the closure.[52] Earlier that same year, Wilson advised Claude Desautels to allow publication of a list of proposed Federal Aviation Administration Office closures, but to arrange for seven of them to be reprieved afterwards when Congressmen asked the OCR for help: '. . . as always, I feel we can never get any appreciation from Congressmen by saving them from dangers they never know exist, and it would be a far more effective operation if everybody was given the bad news and we rescued the good guys.'[53]

Congressional goodwill was easily dissipated by administrative error and political misjudgement. Even committed

[51] Wilson to Kelley, 12/11/63, Wilson, Box 18, '1963-1964 Congressional File: G'.
[52] Wilson to Bunn, O'Brien, Box 21, 'Selden, Rep. Armistead (D-AL)'.
[53] Wilson to Desautels, 10/1/64, Wilson, Box 6, 'White House Staff'.

supporters such as Edward Kennedy sometimes quickly took offence when the rules regarding project announcements were not followed. Angered that he had not received prior notification of the HEW funds, Kennedy wrote to Anthony Celebrezze, the then Secretary of Health, Education and Welfare (HEW), in the summer of 1965 about the news of a $2.5 million federal grant by the Mayor of Boston. The matter quickly came to the attention of OCR staff who instructed HEW on the correct procedure to be followed, emphasising the political value of so large a grant. In his reply, Celebrezze acknowledged the serious difficulties which the administrative breakdown had caused (he could do little else) and confirmed that steps were being taken 'to tighten internal procedures in order to forestall the possibility of any recurrence of the mistake'.[54]

A few months earlier, Senator Pat McNamara (D-MI), chairman of the Senate Committee on Public Works, had been asked to be present at an OEO press conference announcing a $1.34 million grant to Michigan Migrant Opportunity, Inc., to establish four regional centres for migrant workers in the state. In the event, he was not told of the grant's details, nor could his staff discover them from OEO itself. McNamara's press and legislative assistant was furious, and wrote a detailed letter to Manatos pointing out the serious political problems which OEO's clumsiness was causing. The senator's anger was the greater since he had been the primary sponsor and floor manager of the Economic Opportunity Act just eight months earlier:[55]

It is nothing less than insulting to invite him [McNamara] to a Press Conference so he can stand around while someone else announces a major project *in his own state* on a program for which he has primary legislative responsibility. . . George Romney, who could well be Pat's opponent in 1966, is cleverly exploiting the Senator's role in the poverty program in Michigan. . .

As far as our office is concerned, unless we receive adequate advance notice of the projects so that the Senator can announce

---

[54] Celebrezze to Kennedy; Cohen to Desautels, 9/7/65, O'Brien, Box 40, 'Senator Edward Kennedy (D-MA)'.

[55] Winge, E. N., to Manatos, 19/3/65, Manatos, Box 15 (1295), 'McNamara, Pat (D-MI)'.

them first with whatever political benefits accrue, there is no point in sending them to us at all. If it is going to be the continuing policy of OEO to announce these projects first, with either concurrent or after-the-fact notification to the Senator, please tell them to cut us off the mailing list.

CONCLUSION

Both patronage and projects were used by the OCR to accumulate a capital fund on which the president and his staff could draw to his benefit. The Congressional leadership and other loyal whales gained disproportionately by way of federal projects, patronage, and favours because of their importance and loyalty to the president's programme. Apart from them, Democrats in general did well, and supportive (mostly liberal) Democrats best of all. Liberal Republicans gained little for their support of the administration; other Republicans did even worse.

The scope for influencing the award of projects was greater than with patronage, a scarce resource, plentiful only during an administration's first few months when it was least useful. Then, as presidents and their staff made political appointments, they could do little more than settle political debts and attempt to fulfil the expectations of important supporters. None the less, used with subtlety and discrimination, patronage and the award of federal projects and contracts could warm the negotiating climate along Pennsylvania Avenue. When OCR staff thought it appropriate and necessary to intervene in individual cases, they did so, but in most instances, the expected returns in the form of general political support and voting were incremental, general, and long-term.

5

SMALL FAVOURS AND LOBBYING

INTRODUCTION

The several constraints upon the use of patronage and projects limited their usefulness. For the most part, the president gained from them only as part of long-term exchange relationships of political accommodation between legislators and his staff. But Johnson had other resources available to him: small personal favours to Congressmen and senators publicised the latters' contact and association with the Head of State and so could be of electoral benefit to Congressmen, preoccupied with biennial elections.[1]

Personal favours of this kind were known to some OCR staff as 'small potatoes'. Yet they often occasioned a more useful political return than either patronage or project awards and, crucially, assisted in the cultivation of fruitful political relationships between politicians with different perspectives, needs, and ambitions—something which OCR staff fully appreciated.[2] They included personal photographs signed by the president, his reception of a senator's or Congressman's important constituents and VIP tours of the White House for them, flights aboard *Air Force One*, trips on the presidential yachts *Sequoia* or *Honeyfitz*, invitations to bill-signing ceremonies, and the gift to members of pens used to sign the bills. All such favours, carefully used to assist supporters and encourage others, helped create bonds of obligation and exchange between the president and the recipient, thereby contributing to productive working relationships in a political system where institutional fragmentation made presidential bridge-building necessary for legislative leadership to succeed. OCR staff intended that small favours of this kind should be

---

[1] Mayhew, David, *Congress: The Electoral Connection*, New Haven, 1974; Fenno, Richard F., *Congressmen in Committees*, Boston, 1978.

[2] Interview with Larry O'Brien, 24/11/79.

interpreted by legislators as indications of the president's wish to be as accommodating as possible; they were expressions of the general interest and concern with Congressmen's fortunes which, in their own political interests, Kennedy and Johnson required of their legislative advisers.[3]

SMALL GIFTS

As other presidents have done, so Johnson kept a stock of small items decorated with the presidential seal to use as personal mementoes and gifts for staff, Congressmen, journalists, and other visitors. Friends and favoured allies received such small presents (ball-point pens, cuff-links, tie-clips, perfume atomisers, charm-bracelets) with a regularity which some found flattering, and others an embarrassment—though Doris Kearns was certainly an unwitting victim of Johnson's humour in receiving twelve electric toothbrushes, each emblazoned with the presidential seal.[4] To Congressmen and senators, Johnson gave such presents with greater seriousness of purpose, as Larry Temple, Special Counsel to the President from 1967-9, emphasised:[5]

. . . the President recognised full well the great respect and awe that people had for the Presidency, as well as for the man who held that position. . . When he gave things that had his name or a Presidential seal on them. . . he was giving an item that had great significance to the people that received it. He did that in full knowledge.

Presents, like all small favours, showed that the president of the United States wanted to give the impression that he thought the recipient worthy of special attention—few in Washington, even among its governing circle, were or are indifferent to such gestures. Small gifts also gilded political relationships with the alluring quality of personal friendship. Members of Congress knew the political advantage of being on personal terms with the president, especially for so long as he enjoyed political success.

---

[3] Interview with Larry O'Brien, 24/11/79.
[4] Kearns, D., *Lyndon Johnson and the American Dream*, New York, 1976, p. 10.
[5] Temple, Larry, Oral History, Johnson Library, Tape no. 5, p. 2.

Accurate information on Congressmen's and senators' lives and politics made effective liaison and lobbying easier and more effective. News with implications for their political circumstances and responsiveness to Johnson's leadership was constantly sought by his staff. Apart from the need to collect intelligence on informal Congressional contacts (as Henry Wilson characterised it, 'who played poker with whom on Friday nights and what was said during the poker games'[6]), staff were anxious to know of opportunities for demonstrating the president's concern with the welfare of members. Early in 1964, Johnson instructed the secretaries of each of the three armed services to inform his liaison staff when a senator or member of Congress was admitted to the Bethesda Naval Hospital or the Walter Reed Army Medical Center. He wished to be informed immediately, 'at any hour of the day or night', so that he could write 'a note, or send out flowers if he wishes to recognise them in this way'.[7]

Staff had little control over the number of small presents which the president gave away, or the flowers he sent to sick senators or Congressmen. But they strictly limited Congressional trips on the presidential yachts *Sequoia* and *Honeyfitz* and on *Air Force One*, and the allocation of pens from bill-signing ceremonies. Desautels kept files of 'Favors Granted' which included lists of all such presidential favours and attentions, and notes by staff of their political value.[8]

MEETINGS WITH THE PRESIDENT

OCR members were often requested by senators and Congressmen to arrange meetings with the president. At times, these were for important constituents or supporters of the politician in question; at others, for the Congressman or senator himself to see the president. The most precious

[6] Wilson, H. H., 'How it Worked when it Worked', unpublished manuscript, 1979, p. 36.
[7] Clifton, C. V., to Secretaries of the Armed Services, 25/3/64, Ex FG 300/A, Box 321, 'FG 400: The Legislative Branch: 22/11/63–14/4/64'.
[8] During John Kennedy's presidency, the OCR maintained a list of favours granted to the vice-president, too.

presidential resource was time. Accordingly, Johnson's meetings with Congressmen or their constituents were limited to
those occasions where he and his Congressional advisers felt
that something could be gained by way of investment, or the
repayment of debts.

Typically, in the spring of 1964, Rep. Richard Fulton, a
Georgian Democrat who (most unusually and courageously
for a southerner) was then giving valuable support to the
administration on the 1964 Civil Rights Bill, asked Henry
Wilson for a photograph of him with the president to alleviate
the pressure on him in the approach to the 1964 elections.
Johnson was naturally grateful for substantial support from
southern Democrats (especially on civil rights), and so Wilson
gladly endorsed Fulton's request. The photograph was taken,
doubtless accompanied by suitably effusive thanks from the
president, ever mindful of the strong local pressures on
southern members' politics.[9] Wilson and his OCR colleagues
were as careful to deny such favours to opponents: photographs
of Congressmen (especially Republicans) hostile to the
president's policies with the president at official White House
gatherings were withheld during an election campaign.[10]
Congressional opponents could in their campaign literature
make much of association with the president; in 1964, many
Republicans were only too willing and anxious to ride free
on the back of a popular Democratic president.

Brief meetings and 'photo-opportunities' also provided an
opportunity for pointed conversations with members about
imminent votes on measures dear to the president's heart and
an integral part of his calculations. This, of course, was
Johnson's special strength. Masterly in the role, he took
legislators by the arm (or lapels, as he thought best) and
sought to persuade them of the bill's merits, arguing that
they could safely support him without endangering their
election chances at home. Meetings with the president were
thus more than favours to Congressional friends and potential
allies. They also provided opportunities for private presidential
lobbying; the dividing line between liaison and lobbying,

[9] Wilson to O'Brien, 7/2/64, Wilson, Box 18, '1963–64 Congressional File: F'.
[10] Manatos to Johnson, 6/4/66, Manatos, Box 14 (1295), 'Pearson, James B.
(R-Kan)'.

often very fine, disappeared here. In a friendly gathering with members and constituents which both had sought, the psychological and political advantages lay with the president, to exploit as he judged appropriate.[11]

If OCR staff did not think it worth the president's while to set aside valuable time for a meeting, Johnson could none the less choose to send a photograph of himself with an appropriate inscription. Interspersed with the sheaves of letters at the signing table behind his desk were a number of photographs and personal notes to be sent to favoured constituents of friendly Congressmen and senators. The pressures on his diary notwithstanding, both Johnson and his senior staff thought this time well spent, as Larry Temple observed:[12]

. . . he could put an inscription on a picture and sign his name while carrying on a conversation. He did that just hours on end and never once did I hear him complain about the time it took. . . That was a part of the office. . . he knew that he could cut off the pictures [and] that a recipient of a picture would put greater store and greater value on it. . . for having the picture signed by the President.

PRESIDENTIAL TRIPS

Use of either of the presidential yachts for evening trips on the Potomac was an old tradition which Kennedy and Johnson continued. They used them frequently, both for their own leisure and to impress colleagues from Congress. Soon after Sanders joined the OCR in 1967, he sought Johnson's support for the idea of spending one evening every week to entertain members and their spouses aboard the *Honeyfitz*. More anxious than ever to bolster flagging Congressional support, the president supported the proposal, and invited his OCR director to use the *Sequoia* in preference to the smaller *Honeyfitz*. Sanders hoped that the trips would provide an opportunity 'to reward and pay some attention to those who support us

---

[11] Wilson to Moyers and reply, 23/3/64, Wilson, Box 19, '1963-64 Congressional File: S'.

[12] Temple, Oral History, Tape no. 5, pp. 4-5.

most of the time', rather than to cultivate the border and moderate southern Congressional Democrats who, because of their less reliable voting record, were those most ardently lobbied by his colleagues.[13]

At other times, the president used the *Sequoia* for his own small parties, frequently inviting two or three members to join Lady Bird and himself on board. The setting was more appropriate to pleasant socialising than to lobbying for votes, but this was no great handicap. The invitation was intended as a signal favour, and usually interpreted as such; those so fêted reacted warmly; even hardened politicians found it more difficult to oppose a president who took such trouble to woo them. The next Democratic president, Jimmy Carter, saved a little money at the price of sorely needed influence when he sold the presidential yachts.

Johnson's routine travel requirements also offered opportunities to impress which OCR staff duly exploited. Some accompanied the president on *Air Force One*, while others were simply invited to be present at his speaking engagements. Such occasions were particularly popular because of the television coverage they afforded: to be at the president's side at a dedication ceremony for a large federal project, such as a new dam, in one's home district or state proved an irresistible attraction for most. Conversely, if someone were omitted from the aircraft's guest list when political and geographic interests required her or his inclusion, embarrassment resulted, damaging good relations between the president and supporters on the Hill. One such incident occurred in 1967 when a dedication ceremony was held in the presence of the president in south-west Texas for the opening of a major bridge. Irvine Sprague compiled an invitation list of Mexican–American guests to accompany Johnson at the ceremony, but omitted Eddie Roybal, a loyal and trusted Californian Democrat on the Interior Committee, as he later recalled:[14]

Roybal was an old friend of mine and he was very upset when he called me the next day and asked what had happened. 'I'm very

---

[13] Sanders to Johnson, 2/6/67, Ex FG 11-8-1: Sanders, Box 113, 'Ex FG 11-8-1/Sanders, Barefoot, 2/6/67–7/6/67'.
[14] Interview with Irvine Sprague, 7/12/78.

sorry, Eddie,' I said, 'I just screwed up, and the president is as mad as hell at me.'

The president told me to get Roybal down to the White House the following day. I looked at the president's schedule, and saw that he had a meeting with city mayors the next day, so I called Eddie and told him that the president would like him to come along. There was a receiving line at the reception, and Johnson spent a few seconds with each guest. But when it came to Eddie's turn, Johnson just threw his arms around him and had an intimate conversation for about five minutes—that solved any problems he might have had with him.

Small restorative displays of goodwill such as this were second nature to Johnson, a show of concern and interest, shrewdly arranged so that others, too, saw how the president regarded a Congressional colleague. They were an appropriate and effective way of repairing administrative errors. For OCR staff, their great virtue (unlike patronage and projects) was being politically uncomplicated. Helpful or aggrieved members of Congress were rewarded or mollified as appropriate by small gestures of friendship, offers of assistance, invitations to state dinners, or to private parties with the president. Again, OCR staff were dependent upon the president's willingness to participate in these constant displays of goodwill. Presidents Nixon and Carter found informal social occasions awkward; for Johnson, they were both easy and pleasurable.

CONGRESSIONAL RECEPTIONS

In addition to meetings with individuals, all members— Democrats and Republicans, liberals and conservatives—were invited to a series of Congressional receptions in the White House. Eisenhower and his predecessors had held receptions and formal balls for members of Congress; President Kennedy altered their format to black tie receptions, and abolished receiving lines.[15] When Johnson was politically successful,

[15] Kennedy also held 'Social Hours' for members at which a few Congressmen and senators would get together with him for an hour or so in the late afternoon, sitting on the balcony overlooking the south lawn if the weather was good, to exchange gossip (interview with Rep. John Brademas,(D-Ind), 18/9/78; O'Brien to President Kennedy, 22/5/63, President's Office Files: Staff Memoranda, Box 64, 'O'Brien, Lawrence: 9/62–11/63', John F. Kennedy Library).

very few of those invited declined but, as his popularity
waned, more sent their regrets. There was then less inclination
to cancel pressing engagements to attend the receptions,
especially when invitees realised that they could ask to come
on a future occasion. It was a sign of Johnson's diminishing
popularity, and of growing Congressional disenchantment.
Irritated, Henry Wilson decided in February 1967 to instruct
the White House Social Office that, when members declined
future invitations, they should not be invited again during
that series of receptions. Wilson none the less took care to
ensure that neither he nor his OCR colleagues were responsible
for telling this to the senator or Congressman concerned.[16]

Sensing the political advantage of an extended programme
of Congressional receptions, Johnson hosted a special event
hailed as a 'Salute to Congress' for Democratic members at
the end of the second session of the 88th Congress, just two
and a half months before the 1964 elections. It was strikingly
successful; the Congressional Democrats delighted in the free
publicity, as the Speaker, bubbling with enthusiasm, told the
president afterwards.[17] In the New Year, Jack Valenti, a
senior aide, recommended that a new series of extended
receptions be arranged to which both members and their
spouses should be invited. Before the reception itself, Valenti
suggested that briefings on foreign and economic policy be
held for the members, and that their spouses be given a tour
of the Mansion's family quarters. It was a novel idea, designed
to impress. He proposed that its political benefits be extended
by arranging for White House photographers to be present,
too:[18]

1. Have Okamoto and Stoughton take candids of the briefing
   and the receptions. Pictures sent to the Congressmen afterwards.
   (Nothing pleases a Congressman more than pictures of his wife
   and him at the White House. We ought to make certain that
   every Congressman and his wife have their picture taken with
   the President and Mrs Johnson.)

[16] Wilson to Sprague, Sprague, Box 8 (1568-9), 9/2/67, 'Congressional Receptions—Briefings'.
[17] McCormack to Johnson, 20/8/64, WHCF Ex FG 300/A, Box 321, FG 400: 'The
Legislative Branch: 15/6/64-24/12/64'.
[18] Valenti to Johnson, 4/1/65, WHCF Ex FG 300/A, Box 321, 'FG 400: The
Legislative Branch: 25/12/64-28/1/65'.

2. Have the wives take a tour of the second floor—and give to each wife a picture of the White House—the same one given to each White House staff member at Christmas time. They will become a little memento.

3. We have a golden opportunity to reap the harvest this time because of the great number of new Congressmen in this session. This briefing and reception at the White House will be a high point in their lives and we should make the most of it.

4. Briefings done by Secretary McNamara, Secretary Rusk, Kermit Gordon or Gardner Ackley, with the President being the anchor man.

The idea was adopted. Throughout Johnson's presidency, briefings at the Congressional receptions were given by Secretaries of State and Defense, and the Budget Bureau Director. Mrs Johnson took charge of showing the wives of Congressmen (arrangements made for the husbands of Congresswomen are, sadly, unrecorded) around the president's quarters of the Mansion and was assisted by wives of members of the White House—especially OCR—staff.[19] As Jean Lewis told Henry Wilson, the Congressional wives did not appear to resent the implications of this domestic excursion: 'No one mentioned a desire to attend the downstairs briefing. . . there was a feeling that the upstairs program had substance and importance.'[20]

Sprague wrote to Wilson after the same reception: 'Maggie [Sprague's wife] said that several Congressmen, unidentified, commented that they would like an opportunity for a quick look upstairs after hearing about it from their wives.'[21]

Although the idea for these social occasions was Valenti's own, OCR staff were solely responsible for organising them. They requested senior colleagues to talk to certain Congressional guests during the evening, and report their views and observations to Henry Wilson or Larry O'Brien by the following day. OCR staff approached the exercise in an appropriately serious fashion, and tried to ensure that the

[19] Jean Lewis to Wilson, Wilson, Box 11, 'Congressional Receptions', 24/2/67.
[20] Jean Lewis to Wilson, 24/2/67.
[21] Sprague to Wilson, 22/2/67, Sprague, Box 8 (1568 9) 'Congressional Receptions—Briefings'.

non-OCR staff already knew the dozen or so members to whom they were assigned. A book of members' photographs was available in OCR offices for them to browse through so that they would at least recognise the faces of those whom they were asked to contact.[22]

The resulting reports of White House staff to O'Brien and Wilson,(and, later, Sanders) showed that most members had no pressing political difficulties with which they needed the president's assistance; very few made specific observations about legislative proposals before Congress. In the latter phase of Johnson's tenure, many none the less expressed their reservations about American policy in Vietnam; some referred to the large quantities of mail they received on Capitol Hill critical of America's failure either to win or withdraw. (Much of this correspondence was hawkish, and most Congressmen and senators reflected this in what they told OCR staff. Johnson, sensitive to Congressional opinion above all, interpreted it as an indication that there was little sentiment in favour of de-escalation or withdrawal.)[23]

The receptions served several useful purposes: the president's staff made a grand show of the respect upon which Johnson insisted; the briefings provided information—which despite its partiality was welcome to many Congressmen who lacked large staff resources of their own. In their newsletters to constituents, Congressmen reported their briefings at the White House; even if their questions did not elicit the answers they wished for, it took little imagination for such occasions to be presented in a favourable light. Sensitive to this, OCR staff lent special assistance to their Democratic supporters, considered the changing views and responses, and also picked up useful Congressional gossip. In essence, Congressional liaison staff regarded receptions as a bridge-building exercise between the president and the legislators whose co-operation he needed. Wining and dining members and their wives in the splendid setting of the East Room of the White House was a lavish social gesture, easing relations, impressing

[22] Wilson to White House staff, 7/2/67, Sprague, Box 8 (1568 9), 'Congressional Receptions—Briefings'.

[23] For example, Watson to Wilson, 23/2/67, Wilson, Box 11, 'Congressional Receptions'; Chuck Roche to Wilson, 24/2/67, Wilson, Box 11, 'Congressional Receptions'.

members (especially the younger ones) with the grandeur of the Head of State's residence, and strengthening the foundations for productive relationships between the branches of government at either end of Pennsylvania Avenue.

As Johnson lost political standing, and his isolation in the White House grew, so the receptions became less popular and the object of criticism: repetition and inflated expectations caused them to lose some of their impact. Relaxing with members on board the *Honeyfitz* during a summer evening's cruise on the Potomac in 1967, de Vier Pierson (a White House staff member brought into Congressional liaison by Barefoot Sanders) listened to a stream of complaints from three liberal Democrats about Johnson's growing remoteness from members of Congress, observations frequently made during the 90th Congress. John Culver, then a Congressman from Iowa, argued that the Congressional receptions and briefings were too stylized and built around Johnson's interest in 'selling us his viewpoint'. Reporting this to Sanders, Pierson suggested that there should be more sessions of an informal kind between members and the president so that he might meet newer members; they could in turn privately discuss political questions with him. It might thereby be possible to build anew the idea and practice of a Democratic 'team'—a president as leader of his party and his colleagues on Capitol Hill. In the heady days of the Great Society's creation, this was relatively easy, but it faded in the last phase of Johnson's presidency. Pierson told Sanders that Congressional dissatisfaction showed again the need for all OCR staff to take a constant interest in senators and Congressmen:'. . . one of the keys to the Kingdom is just what you are doing— paying attention to them [at] other than those frenzied times when you need a vote. There is no doubt that they want to feel like a constant and well respected friend—not an occasional lover.'[24]

BILL-SIGNING CEREMONIES

Elaborate bill-signing ceremonies were restricted to legislation which the president deemed of central importance, and from which he stood to gain. Major bills such as Medicare, Civil

[24] Pierson to Sanders, 3/8/67, Roche, Box 5 (1819), 'Memos to Staff'.

Rights, Federal Aid to Education, were naturally the subjects of televised ceremonies, often held in an appropriately symbolic place. Thus Medicare was signed into law at Independence, Missouri, in the presence of former President Harry Truman, who had first proposed it in 1948, and a host of invited guests, most of them Congressional supporters of the bill.[25] The Federal Aid to Education Bill was signed outside his one-room schoolhouse in Stonewall, Texas, in the presence of his first teacher, Mrs Kate Deadrich Loney.[26] The 1965 Immigration Bill, which abolished national quotas, was signed at the foot of the Statue of Liberty.[27]

Members of Congress benefited from the publicity as much as the president, and OCR staff took their views and needs into account before deciding whether to recommend the president to stage signing ceremonies. Under President Kennedy, the procedures were unclear, and OCR members had little control over them.[28] During Johnson's administration, Joe Califano tried to assume control of recommendations for ceremonies (as of much else). Earlier in the administration, another non-OCR staff member, Horace Busby, had attempted to alter the format of the ceremonies, and to limit Congressional participation in them to 'periodic meetings', a plan which OCR staff resisted. Manatos told O'Brien that the legislators who piloted the president's bills through Congress should be acknowledged, and benefit from the attendant publicity:[29]

I think the present format makes the most sense. It gives the members of Congress who are the ones who work and vote on this legislation exposure to the President and an opportunity to send pictures to their local newspapers. If we were now to embark on a procedure which would bring in members of Congress for select signings [only] I believe we would have a lot of noses out of joint.

---

[25] Marmor, T. R., *The Politics of Medicare*, London, 1970, p. 1.

[26] *Congressional Quarterly Almanac, 1965*, p. 68.

[27] *Congressional Quarterly Almanac, 1965*, p. 479.

[28] Kenneth O'Donnell had attempted to improve the *ad hoc* arrangements, but succeeded only in confusing departmental liaison offices by refraining from giving full responsibility for the ceremonies to the OCR (O'Donnell to all cabinet officers, 28/9/62, O'Brien, Box 31, 'House Material: Misc.') (John F. Kennedy Library).

[29] Manatos to O'Brien, Manatos, Box 2 (967), 27/4/65, 'Manatos: Legislative: 1965: Mr O'Brien (Jan.-Sept.): Desautels'.

Busby and Califano's attempts to alter the procedure for approving ceremonies failed (though few administrative procedures in the White House survived the frequent changes of staff intact). When Sanders came to the White House in 1967, he asked Marvin Watson to decide whether or not there should be signing ceremonies for particular bills, and encouraged him to allow several days between deciding on a ceremony for a bill and the ceremony itself so that there was sufficient time to ensure that guest lists were shrewdly and prudently compiled.

The ceremonies gave Johnson another stage on which to perform. His staff made of them what they wished, suggesting to the president that he identify individual members for special praise as seemed appropriate and worthwhile. For example, the major water project provided for by the Lower Colorado River Bill, so long a subject of bitter contention between California and Arizona, was signed in an elaborate ceremony in the White House on 30 September 1968.[30] At Sprague's suggestion, Johnson proclaimed it 'Carl Hayden Day' as a mark of respect to the retiring Arizona senator who had invested time and political capital in the project over many years.[31] The president also thanked Congressmen Bizz Johnson (D-CA) and Mo Udall (D-AZ) for their contributions to the solution. Even from a lame-duck president, that (together with the publicity the project itself attracted) was thoroughly welcome to Democrats five weeks before an election.

Bill-signing ceremonies naturally provided lobbying opportunities, in much the same way as other White House events did. Occasionally, either on his own initiative or following conversations with his staff, Johnson took Congressional colleagues aside, and urged them to support him on matters of current importance before their committees or on the floor. This task was invariably more difficult in the latter phase of the administration when the electoral reaction against the extension of civil rights legislation into housing policy (in the shape of the 1968 Civil Rights Act) grew more intense, opposition to advancing the frontiers of the Great

---

30 *Congressional Quarterly Almanac, 1968*, p. 444.
31 Sprague, Box 7 (1568), 'Sanders, Barefoot: Memos For', 10/9/68.

Society spread quickly, and the president confined himself to the White House more than he had. Johnson none the less needed no prompting to encourage senators and Congressmen to support him; like Ronald Reagan, Lyndon Johnson made a minute's conversation with the president of the United States seem longer, and strike home.

Pens which the president used to sign bills were sent to those who had helped pass them, especially to major Congressional sponsors and floor managers. Key supporters from important lobbying groups were often favoured with them, too.[32] Johnson used a large number of felt-tip pens in signing each major bill—in the case of the Economic Opportunity Act, no less than seventy-two. Occasionally, he took the advice offered to him by the White House's Chief Clerk, William J. Hopkins, to include the date, time, and place of the signing ceremony in addition to his name so that his signature would be tidier than when he used several pens for each letter of his name. Hopkins told Johnson that other presidents had used this technique: 'President Truman used all of the above legends a number of times. President Kennedy, on occasion, found it necessary to add "President of the United States" in using up the supply of pens.'[33]

Just as the bill signings were used to publicize the Act itself, and to assist the president and members of Congress, so those given the pens made much of them. During Johnson's administration, some Congressional colleagues collected two or three dozen pens which they displayed on their office walls in a glass case to draw the attention of visitors to their support for the president. Underneath each pen, a small inscription indicated the title of the bill which it had been used to sign. During the legislative rush of the 89th Congress, Mike Manatos told Johnson that a number of Democratic senators were keen to have this mark of association with him:[34]

Senators Anderson and Yarborough as well as Congressman Farnum were very much impressed with the pen display you

---

[32] Sprague to Sanders, 30/6/67, Sprague Box 7, 'Sanders, Barefoot: Memos For'.

[33] Hopkins to Valenti, 12/8/64, Reports On Pending Legislation, WHCF LE, Box 5, '1/8/64–26/8/64'.

[34] Manatos to Johnson, 18/1/66, Manatos, Box 15 (1295), 'Yarborough, Ralph W. (D-Tex)'.

showed them and understood you to say if they cared to finance the cost for an exhibit of this kind we would co-operate in having it made. All three of these gentlemen are anxious to purchase such a display even at a cost of $300.00 or $400.00. I saw Senator Anderson this morning in the Senate Office Building and he flatly said that he had to have one of these regardless of the cost. . . They are, of course, particularly anxious to have the plaque at the bottom which indicates that this was presented by you.

CONGRESSIONAL ELECTIONS AND OCR ASSISTANCE

Congressional elections loomed as large in the minds of OCR staff as for their Congressional charges. Much Congressional liaison by White House specialist staff was directed to the strengthening of loyal Democrats' prospects for re-election. Similarly, incumbents sought to turn their relationship with the president to their electoral advantage.

OCR staff also assisted with election campaigns themselves. For allies, much was done: speaking engagements by the president were commonly arranged with the local Congressman standing by, sharing the acclamation for the president. When Johnson visited the home district or state of a loyal supporter, the senator or Congressman was invariably invited to accompany him on *Air Force One*. Cabinet members, too, spoke in the election campaigns of many Democratic candidates. In rural districts, a visit from the Secretary of Agriculture, Orville Freeman, was often welcome; in some western states, the support of the Secretary of the Interior, Stewart Udall, was an asset.

Primary elections were a different matter; Henry Wilson claimed that however hard he worked to promote party members in Congressional elections, it was inappropriate for him or his colleagues to interfere in primary contests.[35] Ever since Franklin Roosevelt's failure to purge certain conservative Democrats in 1938, this had been a sensitive matter for Democratic presidents. The rule was none the less sometimes broken. In the spring of 1964, O'Brien twisted the arm of a

[35] Wilson to O'Brien, 14/4/64, O'Brien, Box 13, 'Cooley, Rep. H.'.

New York City Congressman: 'Congressman Farbstein now wants a picture of the President. I told him that if he was not right on the Farm Bill (which he says he opposes strenuously) he would have to become concerned about the possibility of a Presidential letter to Haddad [Farbstein's primary opponent].'[36]

This was one of the few occasions when O'Brien felt justified in threatening an incumbent, although in jocular form. His judgement was vindicated when, despite his purported opposition, Farbstein voted for the Farm Bill. (He subsequently won both the primary and the general election.) Two months later, O'Brien again brought the weight of the White House to bear in a primary when he asked Johnson to write a letter to Bob Duncan, an incumbent liberal Democratic Congressman in Oregon, as Daly recalled soon afterwards: 'The letter was an investment in future relations with this bright, young Congressman. Further it was designed to insure the defeat of Charlie Porter, who was flashing a letter of endorsement that the President had written when he [Johnson] was majority leader [and Porter the incumbent].'[37] Duncan easily won both the primary and the Congressional election.

LOBBYING

Appeals from OCR staff, and even from the president himself, were likely to be more successful if made to friends rather than strangers, to those with whom he had developed a durable relationship rather than those with whom the elements of one had to be hurriedly built. Aside from legislators' attitudes towards legislation, and their assessments of the political consequences of their votes, the creation of political goodwill towards the president by OCR staff was a prerequisite for lobbying to be effective. Contrary to some caricatures of Johnson's style, he did not spend most of his time on the telephone pleading for the support of Congressional

---

[36] O'Brien to Chuck Daly, 24/3/64, O'Brien, Box 11, 'House of Reps: Misc: 2 of 2'.

[37] Daly to O'Brien, 18/5/64, O'Brien, Box 11, 'House of Reps: Misc: 2 of 2'.

colleagues.[38] Some members (by no means only opponents) never spoke to the president in a private meeting; still less were they telephoned by him regularly for their votes. Staff were reluctant to ask Johnson to make telephone calls to prise bills out of committees, or lobby for swing votes on the floor of either chamber; no aide asked for the president's direct assistance more than was absolutely necessary.[39] The danger was evident: if the administration's most valuable asset, the president, intervened too often, the marginal effect of each call would tend to decline. Private presidential persuasion was not an infinite resource: if a Congressman was telephoned twice by the president in five years, each call was a significant event—if every month, contacts quickly became routine. Besides, news of calls from the president soon spread among politicians and journalists, and expectations rose. Those telephone calls which the president did make to the Hill were mostly to the leadership and committee chairmen, and invariably made at the suggestion of OCR staff.[40]

OCR staff were almost as reluctant to ask the president to make 'thank-you' calls for important votes by a member, even difficult and courageous ones, as to request him to ask for votes in the first place. Eighteen months passed before Henry Wilson asked President Kennedy to thank by telephone any House member except for the leadership.[41] In this regard, Johnson was more resistant to procedural rules and more difficult for staff to restrain than Kennedy had been. Henry Wilson, alive to the danger of the currency of presidential intervention being inflated by Johnson's profligacy, recalled that in the early stages of the administration, the president occasionally broke free:[42]

---

[38] George C. Edwards claims in his book *Presidential Influence in Congress* (San Francisco, 1980) that 'we lack data on the individual level such as whom the President called' (p. 190). This is not so. The files in the Johnson Library provide a near-perfect record of all the president's outside calls: whom he called, the date, time, and duration of the call, and whether it was taped.

[39] Interview with Irvine Sprague.

[40] Jake Jacobsen, aide to Marvin Watson in Johnson's White House Office, Oral History, Johnson Library, p. 22.

[41] Wilson to O'Brien, Wilson, Box 3, 'Memoranda: 1/7/62–9/7/62' (John F. Kennedy Library).

[42] Interview with Wilson, 20/12/78.

One day, in a fit of exuberance, he made three calls to Congressmen because he had seen their birthdays announced, as Congressmen's birthdays were in those days, in *The Washington Post*. A few hours later, I went in to Johnson and asked him why he had sent birthday greetings to the House people. 'Which one of the staff told you I'd called?' asked Johnson. When I told him that no-one had and that the news had got back to me via contacts on the Hill, he was shaken. I told him that if he wanted to make social calls, he should let me know first. And if he made calls for votes, I said 'You've got me in total trouble'. He took the advice.

Occasionally, lobbying produced specific and discernible results. One of the few examples committed to White House notepaper concerns the St John's River Project in Maine in 1965, a hydroelectric power scheme vigorously opposed by regional power and coal interests, but reported out by the House Public Works Committee in a vote of 18 : 15. OCR staff made calls to seven Democratic Members of the committee, and changed four votes, thereby turning defeat into success. Hearing of it, Johnson sent the OCR vote count to Senator Muskie, the Maine Democrat who had strongly supported the project which held out the prospect of cheaper electricity to his constituents.[43] Understandably, Johnson wanted him to know how hard and successfully the White House had worked.

Approaches from the White House for a vote were sometimes solicited by Congressmen and senators caught between district pressures and their own preferences. In the case of the Nasser Amendment in 1965 (a Republican proposal to cut off funding for the export of food to Egypt in retaliation for Nasser's anti-American foreign policy), Congressman Bingham (D-NY) spoke to the whip of the New York Democratic delegation, Abraham Multer. Multer told White House legislative staff that Bingham was unsure whether he could afford to support the president by opposing the amendment, and that it would be useful if the White House could formally request his help.[44] He would then be able to explain his opposition to the amendment by telling constituents that the White House had made a direct appeal for his support. The OCR could thus

[43] WHCF Ex LE, Box 169, 'LE 5 7/5/65-17/1/66'.
[44] O'Brien, Box 12, 'Bingham, Rep. Jonathan B. (D-NY)'.

deflect political criticism from a member and gain an extra vote in the process.

Lobbying and Interest Groups

Interest groups were commonly used by the White House to increase the effectiveness of its lobbying. Johnson's major domestic reforms were supported by labour and liberal interests with whom his liaison staff naturally developed close working relationships. Senior AFL-CIO officials often assisted with White House lobbying for major bills, and were invited to join task forces charged with the responsibility for proposing new programmes for inclusion in future legislation. The OCR's decision on whether to include external lobbying groups in campaigns of their own turned on whether and to what extent such organisations could compensate for White House political weakness, or augment its strengths. The political resources of large, sophisticated, and well-financed lobbies sometimes exceeded the president's, as George Meany, formerly the head of the AFL-CIO, has explained:[45]

Johnson was one President who realized perhaps more than any other. . . the tremendous influence that organised labor has on Capitol Hill. Now we don't brag about that influence but it is very definitely there. We of course spend a lot of time and effort every two years for the Senate and the House elections . . . I can remember him (Johnson) calling me on the telephone on one of the education bills and telling me just where it was, and when the subcommittee was scheduled, how there were one or two votes that were doubtful that he thought I might be helpful on. . .

Much more typical, however, were the regular calls from OCR staff to their many allies in interest groups and organisations asking them to report on the views of certain members towards pending legislative proposals. The large volume of Great Society legislation, quickly written and ardently lobbied through Congress between 1963 and 1968, meant that these contacts were effectively continuous. Labour unions, ethnic groups, educational associations, the churches, liberal businessmen frequently contributed to the OCR lobbies and vote checks; the composition of Johnson's policies made

[45] George Meany, Oral History, Johnson Library, pp. 6-7.

these groups natural allies on a range of issues. None the less, the coalitions of interests which the OCR helped assemble on the president's behalf often went beyond the bounds provided by Great Society legislation. Defence appropriations conference reports often caused the staff to co-ordinate support from, for example, editors of conservative newspapers, labour interests, aerospace companies, and weapons manufacturers.[46] Contacts between the large departmental Congressional liaison offices in the Pentagon and defence contractors were intimate: Jack Stempler, the Pentagon's chief liaison officer, was quite accustomed to arrange for large numbers of telegrams from the contractors and their allies to members of the Defense Appropriations Subcommittees of both chambers in support of the president's views.

Record-Write

Elaborate stratagems had their drawbacks, however. A 'Legislative Support Program', established in the White House at the end of January 1967 under Hardesty's direction, admirably fulfilled Cornford's famous definition of propaganda as 'very nearly deceiving your friends without quite deceiving your enemies'.[47] (Hardesty was nominally a speech writer for the president, but, like other several other non-OCR White House staff members, spent some time assisting Sanders in an attempt to make good some of the OCR's weaknesses.) The group was composed mostly of departmental liaison officers and OCR staff, its remit being to publicise the president's policies, and thereby to supplement lobbying campaigns themselves. Hardesty's and Roche's initial enthusiasm for the cause of 'retaliating with the truth to the expected frequent attacks and criticisms of the opposition' was clear enough, and they enthusiastically pressed the idea on O'Brien: 'There are many vehicles for performing the mission—statements in support of presidential messages, testimony at hearings, debate on the floor, newsletters and news releases, radio and television

---

[46] Sprague to Sanders, 8/9/67, Sprague, Box 7 (1568), 'Sanders, Barefoot: Memos For'.

[47] Roche and Hardesty to O'Brien, 27/1/67, Roche, Box 5 (1819), 'Memos to Staff'. Bob Hardesty enjoyed pointing out that, from Johnson's perspective, it ought more accurately to have been spelt 'Record-Right'. Cornford, F. M., *Microcosmographia Academica*, Preface to the 1922 edition, Cambridge.

broadcasts, news conferences, public appearances outside Washington, contacts with key interest groups.'[48]

The arrangement did not work quite as smoothly as they had hoped, nor was it noticeably effective. It none the less quickly became a lively White House speech-writing office supplying propaganda to legislators.[49] Hardesty and his small band of assistants wrote speeches favouring the president's policies on matters as diverse as open-housing legislation, Vietnam, and the tax surcharge legislation of his final year. Sometimes, senators and Congressmen asked the OCR for a suitable speech they wished to deliver. Usually, however, White House staff sought out members who, if unwilling to read the speeches on the Senate or House floors, were at least ready to insert them into the *Congressional Record*.

The exercise seemed to influence the president more than anyone else. Johnson read the *Record* every day, and in the latter phases of his presidency insisted that a summary of pro and anti-administration speeches be ready for him to read over breakfast. He set great store by commentaries of praise and laudatory editorials, inspired and written by his own staff. It was altogether odd: the president of the United States sponsored a programme to supply prepared material to members of Congress for insertion into a journal which no one except *aficionados* of legislative politics read, and few regarded as especially significant. Yet if upon reading the summary prepared for him Johnson found that critical speeches outnumbered the favourable, Hardesty (like politicians' assistants since time immemorial) bore the brunt of the president's anger.[50] Remarkably, Johnson even instructed cabinet members, already burdened by the huge task of giving leadership to fissiparous departments, to read the products of this strange recycling exercise. In late November 1967, he told cabinet members that they should all spend more time

[48] Roche and Hardesty to O'Brien, 27/1/67.

[49] The attempt was never made to launch a lobbying campaign on television. O'Brien never forgot that Kennedy's speech urging the Congressional passage of Medicare on 20 May 1962 in Madison Square Garden succeeded only in irritating Wilbur Mills. It did not alter the voting balance at all. O'Brien was ever after strongly averse to going over the heads of members of Congress by direct appeals to the electorate (O'Brien, *No Final Victories*, New York, 1974, pp. 133-4).

[50] Interview with George Christian, May 1979 and Apr. 1981.

promoting his legislation. Warming to his theme, he called for greater commitment from those around him to arresting his political decline:[51]

The first thing you should do every day is read the *Congressional Record*. I read it every day, I read all the bad things they say about you. . . All of you get your share of criticism in the *Record*. Now the White House shouldn't have to be your crutch. We shouldn't have to carry you. You should be your own boss and your own best defender.

Call your Assistant Secretaries in and ask them to look in your trade papers, professional magazines and those of your constituencies. . . Put them in the *Congressional Record*. . . If even a small paper praises you, get it in the *Record*. We have a campaign coming. Our opponents are getting 5–6 speeches a day in the *Record* and we're not. . . We're not doing it now. We are oblivious to it. I would like each of you to produce two or three of these items a week. Put in an editorial or two or a speech or something from the *Farm Service Journal* or NIH [National Institute of Health] publications.

CONCLUSION

Johnson's frustrated plea indicates something of his strengths and weaknesses as a legislative leader. These exhortations in November 1967 sprang from his increasing sense of isolation—political and physical—in the last Congress of his presidential term. The arrangement was an indication of Johnson's declining influence with Congress as he lost his sureness of touch, and his OCR fell into some disarray. Whereas his extraordinary knowledge and understanding of Congressional politics aided him greatly in his early presidential years, so the limitations became more apparent later. His injunctions to cabinet members to read the daily edition of the *Record* shows this, for even had they complied (which was most unlikely) the outcome would have done nothing to pass legislation, raise his standing in the opinion polls, or assist his re-election.[52]

[51] The president, Cabinet Papers, Box 11, 'Cabinet Meeting, 1/11/67,(1 of 2)'.

[52] Johnson's enthusiasm for this exercise would have been more appropriate for a senator or representative striving to gain publicity. It was another indication of the extent to which his political perspective remained that of a legislator.

None the less, taking his presidency as a whole, Johnson was the single most important asset to effective liaison and lobbying in the White House. By November 1963, OCR staff knew the components of success, appreciated the constraints upon them, understood Congressional procedure, and, much more significantly, knew the foibles, views, and weaknesses of individual Congressmen and senators. Coupled with Johnson's unrivaled legislative skill and experience, this enabled the White House to employ small favours shrewdly and subtly to win the confidence of members; the weakness of Congressional parties made it all the more important for the president to add to his store of political capital with them as individuals. Access to the president, whether for full meetings, social occasions, or quick campaign photographs, was politically valuable, especially in the early days when Johnson was powerful and popular. Even then, with large Congressional majorities, liaison was a necessary foundation for successful lobbying. Presidential or staff lobbying when votes were needed was much more likely to succeed on the foundations of a long-standing relationship between the White House and individuals. OCR staff rarely had to ask twice (and often not at all) for favours to be returned; the exchange process was continuous.

Small favours do not rank high in the scale of liaison and lobbying mythology. The major levers of persuasion, patronage, and projects are better known, though often misunderstood. But Johnson considered small favours an effective demonstration of his attention to individual Congressmen and senators, a symbol of his gratitude to supporters, and an important source of his influence over Congress. His OCR staff rightly regarded them as a prized addition to his limited resources, and their prudent deployment a boost to the president's prospects of bridging the gap between executive and Congressional branches to his political advantage.

6

THE INCOME TAX SURCHARGE

INTRODUCTION

Of Johnson's three major policy concerns—civil rights, the Great Society programmes, and the Vietnam War—only the first made little claim on the federal budget: the mix of welfare and education programmes, and especially the massive commitment of military force abroad, were hugely expensive. None the less, had it not been for Vietnam, the growth of federal domestic expenditures could certainly have been contained because the income tax cut of 1964, passed in the wake of President Kennedy's death, quickened the pace of economic activity considerably in mid-decade.[1] Unemployment fell from 5.7 per cent in 1963 to 4.7 per cent in 1965; the 1964 tax stimulus added some $24bn. to GNP (on an annualised rate) by the second quarter of 1965; prices were relatively stable, increasing by just 1.5 per cent per annum in the spring of 1965, and unit labour costs actually fell slightly.[2] 'New Economics' had apparently come to full flower. It was accepted as the official orthodoxy throughout the government—not only in the Council of Economic Advisers (CEA), where Walter Heller had long advocated fiscal stimulus to achieve a low unemployment rate of 4 per cent, but in the Treasury too. It had even some following in that citadel of financial caution, the Federal Reserve Board.[3]

Intent upon avoiding the political conflict which he anticipated would result, Johnson declined to set clear budgetary priorities as Vietnam spending increased with the bombing programme and the commitment of ground troops in the spring and summer of 1965.[4] Financing the Great Society programmes, the president's first concern, increased

[1] Okun, A., *The Political Economy of Prosperity*, Washington, DC, 1970, pp. 47–8.
[2] Okun, A., *The Political Economy of Prosperity*, pp. 47–8.
[3] Tobin, J., *The New Economics One Decade Older*, Princeton, 1974, p. 34.
[4] Schick, A., *Congress and Money*, Washington, DC, 1980, p. 25.

budgetary and inflationary pressures. In his 1967 Fiscal Year (FY 67) budget, issued half-way through the halcyon days of the 89th Congress, Johnson confidently asserted the country's ability to wage a foreign war and develop domestic welfare.[5]

Later in 1966, his economic advisers began to discuss with him the need for fiscal restraint; Johnson in turn explored the possibilities with Wilbur Mills, the chairman of the House Ways and Means Committee.[6] With no encouragement from Mills, the president none the less decided to request a surcharge on personal and corporate income tax of 6 per cent in his 1967 State of the Union Message.[7] Attempting to insulate his domestic programmes, and appealing to patriotism in support of an unpopular fiscal measure, he requested the surcharge only 'for so long as the unusual expenditures associated with our efforts in Vietnam continue', thereby sweetening the pill by implying that the increase was exceptional and temporary. The budget deficit actually incurred in FY 1967 was $8.7bn., an increase of $4.9bn. over 1966.[8] Government forecasts indicated that the deficit would rise further in 1968.

This chapter is a study of the passage of the income tax surcharge (the Revenue and Expenditure Control Act, 1968, HR 15414) through Congress viewed from the perspective of White House lobbying and the OCR. It does not provide a detailed legislative history but considers those aspects of the operation of the OCR which the bill's passage highlights. After an introductory section which sets the economic and historical context, the chapter analyses the administration's Congressional liaison and lobbying campaign. The importance of presidential leadership through the OCR, the Department of the Treasury, and, to a lesser extent, the cabinet, is emphasised. The contributions of these agencies are themselves then considered in the light of the co-ordination and friction between them. White House lobbying is assessed in the light of four main factors: the relative weakness of the president

[5] *Congressional Quarterly Almanac, 1967*, Washington, DC, p. 6A.

[6] Pierce, L. C., *The Politics of Fiscal Policy Formation*, Pacific Palisades, 1970, p. 148; Ackley, G., Oral History, Johnson Library, Tape no. 1, p. 33.

[7] *Congressional Quarterly Almanac, 1967*, p. 6A.

[8] Schick, *Congress and Money*, Table 3, p. 27; *Congressional Quarterly Almanac, 1968*, p. 265.

and of the OCR's staff and its procedures late in Johnson's presidency; the caution of Congress in an election year; and the powerful position of key Congressional whales, most especially Wilbur Mills. It also illustrates the complexity of the American legislative process which renders presidential leadership both essential and difficult.

The president sent Congress a message requesting passage of a tax surcharge twelve months after his economic advisers had urged it upon him, and late in his presidency. The government's economic forecasts indicated continuing growth of the budget deficit; the request was therefore for a 10 per cent rather than a 6 per cent surcharge on the basic rate (not a tax increase of 10 per cent).[9] Unlike the tax cut of 1964, this one contained no redistributive clauses. This, coupled with the absence of any tax reform, and perhaps its justification as finance for an unpopular war, reduced liberal support in Congress.[10] Many liberals, anxious to support a Democratic president, urged that the package should include some move of this kind, if only a promise of future action. Without it, their support could not be assumed. To placate liberals, and preserve his cherished programmes, Johnson proposed no spending cuts, but Congressional conservatives, and in particular Wilbur Mills, opposed a tax increase without them.

Even by the standards of the pre-reform Congress, Mills was an unusually powerful chairman, matching fine political judgement with a complete understanding of his committee's work. Without expenditure reductions, he was not prepared to allow the surcharge proposal out of Ways and Means in 1967: he claimed that the House, which has the constitutional responsibility of initiating all revenue legislation, would not support an increase on such terms. On 3 October 1967, the committee voted 20:5 in favour of tabling the surcharge until the administration produced an acceptable programme of reductions in federal expenditure.[11] Disappointed by the steady growth in non-defence spending since the 1964 tax cut, despite presidential pledges of restraint, Mills was determined in early 1968 to hold the tax surcharge hostage

[9] Pierce, *The Politics of Fiscal Policy Formation*, p. 149.
[10] See p. 122.
[11] *Congressional Quarterly Almanac, 1967*, p. 643.

until his price of significant spending cuts was agreed to, and the entire package assured of majority support on the floor. If the president really wanted a tax increase, he would be obliged to address the question of expenditure. Only in this way could Mills exert pressure on the president: because Appropriations disbursed, and Ways and Means taxed, there was no institutional forum in which the budget as a whole might be considered.

In the ensuing months, this disaggregated process caused difficulties of a kind which advanced the cause of budgetary reform, issuing eventually in the establishment of the Congressional budget committees under the provisions of the Budget and Impoundment Control Act of 1974.[12]

CONGRESSIONAL ATTITUDES TO THE SURCHARGE

The president's budget for FY 69 increased expenditures from $175.4bn. to $186.1bn., a small increment considering that 60 per cent of the budget was 'uncontrollable' expenditure, and that war spending was rising quickly to high levels: by January 1968, spending on Vietnam accounted for 3 per cent of GNP. Significantly, the phrase 'War on Poverty' was dropped from the Office of Economic Opportunity's five-page press release, three pages of which recorded financial and programme retrenchment for FY 69.[13] In January 1968, Mills was almost persuaded by the evidence put by senior administration witnesses from the Troika (the heads of the Treasury, the Council of Economic Advisers, and the Bureau of the Budget, all close economic advisers to the president) and the Federal Reserve Board, to report the surcharge out in order that the dollar might be supported; Charles Schultze, the Director of the Bureau of the Budget (BOB), assured Mills that the federal budget was under strict control. Finally, however, the chairman remained unconvinced and sent Schultze and Secretary of the Treasury Henry Fowler away to pare spending further.[14] The administration soon reached

12 Schick, *Congress and Money*, chapter two.
13 *The Washington Post*, 30/1/68.
14 *The Washington Post*, 24/1/68.

an impasse with Mills and his committee, as Pierce observed: '. . .Mills was stuck. He could not force the President or the Chairman of the Appropriations Committee to ask Congress to cut expenditure. Neither could the President force Mills to report out the Bill, so long as Mills believed it would be defeated.'[15]

These procedural and political difficulties were overcome in the Senate. During Finance Committee hearings there on a bill extending excise taxes on telephones and cars, passed by the House on 19 February, Senators Williams (R-DE) and Smathers (D-FL) proposed to attach the tax surcharge to the Excise Tax Bill.[16] Senator Long (D-LA), chairman of the Finance Committee, opposed the connection on the grounds that it would violate the constitutional provision requiring all tax bills to originate in the House, and the Smathers–Williams amendment was defeated in the Finance Committee by one vote on 14 March. Like his liberal allies, Senator Fred Harris (D-OK) knew that Senator Williams was trying to embarrass the Democrats by attaching to the surcharge spending cuts so severe that many could not then support it, and so voted against.[17] None the less, it was voted through on the Senate floor on 2 April by 53 : 35.[18] It included the 10 per cent surcharge (linking it with a total cut in New Obligational Authority of $10bn. in order to achieve a spending cut of $6bn.), and placed limits on the growth of federal employment.[19] Mills did not object to this unusual procedure for, without it, his objective of expenditure reductions might not have been achieved. The new question was how great an expenditure reduction Mills could force on Johnson. For the president, the Senate's $6bn. figure was an ominous sign since it was unlikely that Mills and his conservative allies would now accept less.

The vote was taken just two days after Johnson withdrew from the 1968 election. Although his speech of withdrawal had dealt mostly with Vietnam, Johnson also urged that the tax bill should be passed, with the 'expenditure control that

15 Pierce, *The Politics of Fiscal Policy Formation*, p. 161.
16 Unlike the House, the Senate has no rule of germaneness.
17 WHCF Ex FG 400 1/1/68, Box 326, 'FG 400: 15/3/68–28/3/68'.
18 *The New York Times*, 3/4/68.
19 *Congressional Quarterly Almanac, 1968*, p. 269.

the Congress may desire and dictate'.[20] As in his State of the Union address two months before, he couched his plea in patriotic terms—the defence of the dollar.[21] The devaluation of sterling in November 1967 had caused increasing instability in the international monetary system and put heavy pressure on the US dollar, intensified by speculation on the international gold market. This ceased only in mid-March with an agreement among finance ministers and central bankers to establish a two-tier gold system for gold transactions. Official sales of gold were separated from industrial and commercial sales, and the US government agreed to continue to sell gold—on the official market—at the old price of $35 an ounce.[22] In addition, a provision requiring all US Federal Reserve notes in circulation to be backed by gold to 25 per cent of their face value was rescinded, thereby making $10.7bn. of gold available if needed on the official market. Henceforth, SDRs, and not gold, would be used to enlarge monetary reserves.[23]

After the vote on the Senate floor, the bill went to conference committee, the Joint Committee on Internal Revenue Taxation. But the administration took no stand on whether the $6bn. expenditure cut was too great; George Mahon, chairman of the House Appropriations Committee, was therefore unwilling to present a programme of cuts to it. He declined to assume that presidential responsibility and run the risks of pressing ahead alone.

Mills none the less insisted that Mahon's Committee act first in producing the cuts required before he acted on the surcharge. On 1 May, Appropriations unanimously passed an administration-backed resolution, that FY 69 aggregate spending be cut by 'not less than' $4bn., new projected obligational authority for FY 69 by $10bn., and unspent appropriations by $8bn.[24] The package was sponsored by the president, attempting to avoid an expenditure cut of $6bn. which most Republicans would have been pleased to secure. The 10 per cent tax surcharge, linked to an expenditure cut

[20] Johnson, L. B., *The Vantage Point*, New York, 1971, p. 452.
[21] Johnson, *The Vantage Point*, p. 452.
[22] Johnson, *The Vantage Point*, pp. 316–19.
[23] *Congressional Quarterly Almanac, 1968*, p. 170.
[24] *Congressional Quarterly Almanac, 1968*, p. 274.

of at least $4bn., was then approved by the Ways and Means Committee on 6 May after a Republican attempt to link the surcharge to a $6bn. cut was defeated on a straight party-line vote of 15:10.[25] But to the surprise and evident annoyance of the president and his staff, Mills and Senator Long engineered conference committee approval of a $6bn. cut in expenditures (having previously agreed on a $5bn. compromise with the president), citing the Appropriations Committee's use of the phrase 'not less than $4bn.' in their support.[26] Conference committee Republican members had themselves already passed a party resolution in support of $6bn.[27] Conference Reports traditionally returned to both Houses with floor procedures precluding amendment.

For most of May, the president's view of the report was unclear; opinion among his staff and cabinet colleagues was sharply divided on the wisdom of accepting large cuts in a small, but politically important, part of the budget. Fowler lobbied hard to secure passage of the surcharge, and was readier than the OCR staff to concede larger expenditure cuts as the price of passage. Sanders supported Johnson's private view that the price demanded was excessive, but the president was willing to accept a higher price from Mills because he shared the view of Wilbur Cohen, the Secretary of Health, Education and Welfare (HEW), that the specification of the cuts by Appropriations subcommittees would cause so severe a political response from those affected by them that the cuts would be restored. At a cabinet meeting in mid-May, when Johnson had reluctantly concluded that he would have to agree to $6bn. if the surcharge was to be approved, he observed that: 'The roof is going to come off when we cut out impact school areas, REA, Engineer Corps projects. I have always thought that they will put it back in. . . When the telegrams start coming in, they'll act to put the money back.'[28]

Johnson left none of his cabinet colleagues in any doubt as to his view: 'We have to try to get this thing. . . I'm willing to do pretty near anything for the tax bill.'[29]

[25] *Congressional Quarterly Almanac, 1968*, p. 276.
[26] Pierce, *The Politics of Fiscal Policy Formation*, p. 168.
[27] Pierce, *The Politics of Fiscal Policy Formation*, p. 169.
[28] Cabinet Papers, Box 13, 'Cabinet Meeting, 1/5/68, (4 of 4)'.
[29] Cabinet Papers, Box 13, 'Cabinet Meeting, 1/5/68, (4 of 4)'.

The controllable portion of the budget was quite small, even in 1968. Since Vietnam expenditures were protected, the cuts fell disproportionately on urban and anti-poverty programmes, the lodestone of the Democratic Party's pledge to the underprivileged.[30] To reduce these commitments in 1968 ran against Johnson's judgement and preferences; it weakened him in the eyes of blacks and liberals (as it would Humphrey in his campaign for the presidency), and strengthened Robert Kennedy. The war was to blame, as Arthur Okun later concluded:[31]

In the fiscal years 1964 and 1965, the declining defense budget was a key catalyst in producing Lyndon Johnson's magic compound of great new social programs, tax cuts, and tight control on the total of the federal budget. Once the Vietnam buildup began, however, the same paradox squeezed nondefense spending and yet generated complaints about reckless government civilian spending.

The liberal response came at the end of May when James Burke, a Democratic Congressman from Massachusetts, introduced a motion in the House directing the conferees to reduce spending cuts to $4bn. The Treasury was only lukewarm in its support, but the White House backed it.[32] None the less, 92 Democrats opposed the proposal, and it was defeated by 137 votes to 259.[33] With the options now clarified, the president prepared his staff and colleagues to support the $6bn. figure, as the only means by which a tax increase might be secured.

Burke's move reflected widespread liberal unease, both in Congress and outside, at the political implications of the cuts. The Speaker, too, was disquieted, and unwilling to support Mills's package until he was certain that no chance remained of reducing their political impact and substantive effect. The Democratic Study Group (DSG), normally content to follow the lead of OCR staff on domestic policy, now scattered: some, such as the Illinois Congressman James O'Hara, were willing to organise against the Conference Report, even after Sanders had explained the grave consequences of defeating

30 Schick, *Congress and Money*, p. 37.
31 Okun, *The Political Economy of Prosperity*, p. 127.
32 *Congressional Quarterly Almanac, 1968*, p. 276.
33 *Congressional Quarterly Almanac, 1968*, p. 276.

it.[34] Others, such as Dan Rostenkowski and Frank Thompson,
liberals from Illinois and New Jersey, were content to be seen
to support the smaller cuts in the Burke motion, and then to
vote for the Conference Report. Thus the battle over the
administration's eventual acceptance of the $6bn. cuts was
one between left, centre, and right—between those who
thought the price of deeper cuts in urban and anti-poverty
programmes too high, those who thought them painful but
necessary, and those who welcomed them as an opportunity
to undo liberal excesses.

The House adopted the Conference Report by a 268:150
roll call vote on 20 June, and the Senate followed the next
day with a 64:16 vote of approval. The president signed the
bill into law on 28 June.[35] In addition to the $6bn. spending
cut, the Act provided for a $10bn. reduction in new
obligational authority; an $8bn. rescission of unobligated
balances; selected reductions in federal employment; accelerated collection of corporate taxes; and sundry other
measures. The net effect of the package eliminated the deficit
of $25.3bn. in FY 68, producing a surplus of $3.4bn. in FY
69, Johnson's last budget.[36]

THE WHITE HOUSE LOBBYING

The divisions of opinion within the administration and among
its usual supporters made lobbying complicated, especially in
the light of the OCR's fewer (and mostly less able) staff. The
lobbying campaign was marked by Johnson's typically close
personal involvement, and also by the different parts played
by the OCR, other senior administration officials, and cabinet
officers. From the moment the surcharge was first sent to
Congress, the president supervised the lobbying, and insisted
that he be kept informed of all the contacts made by Treasury
and OCR staff. Barefoot Sanders frequently asked Johnson
for advice but did not normally trouble him with detailed

[34] Sanders to Johnson, 22/5/68, WHCF Ex LE/FI 11-4, 1/5/68, Box 54, 'LE/FI
11-4: 16/5/68–27/5/68'.
[35] *Congressional Quarterly Almanac, 1968*, p. 278.
[36] Pierce, *The Politics of Fiscal Policy Formation*, p. 172.

reports about the views of individuals—although junior OCR staff, such as Sprague and Gonella, prepared some reports on Congressional intelligence and conversations for Sanders who used them as a basis for lobbying waverers.[37]

Even towards the close of his presidency, Johnson was still able to draw on party ties and feelings of personal loyalty although they were less marked among committed liberals, reflecting their widespread distrust of him in the last phase of his presidency, and returning his former lack of regard for them. Soon after the Conference Committee decided in early May to cut expenditure by $6bn., OCR staff found strong objections to Mills's preferred price but reported that many were willing to support Johnson provided that he would assume the risks of a public declaration, as Sprague reported to Sanders on 9 May:[38]

Harley Staggers. . .'I'll do whatever the President wants. Just tell me'. *Mo Udall.* . . 'I can go either way. The $6bn. is too high, but I'll support it if the President wants it.' *Bizz Johnson.* . .Bizz will vote for the bill: 'I only hope the President goes easy on Public Works cuts. That's all I have in my district'. Bizz thinks the $6bn. is far too high.

The following day, Gonella reported that he had spoken to Henry Helstoski, a liberal Democratic Congressman from New Jersey: 'He asks the same question as the others: "What is the President's position, because I always like to go with him as far as I possibly can?" '[39]

As president, Johnson was powerfully placed to exert influence over Congressmen of his own party by public appeals and statements, and by persuading them privately of his need for their assistance. Notwithstanding this, his task in the House was enormous, for Mills had built his legislative reputation on his sure ability to judge its mood. OCR members therefore had to ensure sufficient floor support for

[37] There were, of course, exceptions to this. See, for example, the note from Califano to the president on 10 May 1968: WHCF Ex LE/FI 11-4, 1/5/68, Box 54, 'LE/FI 11-4: 1/5/68-15/5/68'.

[38] 9/5/68, Sprague, Box 7 (1568), 'Sanders, Barefoot: Memos For'.

[39] Gonella to Johnson, 10/5/68, Sprague, Box 7 (1568), 'Sanders, Barefoot: Memos For'.

an alternative if there was to be any prospect of Mills's calculation altering.

These were not ideal circumstances for Johnson's peculiar talents. He was a product of the Senate rather than the House, and not nearly as skilled at understanding the nuances and complexities of that larger rule-bound chamber.[40] The Senate leadership attended White House breakfasts, of course, and to that extent were privy to the tactical deliberations of the House leadership, the president, and Sanders. But they were only minor actors in the play. Mansfield kept out of the politicking over the Smathers–Williams amendment; he could not be seen to lend his support to a manœuvre which in Russell Long's opinion violated the revenue origination clause.[41] Once the Senate passed the Smathers–Williams amendment, its role was confined to voting on the Conference Report by which stage OCR staff knew that it would be approved.[42]

By 1968, Johnson had been absent from Capitol Hill for seven and a half years. Although many former colleagues still sat in the chamber at the end of his presidency, the turnover in the House had been high. Since November 1960, 30 senators and 273 representatives had resigned or been defeated.[43] The liberal class of 1964 had come, and partly gone; House politics were shifting away from the forms familiar to him. On the other hand, Johnson's withdrawal from the presidential race in the early spring hampered his effectiveness on the surcharge but little—even if, as some of his staff reckoned, it did so elsewhere.[44] The president viewed the surcharge as essential for the country's stability, and his highest domestic legislative priority; to the extent that he presented his withdrawal as offering an opportunity for the restoration of national unity and as a symbol of the country's peaceful purposes, it may temporarily and marginally have

[40] Interview with George Christian, 22/4/79.
[41] Manatos to Johnson, 22/3/68, WHCF Ex FG 400, 1/1/68, Box 326, 'FG 400: 15/3/68–28/3/68'.
[42] Sanders to Johnson, 14/5/68, Califano, Box 54 (1757), 'Califano: Taxes: 1967–1968'.
[43] Bibby, J. F., Mann, T. E., and Ornstein, N. J., *Vital Statistics on Congress, 1980*, Washington, DC, 1980, pp. 14–15.
[44] Interview with Barefoot Sanders, 24/4/79.

enhanced his leverage.[45] In any case, he had no need to hoard his remaining political capital; to that extent, his political freedom (at least in the spring) was augmented rather than diminished.

The weakened OCR remained the prime source of information and tactical advice to the president, though no longer the dominant element in its management because the erosion of its capabilities had weakened its authority over government departments, a development which Johnson did little to arrest. This decreased the influence of the president over legislators on the Hill, lessening the effect which shrewd deployment of his resources had over their behaviour. Whilst the Office had lost status, prestige, and authority within the White House, Sanders strove to retain as much control as possible over liaison and lobbying strategies and tactics. The OCR was still an important clearing-house for liaison with individual Congressmen, committee chairmen, the leadership, and liberal and labour groups outside Congress.

Sanders had little influence over the Treasury, however, where Henry Fowler was dedicated to a tax increase; Johnson's high regard for Fowler strengthened the Treasury Secretary's political position within the administration. Fowler was accordingly able to resist Sanders's attempts to make effective the authority of OCR director; the rules upon which Kennedy and Johnson rightly insisted when O'Brien led the OCR no longer applied. Instead, Fowler drew freely on well-established contacts with organised business and banking organisations to press for the bill's passage. Relations between the OCR and the Treasury were discordant, made worse by Fowler's manifest determination to pass the surcharge at almost any price Wilbur Mills might set, and not at one which the OCR director understood to be the president's preference. That itself was a symptom of OCR weakness, and an indication of the president's disinclination to restore its strength and authority over nominally subject departments.

Sanders maintained O'Brien's principle that the president should be asked to lobby directly only occasionally although, when Johnson withdrew from the presidential race at the end of March, Sanders's customary caution dissipated a little. He

---

[45] *Congressional Quarterly Almanac, 1968*, p. 90A.

asked Johnson on three occasions to make telephone calls to House members, and once to speak to a member at a judicial reception.[46] Califano, always eager to advise the president on any subject whether in his jurisdiction or not, soon added his support. The advantage of lame-duck status would, he said, quickly disappear, especially if Wilbur Mills pushed the $6bn. package of cuts through: 'I think we should turn loose everything we have to take the Ways and Means Committee away from Mills. This would include not only calls from Barefoot, but perhaps even a few critical ones by you. . .'[47]

This indicates both the seriousness of the battle in which the White House was engaged, and Califano's appreciation of the importance of using presidential interventions with care. None the less, the president was later obliged to intervene even after he had lost the fight for smaller expenditure cuts: on 29 May, the Burke motion to instruct the conferees to reduce spending cuts to $4bn. was defeated in the House. Knowing it would fail, the president told a cabinet meeting at midday that he had no option but to go ahead with $6bn. (though he did not say so publicly until two days later). As part of a general lobbying programme by cabinet members, Johnson added that he would personally call a number of Congressmen himself: 'We'll put a chart up here of our contacts and victories and I'll take my share. In fact, I'll take the cream of the crop so that I will look good next to the rest of you on the chart.'[48]

In the cases of Dan Rostenkowski, William Green (D-PA), and Jim O'Hara (D-MI), Sanders suggested presidential calls because he judged that they were unofficial leaders for delegations or groups. Sanders characterised Green as 'the bell cow in Philadelphia', said that Rostenkowski was similarly influential among the Cook County delegation, and noted that Jim O'Hara carried the greatest weight within the DSG.[49] Of the other seven on Johnson's list, two were listed simply as intending to vote 'wrong', but susceptible to presidential persuasion, one of whom, Jake Pickle, was an old

46 Interview with Sanders.
47 WHCF Ex LE/FI 11-4, 1/5/68, Box 54, 'LE/FI 11-4: 9/6/68-30/6/68'.
48 Cabinet Papers, Box 13, 'Cabinet Meeting, 29/5/68 (2 of 3)'.
49 Sanders to Johnson, WHCF Ex LE/FI 11-4, 1/5/68, Box 54, 'LE/FI 11-4: 28/5/68-28/6/68'.

friend who represented Johnson's former Congressional district in Texas. He eventually supported the president on the final floor vote. Then, on 18 June, Sanders advised him to call Congressman Barrett (D-PA) in an attempt to win not only his vote but those of his Philadelphia colleagues James Byrne and Joshua Eilberg—the three had clearly not followed Green's lead.[50] On the day of the vote itself, 20 June, Sanders suggested that Johnson try O'Hara again, 'not only because of his leadership in the DSG but because we have no Democratic votes in Michigan', Henry Gonzalez, a liberal Texan Democrat whom Johnson knew well, and Jim Burke, the Massachusetts Democrat who had proposed the liberal amendment instructing the conferees. Burke was now being lobbied to vote 'no' by the Industrial Union Department of the AFL-CIO.[51] Johnson was successful in persuading all except Barrett to support him, although O'Hara was the only Michigan Democrat to do so.

Johnson made poor use of press conferences to build public and Congressional support though his difficulty lay partly in the unpopularity of tax increases with the electorate. Further, Mills resented any attempt by the president to play the lobbying game in public; Johnson was in no position to bully him publicly as he had Senator Byrd in 1965 about the scheduling of committee meetings on Medicare. Just as Mills was upset by Kennedy's 1962 speech in New York supporting an earlier Medicare proposal, so he disliked Johnson's two open appeals for the tax bill's passage in November 1967 and early May 1968.[52] Mills's resentment at the bypassing of normal Congressional channels was all the greater for Johnson using such words as 'blackmail' when questioned about Congress's (Johnson's euphemism for Mills's) exaction of the $6bn. expenditure cuts.[53] Moreover, in both November and May, Mills objected to the president's criticism of Congressional 'delay'. After the November 1967 press conference, he indicated his displeasure by declining to attend a meeting at the White House.

[50] WHCF Ex LE/FI 11-4, 1/5/68, Box 54, 'LE/FI 11-4: 9/6/68–20/6/68'.
[51] WHCF Ex LE/FI 11-4, 1/5/68, Box 54, 'LE/FI 11-4: 9/6/68–20/6/68'.
[52] O'Brien, L. F., *No Final Victories*, New York, 1974, p. 134.
[53] *The New York Times*, 4/5/68.

In Congressman Al Ullman's (D-OR) judgement, the press conference of 3 May prevented agreement on a compromise $5bn. spending cut, so hostile was the reaction of many Congressmen to the president's intervention.[54] No OCR member, least of all Sanders, urged Johnson to adopt an unyielding position with Mills and his allies. Johnson's intemperate intervention stemmed largely from Califano's advice the previous evening when he recommended that Johnson should take the offensive and 'give consideration to coming out fighting in your press conference tomorrow evening for the tax package we agreed to Tuesday night [i.e., the package with the $4bn. cuts].'[55]

THE ROLE OF THE OCR

Sanders had a much less effective liaison unit working for him in the White House than O'Brien (who, by early 1968, played little part in the OCR) had enjoyed. Irvine Sprague and John Gonella assisted Sanders with head-counting, but rarely with lobbying. Chuck Roche was busier, and de Vier Pierson spent 'countless hours seeing and re-seeing Congressmen till blue in the face'.[56] Roche sent colourful reports to Johnson, (even occasionally deigning to do so via Sanders) of northern Democratic opinion.[57] Bob Hardesty and Jim Jones, the president's speech-writer and appointments secretary respectively, helped from time to time. Usually, however, Barefoot Sanders shouldered most of the burden; there were few full-time OCR colleagues upon whom he could depend.

Handicapped by the generally mediocre remaining full-time OCR staff, and unable to weld its disparate elements into a cohesive lobbying unit, Sanders had to gather much of the Congressional intelligence himself; he could not depend on his staff to provide him with daily reports and assessments of

[54] Califano to Johnson, 17/11/67, WHCF Ex LE/FI 11-4, 16/9/66, Box 53, 'LE/FI 11-4: 10/10/67–31/12/67'; Sprague to Sanders, 9/5/68, Sprague, Box 7 (1568), 'Sanders, Barefoot: Memos For'.
[55] Califano to Johnson, 2/5/68.
[56] de Vier Pierson, Oral History, Johnson Library, Tape no. 1, p. 23.
[57] Roche, C., Box 3, 'Memos to the President, 1968'.

opinion.[58] Drawing on what he heard, and taking special notice of opinion-leaders and key swing voters, Sanders advised the president of tactical difficulties. Johnson participated in meetings with Congressional whales armed with departmental and OCR briefs and suggestions for the presentation of his position.

Close to Congressional opinion throughout, Sanders's advice was invariably sound. It was he who proposed that liberals should be given a chance to vote on a $4bn. expenditure cut package instead of $6bn.[59] Six days before the vote on this Burke motion, nineteen liberal Democratic Congressmen were invited to the Oval Office to discuss the tax bill with the president. All of the members supported Johnson more than 90 per cent of the time in 1967; eleven gave no less than 98 per cent support. Sanders advised Johnson to stress that much as he loathed the idea of expenditure cuts in domestic programmes, there was 'a compelling and overriding necessity for a Tax Bill as soon as possible', and to state his support for the Burke motion but to leave open the question of whether or not he would support the Conference Report's $6bn. reductions if the Burke motion failed:[60]

I doubt that this is the time or the forum in which to announce a decision on this. The hard sell on the need for a Tax Bill will leave the clear message that the President will be forced to accept the Conference Report. . . I think a better time for announcing a decision to support the Conference Report will be after the Burke motion is defeated. And a better forum would be by a letter to the Speaker or in a meeting with the Democratic Leadership.

The president's judgement was sure to be finer if his 'eyes and ears' in the OCR kept him informed of important Congressional views and gossip. Sanders supplemented the simple messenger role with appropriately shrewd political advice, and was the more valuable to the president because of it. Among other Congressional staff to work for Johnson, only O'Brien and Wilson possessed comparable skills. Like them, Sanders acted as a presidential emissary, not just in

    [58] Confidential interview with a member of the Johnson White House staff.
    [59] Sanders to Johnson, 5/9/68, WHCF Ex LE/FI 11-4, 1/5/68, Box 54, 'LE/FI 11-4: 1/5/68–15/5/68'.
    [60] Sanders to Johnson, 23/5/68, WHCF Confidential Files, Box 23, 'LE/FI 11-4'.

lobbying Congressmen, but in discussing awkward political questions with Congressional allies, especially the leadership and chairmen. Before Johnson's important White House meetings at the end of April with the leadership, Mahon and Mills, Sanders discussed strategy and tactics with all except Mills, urging them to limit expenditure cuts to $4bn. Most of the discussion revolved around the White House's determination to press Mills to accept the administration's formula. Sanders tried hard to persuade Mahon to join in the effort:[61]

I urged him to put the focus on Mills rather than the President— that he should help the President and the Leadership push Mills into buying this formula. I emphasized to George that this was the first step, that if Mills would go it could thereafter be decided whether and to what extent the President would publicly support the cuts.

It seemed that Sanders had succeeded when, on 1 May, the Appropriations Committee arrived at the 'not less than $4bn.' clause; only later was it appreciated that this provided Mills with the excuse to push a $6bn. cut through.

The scheduling of the floor vote on the conference report caused some dissension within the OCR, and with some Congressmen. The New York primary elections were to be held on 18 June, and several incumbents, fearing that it would damage their chances, were reluctant to approve substantial cuts before then. Chuck Roche advised Johnson that, if the vote on the floor could be postponed until 20 June, he would probably secure additional support from the New York delegation. One of their number, Joe Addabbo from Queens, told Roche that Mills was either 'crazy' or 'purposely trying to embarrass New York members by calling up the tax bill six days before the New York primary elections'.[62] Sanders opposed delaying on the grounds that it would be difficult to sustain the lobbying campaign for a further week and that the emotions arising from Robert Kennedy's assassination and the Poor People's March would harm the chances of passage.[63] Carl Albert, the House

61 Diary Backup File, Box 99, 'Appointment File, 29 April 1968'.
62 Roche, Box 3, 4/6/68, 'Sanders, Barefoot: Memos For'.
63 Sanders to Johnson, 7/6/68, WHCF Ex FG 400, Box 327, '1/6/68–19/6/68'.

Majority Leader, decided at an Assistant Whips' Meeting on 6 June to delay the vote until after the primary elections. Although opposed to the move, Sanders acknowledged that the vote might improve as a result.[64] Before Albert held his Whips' Meeting, Johnson had told Sanders that he preferred postponement but that, in explaining it, the White House should 'use some other excuse—the death, or something', referring to Robert Kennedy's assassination.[65]

The White House 'Record-Write' team led by Robert Hardesty was relatively inactive throughout. As part of the Treasury's early lobbying in August 1967, Joe Fowler started a 'speech-writing operation' in the Department, with some assistance from the Council of Economic Advisers. Fowler also asked Califano to ensure that Hardesty's group of writers lent their help. With his characteristic energy, Fowler tried to provide as many speeches as possible for insertion in the *Congressional Record* before the recess.[66] After this initial flurry of activity, litle further happened; the OCR were particularly quiescent. Only once did Sanders refer to the White House's preparation of speeches for use by Congressmen. On 4 May, he told the president that he had discussed tactics with Carl Albert and had asked him to make some 'favourable comments' about Johnson's press conference the previous day when the president had virtually accused Mills of 'blackmailing' him. As part of that campaign, Sanders agreed to arrange for 'a few speeches' to be sent up the Hill praising the press conference; Albert dealt with them.[67]

After the bill was passed on the House floor, the OCR ensured that the Senate attended to it quickly, and on schedule. Even though the House was not in session, Sanders obtained unanimous consent for the bill to be signed by the Speaker. He also ensured that technical matters, such as the enrolling of the bill in the House, were finalised by the time

[64] Sanders to Johnson, WHCF Ex LE/FI 11-4, 1/5/68, Box 54, 'LE/FI 11-4: 28/5/68-8/6/68'.

[65] Sanders to Johnson, 19/6/68, WHCF Ex FG 400, 20/6/68-11/7/68, 'FG 400: 20/6/68-11/7/68'.

[66] Fowler to Johnson, 18/8/67, WHCF Ex LE/FI 11-4, 16/9/66, Box 53, 'LE/FI 11-4: 1/7/67-3/8/68'.

[67] Sanders to Johnson, 4/5/68, WHCF Ex FG 400, Box 327, '27/4/68-17/5/68'.

of the Senate vote.[68] The senior White House clerk made special arrangements to bring the enrolled bill, signed by the Speaker and the vice-president, back to the Mansion for the president's signature.[69]

Sanders advised against a signing ceremony on sound political grounds: the organisational contribution made by financiers and bankers whom Fowler had courted would have to be acknowledged, and some would naturally wish to be present at the ceremony. To grant them and their conservative political allies such as Wilbur Mills, Gerald Ford, and Senator Williams this publicity would do the president and his preferred successor, Hubert Humphrey, no good at all.[70] Sanders advised Johnson that to vote for the tax bill had been an act of courage for many of his liberal supporters; they would not now care for their constituents to be reminded of their support for increased taxes in the months before the elections. No bill-signing ceremony was held, but a signing statement drafted by Okun, Zwick, Fowler, and McChesney Martin, the chairman of the Federal Reserve Board, was released to the press when Johnson finally signed the bill on 28 June.[71]

THE CABINET

The president was not obliged to operate through the OCR, and its weakened state encouraged him to look to cabinet colleagues for support—though, as he doubtless privately anticipated, they did not provide it. No member of the cabinet could reasonably have questioned the importance which the president attached to the measure. Johnson none the less failed to win the concerted backing of his colleagues, and most did little or nothing to help him. In an attempt to persuade them, he lightened the tone of their many discussions

---

[68] Markman to Johnson, 20/6/68, WHCF Ex LE/FI 11-4, 1/5/68, Box 54, 'LE/FI 11-4: 9/6/68–30/6/68'.

[69] Markman to Johnson, 20/6/68.

[70] Sanders to Jim Jones, 20/6/68, WHCF Ex LE/FI 11-4, 1/5/68, Box 54, 'LE/FI 11-4: 9/6/68–30/6/68'.

[71] Sanders to Johnson, 22/6/68, WHCF Ex LE/FI 11-4, 1/5/68, Box 54, 'LE/FI 11-4: 9/6/68–30/6/68'.

with his characteristically vulgar humour. At a cabinet meeting an hour after Henry Fowler testified to the Ways and Means Committee on 1 May, Johnson again emphasised that he shared liberal dislike of the expenditure cuts upon which Mills insisted: 'Maybe we should try and take the bull by the tail and get the tax bill now. I remember the "old timers" in the House used to say, "We just got to take the bull by the tail and look the situation straight in the face." '[72]

Three cabinet secretaries, Stewart Udall, Willard Wirtz, and Ramsey Clark, were among the group dissenting strongly from the president's view; Robert Weaver, Secretary of HUD, was also thoroughly displeased for he knew that the beneficiaries of his Department's urban programmes, and those programmes' administrators, would react badly to the prospect of heavy cuts. Johnson therefore used the meetings to emphasise that he had no wish to cut federal expenditure— on the contrary. But he insisted that in the absence of tax increases, he would have no option but to request Congress for a further increase in the debt limit. He could, he said, secure the surcharge which 'my whole committee of liberal economic advisers tells me' to be necessary for financial stability only if the expenditure reductions of $6bn. were accepted as the price of passage.[73] He reiterated his belief that individual programmes would not suffer greatly when the cuts were specified by the Appropriations subcommittees, although he recognised the immediate political import of large aggregate cuts.

By the middle of May, Johnson's view was clear, but he succeeded in persuading his cabinet colleagues neither of the bill's merit, nor of the need to pass it quickly. At the last cabinet meeting in May, Johnson again impressed on everyone the need for a united response and stressed his political commitment to it, urging departmental heads to work with all their lobbyist and Congressional allies and the OCR in order to win over wavering Congressmen. The rhetoric was powerful:[74]

---

[72] Cabinet Papers, Box 13, 'Cabinet Meeting, 1/5/68 (4 of 4)'.
[73] Cabinet Papers, Box 13, 'Cabinet Meeting, 14/5/68 (2 of 3)'.
[74] Cabinet Papers, Box 13, 'Cabinet Meeting, 29/5/68 (2 of 3)'.

. . . we have to get off the pot. We have stalled around too long. I have [had] all kinds of Congressmen in here this week and I was talking to the Labor people before I got out of bed this morning. . . I want painless dentistry, but sometimes you can't get it. . . I want to ask this Cabinet to do what I have asked you to do before. Sit down with these Congressmen, with these 250 men, and take out these charts from this meeting. Tell them we're all in trouble as a nation. . .

I want to say to all you liberals and progressives in this Cabinet that I can take this $6bn. and walk and breathe and live if I get a $10bn. tax bill. I want to tell you that you are going to be hurt if I have to take $6bn. and no tax bill. If I can get $10bn. you'll hurt less. So let us get to work today and tomorrow. We'll look like Hoover if we don't use all the horsepower we've got. This is a question of survival. It is not Democratic or Republican. It is not public relations, it is a matter of survival for the country. So I ask all of you to get with Barefoot Sanders and work on these Congressmen now.

Despite his pleas, and the studied presentations of Henry Fowler, Charlie Zwick, and Art Okun at the cabinet meeting two weeks before, the president and Sanders won little support.[75] The Treasury's prolonged efforts apart, there were few attempts by other departments to build support for the surcharge from their regular supporters among Washington's lobbyists. Such limited attempts as there were sprang from attempts more to placate the White House than to make a genuine effort to pass the bill.[76] As Sanders acknowledged, even departmental Congressional liaison specialists played little role.[77]

Sanders organised a meeting in June between some of his colleagues and 'selected Congressional Relations people from a few other agencies' for a definitive headcount.[78] Charged with the responsibility of securing funding for their programmes, departmental lobbyists were understandably not disposed to press for the adoption of a fiscal measure which would make

[75] Cabinet Papers, Box 13, 'Cabinet Meeting, 14/5/68 (2 of 3)'.
[76] Memo to Califano, 4/5/68, WHCF Ex LE/FI 11-4, 1/5/68, Box 54, 'LE/FI 11-4: 1/5/68–15/5/68'.
[77] Sanders to Johnson, WHCF Ex LE/FI 11-4, 16/9/66, Box 53, 'LE/FI 11-4: 1/1/58–31/1/68'.
[78] Sanders to Johnson, 11/6/68, WHCF Ex LE/FI 11-4, 1/5/68, Box 54, 'LE/FI 11-4: 9/6/68–30/6/68'.

that task more difficult. The division between the presidency
and the executive branch, with a loose collection of virtually
independent departmental heads effectively free of presidential
sanction, makes it difficult for presidents to secure active,
united, support for their chosen course where departmental
interests are threatened. Self-interested departmental perspectives invariably stifle White House pleas for collective
political action.

Even after Johnson's request on 29 May, no cabinet
secretary volunteered to help. That same evening, in his
'Congressional Contact' report to Johnson, Sanders noted
that, because of the lack of volunteers, he would ask for a list
from departmental heads of those Congressmen with whom
they were 'best acquainted', which Sanders then used for
assignments.[79] These having been made, the secretaries all
submitted their reports by 5 June except, ironically, for Henry
Fowler, who was a little late reporting on his Virginia and
North Carolina Democrats. Ramsey Clark was unable to
complete his headcount because of his preoccupation with the
events surrounding Robert Kennedy's assassination.[80] Sanders
also made similar assignments of Republican Congressmen
still thought to be 'undecided', and whom he thought he
might yet persuade.[81]

TREASURY LOBBYING

Under both O'Brien's and Wilson's leadership, departmental
legislative liaison offices were subordinate both in theory and
practice to the White House. In the last phase of Johnson's
presidency, however, lines of authority were confused, as
the tax surcharge showed especially well. Here, the Treasury
was much the most important of the lobbying departments.
Fowler drew on his close relationship with the president to
deal with him directly and usually ignored Sanders. The
Treasury Secretary's dealings with Johnson throughout the

[79] WHCF Ex FG 400, Box 327, 'FG 400: 18/5/68–31/5/68'.
[80] Sanders to Johnson, 5/6/68, WHCF Ex LE/FI 11-4, 1/5/68, Box 54, 'LE/FI 11-4:
28/5/68–8/6/68'.
[81] Sanders to Johnson, 5/6/68, WHCF Ex LE/FI 11-4, 1/5/68, Box 54, 'LE/FI 11-4:
9/6/68–30/6/68'.

spring of 1968 show that he led what amounted to a separate lobbying organisation, negotiating personally with Mills and Mahon, and rarely bothering to consult with the head of the OCR. This made the position of OCR staff immensely difficult. It was further complicated by Fowler's willingness to offer larger cuts in expenditure in return for an undertaking from Mills that the bill would be reported out of committee with his support. Fowler's enthusiasm for passing the tax bill led him to draw up a table on 22 April explaining how $6bn. in expenditure cuts could be made without affecting Great Society programmes. Sanders sent a copy to Charles Zwick, the Budget Director since Charles Schultze's resignation in January, asking him to comment on Fowler's proposals and to send them to the president. Zwick did so, criticising Fowler's note (as Sanders knew he would, and wanted him to do) for being 'unrealistic', concluding: '. . .we can only have $6bn. expenditure reductions if we are willing to slash key social programs and rescind at least $1 billion of the [Federal civil servants'] pay increase. If we cannot touch pay, an expenditure reduction in the $4 billion is all that is feasible.'[82]

Within the Treasury, Fowler personally directed the campaign; Joseph Bowman had formal liaison responsibilities in the Department, but played no major role here. In late April, Sanders's irritation with Fowler's willingness to support deep expenditure cuts prompted him to urge the president to impress upon Fowler the 'uniform administration position'—that nothing in excess of $4bn. would be acceptable.[83]

Sanders also told Fowler directly that 'under no circumstances' should he give Mills the impression that the president would accept deeper cuts than $4bn.[84] Just four days later, however, Mills engineered the $6bn. cut through the conference committee, using Appropriations' approval of 'at least' $4bn. as the vehicle. Fowler then sought to have a simple vote on the Conference Report and opposed, with

[82] Zwick to Johnson, WHCF Ex LE/FI 11-4, 16/9/66, Box 53, 'LE/FI 11-4: 1/2/68–30/4/68'.
[83] Sanders to Johnson, WHCF Ex LE 11-4, 16/9/66, Box 53, 'LE/FI 11-4: 1/2/68–30/4/68'.
[84] Sanders to Johnson, 4/5/68, WHCF Ex LE/FI 11-4, Box 54, 'LE/FI 11-4: 1/5/68–15/5/68'.

Mills and Minority Leader Gerald Ford, the moves developing among OCR staff to arrange a vote on the Burke motion beforehand.[85] As late as 17 May, Sanders told Johnson that he and Fowler continued to disagree about the smaller reduction.[86] The Burke motion went ahead over Fowler's objection. After its defeat, there were no longer grounds for dispute within the administration; OCR and Treasury staff actually collaborated with the OCR on two vote counts in the middle of June shortly before the final vote on the Conference Report.[87]

Poor tactical and policy co-ordination between the OCR and the Treasury handicapped the chances of securing the bill's passage with few spending cuts. But Treasury officials had strengths and contacts which OCR staff did not. Just as the latter had over the years developed close working relations with labour, urban, and ethnic groups, so Treasury officials worked closely with financial and business organisations. Fowler's own background (and future) lay, like Treasury Secretaries before and after him, firmly in the corporate world.

The Treasury's organisation of the business and financial lobbies was within its own terms comprehensive and strikingly efficient. By the middle of August 1967, four senior officials, including Fowler, had already made twenty appearances before approximately 125 organisations to present their case for a surcharge.[88] In the case of the American Bankers' Association, the National Association of Manufacturers, and the US Chamber of Commerce, Fowler arranged for the chairman of the CEA, Gardner Ackley, and Charles Schultze, the Budget Director, to join in the presentation.[89] During May and June of 1968, as lobbying intensified, the Treasury's efforts prompted a frenetic campaign by business groups. After the Burke motion's defeat, eleven major financial,

---

[85] Sanders to Johnson, 11/5/68, WHCF Ex LE/FI 11-4, Box 54, 'LE/FI 11-4: 1/5/68–15/5/68'.

[86] Sanders to Johnson, 17/5/68, WHCF Ex FG 400, Box 327, '18/5/68–31/5/68'.

[87] Sanders to Johnson, 11 and 13/6/68, WHCF Ex FG 400, Box 327, '1/6/68–19/6/68'.

[88] Fowler to Johnson, 18/8/67, WHCF Ex LE/FI 11-4, 16/9/66, Box 53, 'LE/FI 11-4: 1/7/67–31/8/67'.

[89] Fowler to Johnson, 18/8/67.

insurance, banking, construction, farming, and manufacturing organisations urged support for the Conference Report.[90] A group of 500 businessmen and financiers, who had supported the tax surcharge from the moment of its submission to Congress, were still being asked to lobby actively in June, led by a steering group of seventeen senior corporate executives who co-ordinated their efforts with the Treasury.[91] Fowler, determined to restore confidence in the dollar, was seeking to pass the tax bill by 'a very substantial margin', and he used the steering group to lobby marginal Congressmen in the week before the final vote.[92] Two days after Johnson was told of this, a cabinet meeting was held at which Sanders (in Fowler's presence) acknowledged Fowler's success: 'The Secretary of the Treasury has stirred up the business community to a point of surprising fervour. It is almost fanaticism, the way they are in favour of this bill now.'[93]

OCR LINKS WITH NON-GOVERNMENT LOBBYING ORGANISATIONS

The shape of the president's non-congressional support on most Great Society and civil rights matters was broadly similar; the tax surcharge broke that pattern of consistent support. Most liberal lobbies, like their Congressional allies, were opposed to both its regressive character and the accompanying reductions in federal spending.[94] Not only did many organisations find the cuts in domestic programmes distasteful in principle but the political implications alarmed them. For once, the White House could not expect to benefit from these groups' resources and contacts.[95]

---

[90] Fowler to Johnson, 6/6/68, WHCF Confidential Files, Box 63, 'LE/FI 11-4'.
[91] Fowler to Johnson, 6/6/68.
[92] Fowler to Johnson, 10/6/68, Diary Backup, Box 104, 'Appointment File-10th June 1968'.
[93] Cabinet Papers, Box 14, 'Cabinet Meeting, 12/6/68 (2 of 3)'.
[94] Sanders to Johnson, 7/2/68, WHCF Ex LE/FI 11-4, 16/9/66, Box 53, 'LE/FI 11-4: 1/2/68–30/4/68'; de Vier Pierson to Sanders, 11/5/68, WHCF Ex FG 400, Box 327, 'FG 400: 27/4/68–17/5/68'; Sprague to Johnson, 2/5/68, WHCF Ex LE/FI 11-4, 'LE/FI 11-4: 1/5/68–15/5/68'.
[95] Sanders to Johnson, 17/5/68, WHCF Ex LE/FI 11-4, 1/5/68, Box 54, 'LE/FI 11-4: 16/5/68–27/5/68'.

The most important of these organisations was the AFL-CIO; its opposition to the tax bill's expenditure-cut riders was therefore especially serious. Together with groups such as the National Education Association, the League of Cities, the National Council of Churches, and the Urban Coalition, it was 'reluctantly' prepared to accept a spending cut of $4bn; in mid-May all affirmed their opposition to the $6bn figure.[96] This view was particularly important in major northern cities where Democratic Congressmen had firm links with them. This in turn made the timing of the New York Democratic primaries all the more significant since it was on urban and poverty programmes that the burden of the cuts would fall. Sanders knew that the opposition of mayors from major cities would damage the president's chances: five of the nine Cook County Democratic votes could, he calculated, be lost.[97]

Once Mills succeeded in attaching his $6bn. price-tag to the bill, Sanders knew that there was no hope of securing AFL-CIO support; their hostility to 'the meat-axe approach to cutting the budget' was well known.[98] Biemiller sent a statement of the AFL-CIO's views to every member of Congress; after seeing a copy, Sanders told Califano that labour could, if they chose, defeat the bill, and minuted the president to tell him that Biemiller had intensified their lobbying: '. . . he and his troops are going actively to work today to obtain commitments against the Conference Report.'[99]

But Sanders calculated that Biemiller might be persuaded to withdraw his active opposition. Like many Congressmen, the unions wanted the opportunity of a vote on a smaller reduction, and discussed with Sanders how to effect it. Biemiller's preference was for the Rules Committee to allow two consecutive votes: firstly on the surcharge with a $4bn.

[96] Sanders to Johnson, 17/5/68, WHCF Ex LE/FI 11-4, 1/5/68, Box 54, 'LE/FI 11-4: 16/5/68–27/5/68'.
[97] Sanders to Johnson, 16/5/68, WHCF Ex LE/FI 11-4, Box 54, 'LE/FI 11-4: 16/5/68–27/5/68' (eight of the nine were eventually 'right', voting 'aye').
[98] Califano to Johnson, 13/5/68, WHCF Ex LE/FI 11-4, 1/5/68, Box 54, 'LE/FI 11-4: 1/5/68–15/5/68'.
[99] Sanders to Johnson, 15/5/68, WHCF Ex LE/FI 11-4, 1/5/68, Box 54, 'LE/FI 11-4: 1/5/68–15/5/68'.

cut, and secondly with $6bn.[100] This in itself was a concession by labour to the OCR, for if the rule were granted, labour could campaign for the Burke motion leaving aside the question of the Conference Report's $6bn. It would have adeptly avoided the need to oppose the president. The Speaker, however, was unwilling to instruct the respected House Parliamentarian, Lewis Deschler, to write such a rule since Deschler claimed that it would constitute an unacceptable precedent. The rule was not granted.[101]

Whilst OCR staff did not secure a commitment from Biemiller for the AFL-CIO to halt completely its lobbying against the bill, Sanders gained the impression that labour were increasingly fearful of the financial implications of it being defeated. He inferred from this that in the event of the Burke recommittal motion being lost, 'labor would not lobby members to vote against the conference report'. And so it proved. Even with the three-week gap between the Burke motion and the floor vote on the conference report, Sanders's persistence caused Biemiller to modify his position almost to neutrality. Having lobbied heavily in favour of the Burke motion, he discreetly moderated his efforts and those of his colleagues.[102] On 13 June, Biemiller informed OCR staff that he was going to Europe and would not return until just before the floor vote. To Sanders's relief, he even revealed the latest intentions of two wavering marginal Congressmen, as he told the president: 'Andy and his people have been very quiet on the Tax bill, and this has been very helpful'.[103]

THE CONGRESSIONAL LEADERSHIP

Just two members of the leadership were of material assistance to the OCR staff here: the Majority Whip, Hale Boggs, although a member of the Ways and Means Committee,

[100] Sanders to Johnson, 21/5/68, WHCF Ex LE/FI 11-4, 1/5/68, Box 54, 'LE/FI 11-4: 16/5/68–27/5/68'.
[101] Sanders to Johnson, 20/5/68, WHCF Ex LE/FI 11-4, 1/5/68, Box 54, 'LE/FI 11-4: 16/5/68–27/5/68'.
[102] Sanders to Johnson, 29/5/68, WHCF Ex FG 400, Box 327, 'FG 400: 18/5/68–31/5/68'.
[103] Sanders to Johnson, WHCF Ex FG 400, Box 327, 'FG 400: 1/6/68–19/6/68'.

rarely attended hearings, and his political judgement did not inspire confidence in the White House.[104] Albert, the House Majority Leader, was crucially important. In the autumn of 1967, he strongly supported the tax proposal, while doubting that Mills could be persuaded to report it out of committee— something neither he nor the president could do much about.[105] In the following spring, Sanders saw Albert regularly, discussed strategy and tactics with him, and ensured that Johnson always knew his views.

Nevertheless, Albert became frustrated when Mills gained the upper hand during April, and the likelihood grew of a $6bn. expenditure cut; he deeply resented Mills's decision and behaviour. Albert collaborated closely with Sanders on the timing of the Burke motion, and successfully persuaded Mills not to file the Conference Report until it was voted upon.[106] If the vote on the $6bn. cuts had come first, liberals would have been bound to vote against, and Mills's cherished expenditure cuts would have failed. Honour having been partly satisfied after the defeat of the $4bn. alternative, Albert supported the $6bn. price-tag as the unavoidable price of passage. In doing so, he split with those who continued to look for something more to justify an unpopular vote with their constituents. Like other liberals, John Brademas eventually voted against the Conference Report because it included no reference to tax reform. As late as 14 June, Sanders reported that an increasing number of liberal Congressmen were calling for tax reform—or a promise of it to ease their political difficulties: 'By and large, these men simply want some action or semblance of action to point to.'[107]

The Speaker shared many of their sentiments. He was much more equivocal in his support than Albert, and thus in his usefulness to the White House, especially in early May when it still seemed possible that expenditure cuts on only $4bn. might be won. Whilst his limitations as Speaker were well

[104] Roche to Johnson, 4/5/68, Roche, Box 3, 'Memos for the President, 1968'.

[105] Califano to Johnson, WHCF Ex LE/FI 11-4, 16/9/68, Box 53, 'LE/FI 11-4: 16/10/67–31/12/67'.

[106] Sanders to Johnson, 21/5/68, WHCF Ex LE/FI 11-4, 1/5/68, Box 54, 'LE/FI 11-4: 16/5/68–27/5/68'.

[107] WHCF Ex LE/FI 11-4, 1/5/68, Box 54, 'LE/FI 11-4: 9/6/68–30/6/68'.

known to OCR staff, he was an enthusiastic supporter of the Great Society programmes, and consequently unhappy at the prospect of cuts. In early May, McCormack told Sanders not to ask for his support for a $6bn. cut. He conceded that Mills had played his strong suit skilfully, but was angry that the president and the House leadership should be dictated to by the chairman:[108]

The Speaker feels—quite vocally—that the President and the Democratic Leadership are being 'blackmailed' by Mills with the $6bn. expenditure reduction. He says, in effect, that since Mills has taken over the leadership of the House, he can get his own Rule out of Committee and get his own votes on the Floor for the Conference Report.

The Speaker was unwilling to support Johnson by challenging Mills; Sanders concluded by mid-May that his preferred course of letting Mills and the Republicans argue the case for the $6bn. cuts without his help was the best option. Without the Speaker's support, the president could do little, either. To have backed the Conference Report would, in Sanders's view, have been to capitulate publicly to Mills, to damage the president's leadership on other matters before Congress, to split with a loyal Democratic Speaker, and to run the risk of being 'accused by liberals of abandoning the Great Society'.[109]

The Burke motion enabled the leadership and the president to extricate themselves from the corner into which Mills had painted them. After its defeat, there was clearly no escape from the dilemma except to vote for or against the surcharge with the $6bn. cuts. No other options remained. Both the Speaker and Albert appreciated that Sanders had lobbied strenuously for the Burke motion, but McCormack was initially reluctant to support the conference report without a public lead from the president.[110] Nevertheless, both he and Albert eventually backed the president's decision to support

---

[108] Sanders to Johnson, 9/5/68. WHCF Ex LE/FI 11-4, 1/5/68, Box 54, 'LE/FI 11-4: 1/5/68–15/5/68'.

[109] Sanders to Johnson, 11/5/68, WHCF Ex LE/FI 11-4, 1/5/68, Box 54, 'LE/FI 11-4: 1/5/68–15/5/68'.

[110] Sanders to Johnson, 29/5/68, WHCF Ex FG 400, Box 327, 'FG 400: 18/5/68–31/5/68'.

the surcharge with Mills's attached heavy cuts. In the days before the vote, Sanders worked in the Speaker's office to check that their headcounts tallied. McCormack even spoke to Gerald Ford, to assess the strength of Republican support, and lobbied as many Democrats as the White House asked him to: 'I had prepared a list for the Speaker to call and he called every person on that list—he is really working hard on this one. . . We agreed to meet again Wednesday for the Speaker to call the New York Democrats since their primary will be over tomorrow.'[111]

Sanders's frequent contacts and discussions with the leadership were supplemented in the usual way with the White House leadership breakfasts where, on 15 May, the leadership asked for an initiative, claiming that they were actually uncertain of his views. Knowing just how little freedom of manœuvre everyone had, Sanders feared that without a presidential lead, the leadership might split, with Boggs supporting the Conference Report, McCormack and Albert opposing it. But this did not happen. Johnson used the meetings to present the options to the leadership, discussing with them submissions from the Budget Bureau and the Treasury.[112] He indicated his support for the Burke motion, which he knew would be defeated, but affirmed the 'distasteful' necessity of supporting a tax bill, even with the larger cut.[113]

George Mahon, the House Appropriations chairman, maintained throughout his willingness to support whatever level of cuts the administration would publicly back.[114] Mahon, a conservative Texan who had usually supported Johnson on important issues, was no willing accomplice of Wilbur Mills. On the contrary, he allied himself with Sanders and his staff, discussing how best to deflect the political damage from the president and his own committee. He had no wish to play a risky hand without an assurance of presidential support.

[111] Sanders to Johnson, 17/6/68, WHCF Ex LE/FI 11-4, 1/5/68, Box 54, 'LE/FI 11-4: 9/6/68–30/6/68'.
[112] Califano to Johnson, 20/5/68, Califano, Box 54 (1757), 'Califano, Taxes: 1967–1968'.
[113] Sanders to Johnson, Diary Backup, 21/5/68, 'May 21, 1968'.
[114] Sanders to Johnson, 27/4/68, WHCF Ex LE/FI 11-4, 16/9/66, Box 53, 'LE/FI 11-4: 1/2/68–30/4/68'.

The major tactical difficulty which Mahon and Sanders faced during April was that neither knew what cuts Mills wanted or would agree to. By the end of the month, Mahon knew that Mills would neither accept expenditure cuts of only $4bn. nor commit himself to support a $5bn. reduction. Mahon was 'extremely upset' by Mills's clever manœuvering in successfully winning a $6bn. cut, and agreed with Zwick that the Appropriations Committee simply could not achieve reductions of that size. He was correct. Actual spending for FY 69 was $4.5bn. above the limit set in Mills's package.[115] But the size of the eventual outlays mattered little. The immediate political significance lay in the nominal cuts which Mills finally won. It was this key political battle which Mahon and the administration lost.

Notwithstanding the great powers his chairmanship gave him, Mills's achievement was remarkable: he exploited to the full his institutional advantage. It was he around whom the president's and Sanders's tactical considerations hinged. Without his approval, nothing could be done. He retained complete control of his committee while pressing his fiscal and political preferences to remarkable effect; floor defeat was unthinkable for him. He temporised, and waited for the wind to change, unmoved by the view that Keynesian demand-management techniques required the House's revenue-raising committee to respond quickly to executive branch requests for fiscal adjustment in the name of fine-tuning. (He had taken a long time to be persuaded of the virtues of the tax cut which John Kennedy had proposed in 1963, and believed his standing had been injured when, after agreeing to the suspension of the 7 per cent Investment Tax Credit in September 1966, the president asked him to reinstate it shortly afterwards. He was this time determined not to move quickly in more promising political circumstances.[116])

There was no easy way around the obstacle he presented. Theoretically, the Rules Committee could have passed a resolution making consideration of the tax bill in order on the floor, a possibility which, in the winter of 1967-8 when the chances of Mills acting were (correctly) felt to be slim,

[115] Schick, *Congress and Money*, p. 37.
[116] Pierce, *The Politics of Fiscal Policy Formation*, p. 152.

the OCR seriously entertained. Richard Bolling, a devoted student of Congressional procedure, perspicacious legislator, and in later years himself the Rules chairman, explained to Sanders that in 1953, Speaker Joe Martin (R-MA) had threatened to take a bill away from the then Ways and Means Committee chairman Daniel Reed (R-IL) and clear it through the Rules Committee for immediate floor debate. Bolling recalled, with evident relish, that 'the threat was sufficient to blast the bill out of Reed's committee'.[117] But McCormack was, as Carl Albert remarked, unlikely to try to do the same now. In any case, Sanders felt that a 'considerable number of people. . . would be angered by the bypass of the regular Committee route', and that the Speaker would be reluctant to oppose Mills and challenge his authority in this way.[118] Where the Speaker was reluctant to try, the OCR were incapable of defeating Mills because of the latter's dominance of his committee. All were agreed that there was no possibility of a committee rebellion against him. Such was the power of the most able chairmen of key pre-reform committees.[119]

White House influence was reduced still further by the nomination of Thurgood Marshall to the Supreme Court. Astonishingly, Mills had himself aspired to a place on the Court, and believed scattered rumours in the press that Johnson would nominate him. Jim Jones told the president that Mills's voting record since Marshall's nomination 'attests to this disappointment he obviously still feels'. Jones added, ironically perhaps, that if the president wanted to pass the tax surcharge, he should find a Supreme Court place for the chairman.[120] Coincidentally, Earl Warren announced his retirement less than a month later, but by that time it was too late to sway Mills. In any case, Johnson certainly would not have attempted to influence Mills by offering him a place on the Court, a valued prize. Relations between the two, never intimate, had soured because of the latter's in-

[117] Sanders to Johnson, 24/1/68, WHCF Ex LE/FI 11-4, 16/9/66, Box 53, 'LE/FI 11-4: 16/10/67–31/12/67'.
[118] Califano to Johnson, 17/11/67, WHCF Ex LE/FI 11-4, 16/9/66, Box 53, 'LE/FI 11-4: 16/10/67–31/12/67'.
[119] Sanders to Johnson, 31/8/67, WHCF Ex LE/FI 11-4, 16/9/66, Box 53, 'LE/FI 11-4: 1/7/67–31/8/67'.
[120] Jones to Sanders, 23/5/68, WHCF FG 400, 'FG 400: 15/5/68–31/5/68'.

transigence, and what Johnson regarded as his duplicity over the $5bn. compromise. Moreover, it would have been thought a poor nomination by most of Johnson's allies, and probably have pitted his usual allies and senatorial supporters against it.

CONCLUSION

The tax surcharge reveals especially well some of the weaknesses of White House liaison with Congress in the last phase of Johnson's presidency. The sure touch of the OCR under O'Brien, together with the acknowledged lines of the responsibility and authority within the Office, and between it and the departments, had gone. So had the liberal majority of the 89th Congress, and much of the president's stock of political capital.

The circumstances were so unpropitious, however, that, even with a highly skilled White House liaison team, it is unlikely that the result would have been better. The president wanted to pass the surcharge as quickly as possible, having been convinced of the need for a tax increase; Wilbur Mills was equally determined that it should not pass without large expenditure cuts. His position as chairman of Ways and Means was impregnable, and Johnson's sanctions few. Furthermore, the president's (and therefore the OCR's) customary supporters and lobbying partners—the Congressional leadership, the liberal, urban, and labour lobbies, and liberal Democratic congressmen—greatly disliked the idea of social spending cuts; liberal politicians were wary of voting for a tax increase in an election year, and Republican and conservative opponents seized on the chance to wound a liberal Democratic administration with elections not far off.

The tax surcharge none the less illustrates several of the techniques which OCR staff used to lobby members of Congress and the constraints upon them. It shows the advantages and drawbacks of detailed presidential supervision and a departmental lobby effectively outside OCR influence: Johnson showed neither the will nor the capacity to insist anew on the supremacy of a well-organised OCR within the White House Office, and of its authority over departments with sectional, not necessarily presidential, interests.

More generally, the surcharge and the associated spending cuts symbolised the failure to realise the grander dreams of the Great Society's protagonists, and in particular those of its presidential architect, Lyndon Johnson. The Vietnam War was the main source of the crippling budgetary problem; the surcharge would have been unnecessary had it not proved a huge financial drain as well as a ghastly military and political failure. Vietnam did not only destroy the president, it tarnished his Great Society in the eyes of committed supporters. With Johnson's presidency, the face of American politics and policy had changed; the status quo had been transformed into a liberal order in which the state's roles of service, redistribution, and intervention had grown considerably despite skilful political resistance, especially in Congress. The price of passage of the tax bill meant that the OCR, which had been used just three years before to help achieve a liberal legislative revolution, was now engaged in the politically unwelcome task of arresting its growth.

Its consideration by Congress none the less allowed the president and his staff the prospect of negotiations with conservatives. Supreme Court nominations in 1968, by contrast, were a zero-sum game. Weakened liberal representation in the 90th Congress, coupled with growing public antipathy to the much-publicised protests of student radicals and black ghetto dwellers, resulted in a more conservative approach. Public concern with the rising rate of violent crime was heightened by the assassinations of King and Kennedy, and more particularly by the widespread rioting which followed King's death. Such circumstances provided an unpropitious setting for the Senate's consideration of Johnson's two Supreme Court nominees in the summer. Many southern senators adopted the politically convenient line (for them) that the decisions of the Supreme Court's liberal majority had fostered the growth of crime. In this way, conservatives tried to discredit the generally accepted civil rights and reapportionment decisions which struck at the heart of the old conservative power base, by tarring the Court's liberal members with the stain of social disorder and criminality.

7

THE SUPREME COURT NOMINATIONS

INTRODUCTION

On the tax surcharge, the president had the disadvantage of having to bargain with the House, which he understood less well than the Senate, on a matter that divided his supporters. He secured his fiscal legislation only at a high political price. With the Supreme Court nominations of Associate Justice Abe Fortas to Chief Justice and Homer Thornberry to Associate Justice made in June 1968, he had to deal only with the Senate, and enjoyed the advantage of support from the labour and civil rights lobbies. Despite strong White House lobbying (which he closely supervised) no vote was taken on the nominations themselves: they were withdrawn in the early autumn of 1968 when a motion to impose cloture on further Senate debate failed to secure the necessary two-thirds majority of senators present and voting.[1]

Abe Fortas's Supreme Court career ended within a year of his nomination to the Chief Justiceship. He resigned on 14 May 1969 (the first instance of its kind in the history of the Court) amid charges of financial impropriety arising from his having accepted $20,000 from a charitable foundation controlled by Wolfson, then under federal investigation for illegal stock trading.[2] (President Nixon in turn nominated Judges Haynsworth and Carswell, withdrew the nominations when each came under sustained criticism, and finally nominated Judge Harry Blackmun, overwhelmingly confirmed by the Senate on 12 May 1970.[3])

[1] Most papers in the Johnson Library referring to the 1968 Supreme Court nominations have been drawn from various sources into a special file entitled 'Files Pertaining to Abe Fortas and Homer Thornberry'. Footnotes to this chapter cite this collection by quoting 'Fortas, Box "x" . . .'.

[2] Massaro, J., 'LBJ and the Nomination for Chief Justice', *Political Science Quarterly*, vol. 97, no. 4, winter 1982–3, p. 603.

[3] Abraham, H. J., *Justices and Presidents*, 2nd edn., New York, 1985, pp. 13–23.

The chances of the liaison staff making the crucial marginal difference between success and failure lessened as opponents exploited the adverse circumstances surrounding the confirmation, and by the middle of September, the prospects of confirmation had almost entirely disappeared. None the less, the difficulty of securing confirmation, evident soon after submission of the nominations, meant that Johnson and his staff brought a wide range of presidential resources to bear; it is in consequence a rich, as well as an important, field for study. Two other important factors also emerge: the close supervision of White House lobbying by the president, and the importance of Senate whales in the days before reform. The resignation of Chief Justice Warren and the closely related question of Fortas's nomination were inseparable from the ebbing of Johnson's power, as his presidency drew to its end, and his weakened judgement, as his desperate attempt to buttress his legislative achievements by judicial means shows well.

At first sight, most lobbying staff in the White House thought confirmation seemed assured. The Senate was strongly Democratic, and Fortas, the nominee for Chief Justice, appeared a strong candidate. But the political composition and mood of the Senate was less liberal than three or four years before, and there were widespread anxieties in the country about rising crime. Since his confirmation as Associate Justice in 1965, Fortas had identified himself closely with the Court's liberal majority on almost all major decisions affecting the rights of suspects under interrogation and in police custody. He was therefore a prime target for criticism by those who claimed that such decisions were partly responsible for the increase in crime. Many candidates running for office in 1968, and powerful conservative incumbents, drew precisely this connection; Richard Nixon and George Wallace made law and order key parts of their campaigns for the presidency.

Concern over rising crime was not confined to conservatives. The assassinations of Martin Luther King and Robert Kennedy were felt acutely in liberal circles. The administration's proposed anti-crime legislation arose as much from liberal as from conservative concerns, and reflected widespread public fears. The bill had included strict gun-control measures

and licensing requirements but the Act finally passed by
Congress in 1968 contained no registration requirement and
had few liberal or reforming provisions. Besides authorising
$100 million to the states for the improvement of police forces,
it granted broad wiretapping authority to both federal and
state government agencies. Congress's view of the Warren
Court's decisions on the rights of suspects in police custody
was clearly indicated by the Act's weakening of a number of
important Supreme Court decisions.[4]

The powerful position of the Judiciary Committee chairman,
Senator James Eastland, increased the possibility that the
nominations might be seriously delayed before they reached
the floor; the hearings provided a focus for anxieties about
crime and its relationship to the decisions of the Court, as
Fortas's opponents in the Senate intended they should.
Judiciary Committee conservatives had suffered a significant
defeat the previous year when, after protracted committee
hearings, Thurgood Marshall was eventually confirmed as the
first black member of the Supreme Court.[5] With the
approaching elections weighing heavily in their minds, this
earlier setback increased the determination of conservatives
and Republicans to defeat Fortas, and preserve the opportunity
for Richard Nixon (the likely victor) to nominate.

As it usually does, the structure of American government
gave the advantage to the procrastinators: once on the Senate
floor, the danger of a filibuster increased as time passed
and the November elections approached. In any case,
the president's influence with southerners, liberals, and
Republicans was in decline. Many southerners resented the
enactment of Great Society programmes and Johnson's failure
to win the war in Vietnam. Liberals increasingly opposed the
war effort in principle, and were bitter about the squeeze on
social spending which it caused. Most Republicans steered
clear of a weakened lame-duck president in an election year.
Senator Griffin's (D-MI) ambitions to be Minority Leader
encouraged him to take a lead against Fortas's confirmation
ostensibly on the grounds that the incumbent president ought
to leave the nominations to the next chief executive. Griffin

[4] *Congressional Quarterly Almanac, 1968*, pp. 117–18, and p. 142.
[5] *Congressional Quarterly Almanac, 1968*, pp. 1164–5.

won the support of eighteen Republican Senate colleagues on 26 June, opposing (once again on the grounds that he was a lame duck) the president's right to nominate anyone to the Supreme Court.[6] The charge had no constitutional warrant, but contained important grains of political truth.

Fortas's moral probity was increasingly called into question as the summer wore on. This proved a devastating blow to his supporters. Further, the OCR's reduced size and inferior quality was such that an *ad hoc* lobbying unit was hastily created which, under the president's fitful leadership, lacked organisational coherence and political authority.

THE RESIGNATION OF EARL WARREN

June 1968 was therefore an unpropitious time at which to make two liberal Supreme Court nominations, made more difficult by the tight limits which the summer and autumn of a presidential election year placed upon the Senate timetable and hence upon White House lobbyists. The president, fearful that the nominations might receive especially thorough scrutiny by committee conservatives skilled in the arts of parliamentary manœuvre and delay, was intimately involved with the announcement of Warren's resignation. His manœuvering gave Senate opponents a further reason to work for the defeat of the nominations.

Supreme Court resignations normally take effect on a particular date. Warren's, however, was 'to be effective at your [i.e., the president's] pleasure', an unusual procedure conceived by Johnson and Fortas, acting together; Johnson had met Warren for nearly forty minutes in the Oval Office on 13 June, the day the letter was sent.[7] The manner of Warren's resignation was discussed at this meeting together with Johnson's preferred phrasing of it. The president seized the chance: 'With your agreement,' ran his reply, 'I will accept your decision to retire effective at such time as your successor is qualified'.[8] Despite the White House's subsequent

---

[6] *Congressional Quarterly Almanac, 1968*, p. 531.
[7] Daily Diary, 13/6/68.
[8] Christopher to Temple, 20/12/68, Fortas, Box 3, 'Chron File: 1/10/68–20/12/68'.

---

attempts to gloss over its significance, a long record prepared much later in the year by Warren Christopher notes that the president had told Ramsey Clark, the Attorney-General, to take 'great care' in formulating a reply to Warren. The president had stressed 'that he would like to accept the retirement in a manner to make it effective upon the qualification of Warren's successor, and to enable the retirement to be withdrawn if necessary.'[9]

The contingent nature of the acceptance of Warren's resignation caused the White House great difficulty: the only precedent which the Justice Department was able to discover was that of Justice Gray in 1902, though he died before his successor, Justice Holmes, was confirmed.[10] Plainly, Johnson was politicking, though Fortas's part in the affair was not known at the time. Some senators opposed to Fortas's nomination claimed that there was no vacancy for him to fill since Warren was still Chief Justice at the time of the Senate Judiciary Committee hearings. If his successor were found to be unqualified, Warren would, they claimed, therefore be perfectly entitled to continue to preside over the Supreme Court at the beginning of the Court's new term in October.

The White House relied on Professor Charles Fairman, a retired law professor, for support. Fairman wrote that the 'no vacancy' argument raised against Fortas's nomination by Senator Ervin was 'so unsubstantial and Ervinesque' that 'to state the proposition is to refute it'.[11] This was not so. Ervin argued that even if Fortas were confirmed by the Senate, his commission signed by the president, Warren could actually refuse to relinquish the Chief Justiceship, and thus determine when the Chief Justice-elect succeeded him. A constitutional crisis would inevitably result. Fairman would surely have been startled to know that the 'no vacancy' argument represented the president's reserve position. Johnson asserted in public that Ervin and Thurmond's inflexible 'no vacancy' argument was absurd, and yet privately relied on the strength of it to ensure that, should Fortas's nomination fall, Warren

[9] Christopher to Temple, 20/12/68.
[10] Warren Christopher to Larry Temple, 2/7/68, Fortas, Box 2, 'Chron File: 1/7/68–6/7/68'.
[11] Christopher to Temple, 20/12/68.

could safely remain on the Court—thanks to a manœuvre which Johnson had requested, finally approved, and which Fortas had helped draft.

The lengths to which Johnson thus went to ensure that the Supreme Court would remain a bastion of liberalism revealed the underlying reason for Warren's resignation. Although in good health, Warren was 77 years old and obviously could not be sure that he would be able to stay on the court until the end of a two-term Nixon presidency.[12] Like Johnson, he was fearful that Humphrey would be defeated in November; it was therefore important to prevent Richard Nixon (an old political opponent) nominating the next Chief Justice. Nixon's choice would certainly be a judicial conservative, and perhaps lead the Court to undo much of Warren's work. Hence his carefully worded resignation and the equally measured reply from the president twelve days later. Johnson was anxious to consolidate his domestic reforms by bolstering liberal opinion on the Court for years to come.

Having devoted such careful attention to Warren's resignation, creating additional difficulties for himself in the process, Johnson's choice for Chief Justice was unsurprising. Abe Fortas's career had been closely linked to Johnson's for thirty years. As Johnson's lawyer, Fortas had persuaded Justice Black that the result of the 1948 Texas Democratic State primary election should be allowed to stand. (Johnson won by 87 votes out of 988,295 cast—thanks to a late, fraudulent, return from precinct no. 13 in Jim Wells County which gave Johnson 202 votes.[13]) The junior senator from Texas owed his brilliant lawyer his career.

Equally, Fortas had in Lyndon Johnson a most powerful ally. Johnson's strong support for his nomination to Associate Justice in 1965 had outweighed his lack of judicial experience. (Fortas was the first nominee to be elevated directly from private practice since Owen Roberts was nominated by Herbert Hoover in 1930—not an altogether happy precedent.) No one else was seriously considered for the vacancy in 1968, and his colleagues anticipated it. Justice Douglas, to whom

[12] Warren almost outlived Nixon's shortened second term. He died on 10 July 1974.
[13] Dugger, R., *The Politician*, New York, 1982, pp. 332–41.

Fortas had always been close, both professionally and personally, strongly urged Fortas's name upon the president. 'I hope you make Abe our new Chief', Douglas wrote to Johnson on 18 June, 'he'd be superb'.[14] By the time that Johnson became president, his relationship with Fortas had developed into one of close political and personal friendship. Johnson's closeness to Fortas was well known in Washington, and opponents duly attacked the nomination as cronyism. Robert Shogan's observation on the relationship hints at its importance: '. . . while every Washington lawyer had friends in high places, no one else had such a good friend in such a high place as Abe Fortas had in Lyndon Johnson'.[15] Johnson behaved towards Fortas as he often did towards close friends, showering gifts on both him and his wife with embarrassing frequency. Scarcely two months passed without Johnson sending a present of some sort, often a collection of photographs. In return, Fortas thanked him in cloying correspondence which, in any other context, would have seemed ridiculous. In late February 1967 (as Justice Fortas), he wrote to Johnson:[16]

My dear Mr President—dear Boss—dear Friend—I can't adequately tell you how much Carol and I have enjoyed the album of marvellous photographs. They will be a treasure forever, and a reminder of a warm, generous and great human being and of our friendship. Abe

As president, Johnson valued Fortas even more than before. With Clark Clifford and Senator Richard Russell (whose closeness to Johnson diminished later in the presidency), Fortas became one of Johnson's principal unofficial advisers, and continued in this role after joining the Court in 1965. Opponents of his nomination in the Senate repeatedly charged that by acting in this way, he had violated the separation of powers between the executive and judicial branches. He tendered advice on many subjects, often with the highest security classifications, over a period of several years. This rightly came under scrutiny during the Judiciary Committee

---

[14] William O. Douglas to Johnson, 18/6/68, White House Name File, 'Fortas, Abe: June 1968'.

[15] Shogan, R., *A Question of Judgment*, Indianapolis, 1972, p. 79.

[16] Fortas to Johnson, 23/2/67, Fortas, Box 1, 'Fortas, Abe, 1964-67'.

hearings.[17] There, Fortas hid the full extent of his role, giving
the impression that it was limited to 'that of one who sits in
the meeting while other people express their views' and that
such meetings were relatively infrequent.[18] In fact, Fortas
had attended five meetings on Vietnam policy in the eight
weeks before his nomination, and had participated in crisis
meetings on the Detroit riots, major strikes, and in discussions
on fiscal matters. From the time of his nomination to Associate
Justice in 1965 until 1968, there were eighty-seven recorded
meetings and conversations between Fortas and the
president.[19] When he accepted the nomination to Associate
Justice, Fortas invited Johnson to continue to seek his counsel
on political matters: 'I know that the adjustment will be
difficult for me—made more difficult by the realization of
tasks left unfinished. I can only hope that you will continue
to see me and to call upon me for anything I can do to
help.'[20]

Although there was little White House discussion about the
nomination for Chief Justice, there was rather more about
filling the vacancy which Fortas's promotion would create.
Justice Douglas suggested that Warren Christopher, a law
clerk of Douglas's twenty years before, should be nominated.[21]
Determined on his own choice, Johnson did not acknowledge
Douglas's note. On 22 June, Ramsey Clark discussed the
matter with Johnson. Apart from Homer Thornberry, other
names mentioned were Cyrus Vance, Senator Edmund Muskie
(D-ME), Secretary of the Treasury Henry Fowler, and Albert
Jenner, chairman of the American Bar Association.[22]

The eventual nominee, Homer Thornberry, had been a
friend of Johnson's for many years. He had represented

[17] Senate Judiciary Committee, *Hearings on Abe Fortas and Homer Thornberry*, 1968,
pp. 167-8.
[18] Fortas's testimony before the Senate Judiciary Committee, 17-19 July 1968,
quoted in Maguire to Johnson, 27/7/68, Fortas, Box 7, 'Additional Material not
included in WHCF: 3/7/68-31/8/68'.
[19] List of Meetings, Fortas, Box 7, 'Additional Material not included in WHCF:
3/7/68-31/8/68'.
[20] Fortas to Johnson, 29/7/65, Fortas, Box 1, 'Fortas, Abe, 1964 -67'.
[21] There was little prospect that Johnson would nominate Christopher for
he valued highly Christopher's role as a mediator between himself and the
Attorney-General.
[22] Christopher to Temple, 20/12/68.

Johnson's old Congressional district in Austin, Texas, and, like him, grew less conservative during the 1950s. At Johnson's instigation, President Kennedy nominated him to a District Judgeship. As president himself, Johnson nominated Thornberry to the Federal Circuit. After the announcement of his nomination to Associate Justice, Thornberry received little public attention, and only cursory examination from the Judiciary Committee. Strom Thurmond actually refused to question him on the ground that there was no vacancy to fill. His nomination made confirmation even more difficult for it lent weight to the accusations of cronyism; even among those sympathetic to him there was some doubt that Thornberry was qualified for the post—a suspicion never voiced against Fortas.

The main problems for White House lobbyists in June and July were therefore that the nominations were made by a 'lame-duck' president, that Fortas was a 'crony' of Johnson's whom he had advised while a Supreme Court Justice. These difficulties were considerable but not as damaging as the revelation in August that Fortas had received a $15,000 fee for holding six seminars at The American University in Washington, DC, that summer. Worse still, the sum was raised by Paul Porter, Fortas's former law partner.[23] For many who had supported him in June and July, this incident sowed fresh doubt in their minds, and opinion among previously uncommitted senators shifted against confirmation. The president himself had not known of Fortas's fees, and seemed 'shocked' to hear of them, as Clark later recalled.[24] 'The American University thing was a complete surprise to all of us, and I'm sure to the President. I can remember that that was a surprise to him.'[25]

THE ORGANISATION OF THE LOBBYING UNIT

OCR staff did not manage the lobbying on the Fortas nomination in the usual way. Rather, a special liaison unit was arranged composed of OCR and non-OCR members of

[23] One of the five former business associates from whom the money was raised had a son involved in a federal criminal case at the time (*Congressional Quarterly Almanac, 1968*, p. 531).

[24] Interview with Larry Temple, 9/4/79.

[25] Ramsey Clark, Oral History, Interview no. 5, Johnson Library, p. 11.

the White House staff. It also included (unwisely, under the circumstances) Paul Porter.[26] Barefoot Sanders was obliged to spend most of his time working on liaison with the House, while Mike Manatos, though diligent, was not entrusted by the president with the important role of leading the lobbying campaign. It fell to Larry Temple, the president's assistant on legal matters, to co-ordinate an *ad hoc* liaison team. Its members included Ramsey Clark, Warren Christopher, Special Counsel Harry McPherson, appointments secretary Jim Jones, Postmaster-General Marvin Watson, Joe Califano, Mike Manatos, Barefoot Sanders, and Ernie Goldstein, another member of the staff. The group's meeetings were infrequent, and poorly attended.

The growing fear that Thornberry's nomination might be rejected outright, and that Fortas's might encounter difficulties, confirmed in Johnson's mind the need to establish the special team, and draft extra forces. The weakness of formal liaison arrangements in the last phase of Johnson's presidency, and the exclusive concentration upon the Senate, gave peculiar emphasis to Johnson's domination of the organisation of relations with the Hill. His experience, and strong interest in securing confirmation of his nominees, made his actions especially important, as Larry Temple stressed: 'The president was the quarter-back on this . . . this was really a Johnson operation.'[27]

Temple and Clark played a joint co-ordinating role in the team—Temple from the White House, and Clark from the Justice Department. Manatos continued to assess opinion among senators and their staff, and reported back to his colleagues and the president. He also unsuccessfully used such contacts as he had in the House to win additional lobbying support for the nominations.[28]

The responsibilities of other staff members were determined on the basis of their contacts, interests, and experience. Wisely,

---

[26] In a telephone call to Jim Jones, the president's Appointments Assistant, on the morning of 27 June, Fortas himself said that Porter 'will be the central clearing house on information and assignments'. In the same call, he told Jones that he had persuaded several prominent Jewish friends, including Senators Ribicoff and Javits, to help with the nomination battle (Fortas, Box 4, 'WHCF Ex FG 535/A: 25/6/68–30/6/68').

[27] Interview with Temple, 9/4/79.

[28] Sanders, Barefoot, Oral History, Johnson Library, Tape no. 2, p. 8.

Marvin Watson, a conservative Texan, exploited his political friendships with several southern senators.[29] Irvine Sprague, Sanders's OCR deputy, had links with a number of prominent Californians both in and out of Congress, and others from western and south-western states, and was therefore employed to lobby Senators Murphy (R-CA), Kuchel (R-CA), Fannin (R-AZ), and Fong (R-HA). At the end of June, Sanders asked Sprague to suggest to Rep. Morris Udall (D-AZ) to check 'if there is any way of shaking up Fannin'.[30] Udall spoke to Fannin, but without success. After talking to Udall, Sprague took the view that Fannin, along with Murphy and Fong, 'probably are impossible'.[31]

Harry McPherson and Ernie Goldstein spent some time working on the nomination. McPherson (a practising Episcopalian) continued to play his curious role as Johnson's chief liaison with the Jewish community by helping Goldstein gather support among various Jewish groups. He also contributed on other occasions when the assistance of his friends in the senate and in newspaper editorial offices could be used to advantage.[32] Other members of the administration, including members of the cabinet and their assistants or deputies, were assigned the task of checking senators' views as the need arose, and occasionally of lobbying those known to them personally.

Lobbying staff did not trouble to ask cabinet members to seek the support of senators such as Robert Byrd, James Eastland, and John Stennis, who made their firm opposition known at an early stage, but asked them to concentrate on those who could be persuaded to back the nominees.[33] Whenever possible, old friendships or professional relationships were exploited to the president's advantage. Many senior departmental officials, whether from agency liaison offices or not, drew on political capital accumulated over time with senators they had worked closely with. For example, Senator Jackson's membership of the Armed Services Committee, and

[29] Sanders to Clark, 27/6/68, Fortas, Box 1: 'Chron File: 13/6/68–25/6/68'.
[30] Sanders to Johnson, 28/6/68, Fortas, Box 5, 'WHCF: Subject File'.
[31] Sprague to Sanders, 28/6/68, Fortas, Box 4, 'WHCF Ex FG 535/A: 25/6/68–30/6/68'.
[32] His main contact at the *Post* was Alan Barth, an editorial writer.
[33] Allocation List, Fortas, Box 3, 'Chron File: Undated: 2 of 3'.

his concern with defence and weapons procurement, led to
two officials from the Defense Department (one being the
Pentagon's liaison director) lobbying him.[34] Senator Russell
Long (D-LA), chairman of the Senate Finance Committee,
was visited by Secretary of the Treasury Henry Fowler, whom
he naturally knew well.

Temple and Clark's loose co-ordinating role fell a long way
short of directing the group's ill-defined activities, as Temple
recalled:[35]

. . . the President sort of looked to the Attorney-General and to me
to kind of keep the headcount and be responsible for the nomination.
There were a lot of people doing work. We had a substantial number
of people contacting members of the Senate. For example, even
though Marvin Watson was over at the Post Office Department
then [as] Postmaster General, he was . . . doing some headcount
with Sanders. . . Ramsey [Clark] was; Warren Christopher was;
Harry McPherson did some. Paul Porter, who was the senior
member of the law firm that Justice Fortas practiced with, sat in
on most of our meetings because he was helping to marshall some
of the outside organisations. And we did a fairly good, and I think
accurate, headcount.

Responsible finally only to the president, the team lacked a
staff director experienced in Congressional, especially Senate,
politics with the president's grant of authority to speak on
his behalf. Slack administrative procedures within the group
did the nominees' chances no good at all, and damaged the
prospects of resolving complicating political questions as they
arose. Diffusion of authority within the ill-defined group was
made worse by the absence of regularly scheduled group
meetings to review progress. Sanders confirmed Temple's
assessment: 'The Fortas "task-force" didn't amount to much—
it was an amateurish type of operation with no underlying
strategy and no very obvious chief.'[36]

LOBBYING TACTICS AND STRATEGY

The lobbying unit made a few unfortunate errors, mostly not
serious in themselves, but which together cast doubt on the
fabled political abilities of Johnson's staff. Due to the intimacy

---

[34] Allocation List, Fortas, Box 3.
[35] Larry Temple, Oral History, Johnson Library, Tape no. 5, p. 41.
[36] Interview with Barefoot Sanders, 24/4/79.

of the president's involvement, the errors which were made also raise questions about his declining capacity to lead difficult legislative battles in 1968, and, fundamentally, about his political judgement.

In failing to seek and heed the advice of staff and senators about the choice of nominees, Johnson made the first of his mistakes. Any liberal would have encountered opposition in 1968, but Arthur Goldberg would have been better placed than Fortas to withstand it, as would Cyrus Vance or Warren Christopher.[37] The problem was magnified by both nominees being vulnerable to charges of cronyism, one to doubts about his moral fitness, and the other to doubts about his qualifications. At the end of June, Johnson admitted to his aides that the nominations were in trouble, despite the optimism of some—particularly Manatos whose early estimates of support were wildly optimistic. On 26 June, Manatos found eighty-five votes in favour of Fortas, with slightly fewer supporting Thornberry: 'These nominations have been generally well-received. The only soft areas are among certain southern Democrats, and a small Republican group.'[38]

Sanders later recalled that Johnson was dubious: 'he said he just couldn't see how it could be . . . he could see right then that we were in a hell of a shape.'[39] Shortly after Manatos's first report, W. T. Finley, an Assistant Deputy Attorney-General, contacted all but one senator and estimated there to be sixty certain pro-Fortas votes, with twenty-eight equally opposed.[40] Manatos's optimistic assessment meant that subsequent lobbying ran the risk of being confused and misdirected. When Manatos told a cabinet meeting in early July that 'We are in good shape', the president intervened: 'I think we are going to have rough days ahead on this problem. I think it is clear, that for political reasons, Richard

---

[37] Warden, P., 'Senate Cloture Bid Promised if Court Filibuster Develops', *Chicago Tribune*, 29/6/68. Warden quoted Sentor Griffin, who opposed the nominees on the grounds that Johnson was a lame-duck president, as saying that he would not have opposed the nomination of Arthur Goldberg. The inconsistency of Griffin's position was made the subject of some speeches prepared in the White House for use by friendly senators (Fortas, Box 4, 'Chron File: 3 of 3'). It demonstrated Griffin's anxiety that he might be accused of being anti-Semitic.

[38] Manatos to Johnson, 29/6/68, Fortas, Box 1, 'Chron File: 26/6/68–30/6/68'.

[39] Interview with Sanders, 24/4/68.

[40] 1/7/68, Fortas, Box 4, 'WHCF Ex FG 535'.

Nixon is involved in the effort to thwart these appointments. I think we are going to have a rough time.'[41]

Johnson was also less convinced than Manatos of the firmness of the resolve of the Republican leader, Everett Dirksen. Whether Dirksen really thought in early July that there would be no filibuster by Fortas's opponents is unclear, but Manatos believed him, and duly told the president so.[42] Senator Griffin's efforts to secure prominent Republican signatories to his petition opposing the nominations, which Dirksen worked hard to undermine, were, Manatos said on the same day, 'slowly dying'.[43] Johnson, sensitive to the changing pressures on Dirksen in an election year, was less certain. Griffin's ambition for the Minority Leadership was one of these pressures, that of party unity behind Richard Nixon—who increasingly sought to weaken the nominations— was another. Long committee hearings would wear down wavering Republicans, too, and weaken their support for Fortas as November approached. Dirksen had always to keep in step with his party colleagues, and could not support Fortas if Republican support crumbled, as Johnson well understood: 'We've got to get this thing through, and we've got to get it through early, because if it drags out, we're going to get beat . . . Just take my word for it. I know him. I know that Senate. Ev Dirksen will leave us if we get this thing strung out very long.'[44]

Johnson's worst fears were realised when Dirksen defected to the opposition in September. Having voted for Fortas in committee, he opposed the cloture petition.

As Johnson had manœuvred to ensure a liberal Chief Justice irrespective of whether Fortas was confirmed, so important Senate opponents had little scruple, either: McClellan was determined to investigate the circumstances of Warren's resignation and Fortas's nomination by using hearings, 'real long ones' if necessary, to 'find out about the "deal" which was made'.[45] Ervin spent most of his time during the hearings setting out at inordinate length his view

41 Cabinet Papers, Box 13, 3/7/68.
42 Manatos to Johnson, 2/7/68, Fortas, Box 2, 'Chron File: 1/7/68–6/7/68'.
43 Manatos to Johnson, 2/7/68.
44 Temple, Oral History, Tape no. 5, p. 42.
45 Manatos to Johnson, 26/6/68, Fortas, Box 1, 'Chron File: 26/6/68–30/6/68'.

of the proper role of the Supreme Court. Above all, there was no precedent for the decision by McClellan, Ervin, and Eastland to call a sitting Justice before the committee.

The latter move seems to have prompted no debate in the White House lobbying unit nor consideration by Johnson and his legal advisers, McPherson and Temple, of its constitutional and political implications. Only in the Justice Department was there any discussion about it: after careful consideration, the Attorney-General and his deputy recommended that Fortas should appear.[46] Whilst Thornberry would have to testify before he was confirmed, the White House slipped in agreeing to suggestions from Eastland for the dates of the hearings and those on which he anticipated Thornberry and Fortas would be asked to testify.[47] Despite Fortas's own wish to appear, the president and his lobbyists should have anticipated the dangers which such an occasion presented and advised him accordingly. Fortas would have been on the safest constitutional ground of separation of powers in declining. Ironically, Fortas's own slackness in respecting the separation of powers was to prove a grave weakness in testimony before the committee.

When Fortas was later asked to reappear in mid-September, opinion within the administration was divided on whether he should do so. The president's initial view was that he should return, but the Attorney-General (and Fortas himself) believed that his chances of confirmation had already been so badly damaged that it would be foolish to risk further trouble.[48] Senator Phil Hart, a liberal Michigan Democrat, drafted a letter arguing against his reappearance, which White House lobbyists tried to persuade a majority of the Judiciary Committee to sign.[49] At one stage, it seemed that all the moderate Republicans on the committee would do so, but the approach of the elections caused Senator Scott (R-PA) to change his earlier view; on 12 September he withdrew his signature.[50] Dirksen also refused to sign.[51] Fortas ended the

[46] Confidential interview, 3/5/79.
[47] Christopher to Temple, 20/12/68.
[48] Christopher to Temple, 20/12/68.
[49] Temple to Johnson, 11/9/68, Fortas, Box 3, 'Chron File: 3/9/68–14/9/68'.
[50] Temple to Johnson, 12/9/68, Fortas, Box 7, 'Additional Material not included in WHCF: 1/9/68–8/10/68'.
[51] Temple to Johnson, 11/9/68.

discussion by writing to the chairman on 13 September, declining to return.

Lobbying was occasionally too enthusiastic, and so counter-productive. Intense pressure on a senator might do positive harm, for if his personal dignity was hurt, the battle for his support was often lost and much careful liaison work could be undone. Staff had to deploy the resources of the presidency with tact and discrimination, and not irritate those whose support they required. Several of those thought open to persuasion received many enquiries, and were lobbied by numerous individuals and organisations. Some, such as the Colorado Republican Gordon Allott, resented it. He was subjected to constant pressure from a variety of sources, mostly prompted by White House staff, and, as the commmittee hearings wore on through July, grew increasingly angry, as Sanders told the president: '. . . the Colorado banker who talked with Allott says that Allott is absolutely committed against the nomination and against cloture. The banker further reports that Allott is bitter about the pressure he has been receiving and sees no prospect that Allott will change.'[52]

Undeterred, Sanders told the president in the next sentence that he had arranged for 'the Republican National Com-mitteeman from Colorado' to talk with both Colorado senators at the Miami Convention of the Republican Party.[53] Wallace Bennett, a conservative Republican from Utah, complained to a private lobbyist that he was being called 'by too many people' from the White House which, the lobbyist believed, was 'irritating him rather than influencing his outlook'.[54]

White House staff in the lobbying unit were also guilty of poor political judgement in suggesting, with scanty evidence, that anti-Semitism played a part in the opposition to Fortas: at most, this was a contributory factor in the decisions of one or possibly two southern senators to oppose Fortas. On 10 July, a lobbyist reported that there was little public comment, either: 'The Jewish issue has not been raised in Senate mail. No letters mention it to Senator Byrd of Virginia despite his

[52] Sanders to Johnson, 29/7/68, Fortas, Box 2, 'Chron File: 14/7/68 31/7/68'.
[53] Sanders to Johnson, 29/7/68.
[54] George Reedy to Johnson, 2/7/68, Fortas, Box 4, 'WHCF Ex FG 535/A: 1/7/68–2/7/68'.

mail being against. Senator Kuchel has one letter, and Senator Griffin 2 or 3.'[55]

Goldstein readily admitted that there was no convincing evidence that anti-Semitism was important: 'If evidence exists, I have not seen any.'[56] Sundry extreme right-wing groups, including a Nazi organisation in Virginia, made use of Fortas's Jewishness in their fanatical opposition to him, but it played no part in Senate debate, and little in private calculation or conversation. Ed Weisl, a New York lawyer friend of both Johnson and Califano, remarked in a letter to Califano that charges of anti-Semitism, casually made against certain Republican senators, were greatly resented since it played no part in their judgements. Senator Javits told Weisl that the White House should 'not stress anti-Semitism' since 'a caucus of Republican senators. . . were very upset at this propaganda'.[57] Javits was keenly aware of the electoral damage which might result.

PROJECTS AND PATRONAGE

Members of the lobbying unit made no systematic use of the leverage of patronage and projects in this case. In the two cases in which it was quietly employed, it swayed no votes. Barefoot Sanders recommended that the president should invite George McGovern, the liberal Democrat from North Dakota, to a bill-signing ceremony, S6, which authorised construction of the Oahe irrigation unit as part of the large Missouri River Basin Project. This expensive scheme was particularly important to McGovern, and it was certainly to his advantage to be present at the bill's signing; such publicity was always welcome. Although McGovern's support for Fortas was assured, Sanders saw some value in it for the president, too: 'I realise there are some problems about McGovern, but it might be a good idea in view of the upcoming fight on the

[55] Goldstein to Johnson, 10/7/68, Fortas, Box 5, 'WHCF Ex FG 535/A: 3/7/68–30/7/68'.
[56] Goldstein to Johnson, Fortas, Box 3, 'Chron File, undated: 1 of 3'.
[57] Weisl to Califano, 8/7/68, Fortas, Box 5, 'WHCF Ex FG 535/A: 3/7/68–30/7/68'.

Fortas and Thornberry nominations to cultivate friendly Senators whenever we have the opportunity.'[58]

Marvin Watson's executive assistant in the Post Office Department, Douglas Nobles, told him at an early stage in the lobbying campaign that Senator Russell Long had asked for a prominent constituent, Robert Christ, to be appointed a Deputy Regional Director in the Post Office. He also wanted a 'positive decision' from the Department on the opening of a post office at Shrevesport, Louisana. Nobles suggested that the requests 'might be an opportunity to switch his vote', adding that: 'It might be well to consider bargaining with the Senator on this facility in an effort to secure his vote'.[59] If any White House negotiations with Long occurred, they bore no fruit. He wrote to the president just nine days later stating his firm opposition to Fortas's nomination: 'The Supreme Court, [is]. . . largely responsible for the major increase in crime in this country. . . I would have to vote "no" if we were voting on whether to confirm him again.'[60]

Johnson prudently avoided punishing senior Congressional figures whose support or goodwill he might need, and Long duly received approval for the opening of his post office. Whatever view Long took of the Fortas case, or of any other matter, his chairmanship of a key Senate committee exempted him from retribution for occasional unwelcome votes. In this instance, Johnson did no more than urge Watson, who was to be present at the announcement in Shrevesport on 5 August, to remind the senator of other projects on which he had assisted him: 'Try to soften Russell Long on Abe Fortas. He is interested in Camp Polk—I'm helping him; he wanted Buffalo NY building—I helped him; I need his quiet help. L.'[61]

---

[58] There were three major 'problems' with McGovern. He had been an early opponent of American involvement in Vietnam, had since 1965 been urging Robert Kennedy to run against Johnson, and was Al Lowenstein's first choice for a liberal Democratic challenger to Johnson (Schlesinger, A. M., *Robert Kennedy and his Times*, Boston, 1978, p. 824; Sanders to Jim Jones, 29/7/68, Fortas, Box 5, 'WHCF Ex FG 535/A: 3/7/68–30/7/68').

[59] Nobles to Marvin Watson, 9/7/68, Fortas, Box 7, 'Postmaster General W. Marvin Watson'.

[60] Long to Johnson, 18/7/68, Fortas, Box 2, 'Chron File: 14/7/68–31/7/68'.

[61] Watson to Johnson, 31/7/68, Fortas, Box 7: 'Additional Material: 3/7/68–31/8/68'.

But Long maintained his opposition, and was recorded a week later by Joe Califano and Mike Manatos as being 'hard against' the nomination, together with thirty-one Senate colleagues.[62]

PREPARATION OF SPEECHES AND INFORMATION

The Supreme Court nominations produced one of the best examples of a tactic used quite frequently during the Johnson administration by OCR staff, and described in chapter four: the preparation by specialist speech-writers from outside the lobbying unit of speeches for delivery in Congress. In general, these staff were specialists who wrote speeches for senior administration figures, and especially for the president. For the Court nominations, Bob Hardesty and Leo Janos spent many hours writing material for senators to use. Speeches were either prepared for senators' use in public, on the Senate floor, or simply for insertion in the *Congressional Record*. Wayne Morse, a liberal Republican turned Democrat from Oregon, was in particularly close contact with members of the lobbying unit and often used their prose. As one of the earliest opponents of American involvement in south-east Asia, Morse was valuable as a link to liberal dissenters; unlike McGovern, he had voted against the Gulf of Tonkin Resolution. Alive to political advantage of this kind, Johnson himself suggested the names of senators whose help in this way would be useful to him.[63]

Before the recess in early August, when the nominations had run into serious difficulties, Sanders urged that the effort be increased with prepared speeches, complemented by 'a hard hitting press release' being sent to the Senate to maintain the pressure.[64] This would also give Fortas some welcome favourable publicity after his savaging at the hands of Ervin, Thurmond, and McClellan in committee. Claiborne Pell (D-RI) was one of several who obliged. He gave a speech in

[62] Califano to Johnson, 13/8/68, Fortas, Box 2, 'Chron File: 3/8/68–17/8/68'.
[63] Goldstein to Johnson, Fortas, Box 5, 'WHCF Ex FG 535/A: 3/7/68–30/7/68'.
[64] Sanders to Johnson, 30/7/68, Fortas, Box 2, 'Chron File: 13/7/68–31/7/68'.

the Senate on 2 August, and inserted a favourable editorial from the *New Republic* into the *Congressional Record*.[65]

Larry Temple devised an ingenious variant on the theme of 'Record-Write' for use specifically on Thornberry's nomination. Thornberry was known to most senators in 1968, if at all, simply as a close friend of the president's—not necessarily an advantage by 1968, either with southern conservatives suspecting Johnsonian liberalism on domestic issues, or with some northern liberals who distrusted the president on account of his Vietnam policy, and what they believed to be his retreat from the political values of the Great Society. The judge's views were therefore generally unfamiliar. Temple compiled two groups of Thornberry's opinions: one for liberals, illustrating his progressive views on civil rights, freedom of speech, extension of picketing rights, and freedom from unlawful search. Temple noted in a covering memorandum that this was 'good material for northern and eastern liberal Senators. . . and for the law school people'.[66] For conservatives, he collected a set of Thornberry's opinions on searches and warrants for house-entry, which gave the appearance of his being judicially conservative on matters of law-enforcement. He sent them to Johnson early in the campaign before Fortas's nomination encountered intense opposition, noting that, 'These will be helpful when we talk with some of the southern Senators on Monday.'[67] Alas, there is no evidence in White House files of the effectiveness of these tactics.

INTEREST GROUPS

The lobbying unit systematically organised interest groups to bring additional pressure on senators—a common OCR method, especially important here. Support was sought from a variety of organisations: the judiciary, law school professors, the media, labour unions, Jewish organisations, and businessmen. Black groups did not figure prominently, but

[65] *Congressional Record*, 90th Congress, p. 24973.
[66] Temple to Johnson, 29/6/68, Abe Fortas Name File: 'June 1968'.
[67] Temple to Johnson, 29/6/68.

Clarence Mitchell, Executive Director of the NAACP, approached several liberal Republicans including, unsurprisingly, the liberal black Republican senator from Massachusetts, Edward W. Brooke.[68]

On 29 June, at the outset of the lobbying campaign, Sanders asked Judge Irving Goldberg to urge his colleagues on the Fifth Circuit (covering most of the southern states) to contact their senators and the chairman of the Senate Judiciary Committee specifically to support Thornberry's nomination. The intention was to use southern judges to put pressure on southern senators for Thornberry, a former southern Congressman, and a fellow southern judge. Goldberg promised that he would spend the weekend building support for Sanders's request. The Attorney-General also attempted to assist Thornberry's cause by contacting another Fifth Circuit judge, requesting that he see Judge Griffin Bell to 'activate him with the Georgia Senators'.[69]

On the following Monday, Goldberg told Sanders that he had persuaded colleagues from Florida, Alabama, and elsewhere to contact their senators. Chief Judge Brown of the Fifth Circuit took the view that a round-robin letter was 'inadvisable', but promised to ask them all to write individually in support of Thornberry. Brown also undertook to telephone two Republican members of the Judiciary Committee, Senators Hruska (R-NE) and Scott, even though Hruska's opposition was unqualified.[70] Overall, however, this was something of a coup for Sanders. Clear support for Thornberry from his colleagues on the bench would be most welcome if Fortas's nomination were first confirmed. Since this did not happen, the lobbying on behalf of Thornberry was to no avail. No comparable regional effort was made for Fortas—his lack of judicial experience prior to his becoming a Supreme Court Justice in 1965 prevented White House lobbyists from drawing on a comparable base of support.

Both nominees benefited from the administration's organisation of groups of law school professors and deans, and of a

[68] Sanders to Johnson, 29/6/68, Fortas, Box 1, 'Chron File: 26/6/68–30/6/68'.
[69] Sanders to Johnson, 29/6/68, Fortas, Box 4, 'WHCF Ex FG 535/A: 25/6/68–30/6/68'. Bell was later Jimmy Carter's Attorney-General.
[70] WHCF Ex FG 400, Box 327, '20/6/68–11/7/68'.

large committee of distinguished lawyers from across the country. Not all of those involved with this, and the initiation of various support projects with the American Bar Association (ABA), were members of the lobbying unit. Lloyd Cutler, chairman of the Individual Rights and Responsibilities section of the ABA, and Nicholas Katzenbach, a former Attorney-General, worked with Paul Porter, Larry Temple, and others in an attempt to bring the weight of the profession behind the nominations.[71] Three hundred law school professors and deans sent a telegram, which formed part of the record of the Judiciary Committee's hearings, to Eastland protesting at the use of the 'lame-duck president' thesis.[72] Warren Christopher told Larry Temple on 31 July that he and his senior colleagues in the Justice Department had advised their press office to encourage reporters due to cover the ABA Convention in August to seek comments on the nominations and the Judiciary Committee's hearings from certain senior figures there.[73] All of those whom Christopher named could naturally be relied upon to give full support.

As defeat appeared more likely, another effort was made to demonstrate support from professional colleagues. The statement from the Lawyers' Committee on Supreme Court Nominations opposed both the use of the filibuster against judicial nominees, and Judiciary Committee scrutiny of their judicial decisions. The White House secured the signatures of 151 lawyers from forty-nine states and the District of Colombia, including seven past presidents of the ABA, and twenty law school deans.[74] Lobbying unit staff distributed a press release about the statement to the wire services, Senate Gallery, and Press Club, and to Eastland. Lloyd Cutler spoke to Eric Sevareid of CBS and David Brinkley of NBC, who both hoped to cover the story on their early evening news programmes,

---

[71] Califano to Johnson, 1/8/68, Fortas, Box 5, 'WHCF Ex FG 535/A: 1/8/68–1/11/68'. Lloyd Cutler was later Special Counsel to President Carter.

[72] Telegram to Eastland, Fortas, Box 2, 'WHCF Ex FG 535/A: 1/8/68–1/11/68'.

[73] Christopher to Temple, 31/7/68, Fortas, Box 2, 'Chron File: 14/7/68–31/7/68'. Among the ABA figures was Lloyd Cutler.

[74] Statement of the Lawyers' Committee on Supreme Court Nominations, attached to a memorandum for Johnson from Califano, Fortas, Box 3, 'Chron File: 3/9/68–14/9/68'.

and to correspondents of *The New York Times* and *The Washington Post.*[75]

With exceptions such as Palmer Hoyt, a newspaperman in Colorado who lobbied Senator Allott, individual correspondents from press and television played little role in the lobbying unit's strategy, though *Time* or *Newsweek* journalists sometimes came to the White House to be briefed; on one occasion, the president personally briefed a journalist. McPherson kept in frequent contact with Alan Barth of *The Washington Post*, whose dedication to liberal causes as an editorial writer for that newspaper made him a valued ally.[76] Barth worked hard, giving editorial support for Fortas throughout.[77] After the withdrawal of the nominations in early October, McPherson wrote to Fortas to express his regrets, and added: 'Some day you might. . . want to give Alan Barth a call. He was a tiger for us all the way, and he was altogether responsible for the *Post*'s firm and steady support.'[78]

Lobbying staff used their close ties to AFL-CIO officials and union leaders to contact senators friendly to labour, especially some liberal Republicans.[79] Sanders co-ordinated his contacts with labour through Andrew Biemiller, the AFL-CIO's chief lobbyist, whose assistance had been so welcome in the difficult final stages of the tax surcharge campaign. Less than a week after the nominations were submitted, Sanders persuaded him to send a strong statement, signed by George Meany, endorsing Fortas and Thornberry, to all Democratic Study Group members in the House in the hope that they would help persuade reluctant senators. Biemiller also agreed to arrange for state AFL-CIO groups to send telegrams of support.[80]

[75] Statement of the Lawyers' Committee.
[76] Barth had, according to David Halberstam, an 'unbending belief in civil liberties, an ability to stand back from the heat of contemporary passion and to express his ideas with great force and lucidity' (*The Powers that Be*, New York, 1979, p. 184).
[77] McPherson to Johnson, Fortas, Box 5, 'WHCF Ex FG 535/A: 3/7/68–30/7/68'.
[78] White House Name File, 'Abe Fortas: October 1968', McPherson to Fortas, 4/10/68.
[79] Sanders to Johnson, 27/6/68, WHCF Ex FG 400, Box 327, '20/6/68–11/7/68'.
[80] Sanders to Johnson, 2/7/68, WHCF Ex FG 400, Box 327, '20/6/68–11/7/68'.

In September, labour organisations increased their efforts. Meany tried vainly to get Senator Dodd (D-CT) to sign the letter opposing Fortas's reappearance before the Judiciary Committee. Three days earlier, he had told Biemiller that the nominations were 'the most important matter which Labor has pending in Congress'.[81] Walter Reuther of the United Auto Workers took a similar view and was helpful when in early July it seemed that Senator Griffin represented a major threat. The UAW's strength in Michigan was so great, and Reuther's contacts so numerous, that he had little difficulty in persuading senior business executives to approach Griffin.[82]

Paul Porter tried to win support from business but there was little organised lobbying on Fortas's behalf by business associations or individual firms despite his relatively sympathetic judicial record in economic and financial matters where his approach had not been anti-trust as a matter of principle—indeed, rather the reverse. A brief prepared for Senator Dirksen by his legal advisers stressed this feature of Fortas's judicial philosophy.[83] In a dissent from a decision delaying the merger of the New York Central and Pennsylvania railroads, Fortas declared: 'The Courts may be the principal guardians of the liberties of the people. They are not the chief administrators of their economic destiny.'[84]

Gaither called William G. Miller, president of Textron, and Floyd Hall, president of Eastern Airlines, who promised to use their influence at the headquarters of the National Association of Businessmen to gather support. Gaither reported to Califano on 1 July that his several contacts at the NAB:[85]

. . . have begun a concentrated campaign on behalf of Fortas. They have written and sent telegrams to Hruska, Hickenlooper, Carlson, Murphy, Tower and Eastland. They are also making personal contacts. Their approach, which was developed after some discussions with Paul Porter, is to argue that business and the free enterprise

[81] Sanders to Temple, 10/9/68, Fortas, Box 3, 'Chron File: 3/9/68–14/9/68'.
[82] Walter Reuther to Califano, Fortas, Box 5, 'WHCF Ex FG 535/A: 3/7/68–30/7/68'.
[83] Memo re Fortas opinions, Working Papers, Box 966, The Dirksen Center.
[84] Shogan, *A Question of Judgment*, p. 125.
[85] Later, during the Carter administration, Miller was chairman of the Federal Reserve Board, and then Secretary of the Treasury (Gaither to Califano, 1/7/68, Fortas, Box 4, 'WHCF Ex FG 535/A: 1/7/68–2/7/68').

system are behind Abe Fortas and that he would be an excellent Chief Justice from their point of view.

Fortas's ethnicity enabled White House lobbyists to mobilise the strongly organised and well-connected Jewish groups and networks throughout the country. Once group members realised that Fortas was indeed Jewish (something of which the nominee seemed scarcely conscious), support for him was quickly forthcoming. Harry McPherson recalled that this occasioned some amusement:[86]

I remember on the Fortas thing, when I started to work with Jewish groups, the response was like one-handed clapping. I was often asked 'Is Abe Fortas Jewish?' I recall that Dave Brody [of the Anti-Defamation League] sent me photos of Abe and David Lloyd Krieger playing the violin, and both were wearing Yamulkas. I was very pleased with this and showed them to Johnson. 'That doesn't mean a goddamned thing,' he said. 'I've worn more of them than Abe has!'

The nomination of Thurgood Marshall in 1967 was symbolically important because he was black, the first to sit on the Court. But there had been Jewish Justices before, and it was therefore difficult to portray Fortas's nomination to Chief Justice as a comparable step forward for a beleaguered ethnic minority. Since anti-Semitic sentiment had no weight, Fortas's confirmation or rejection had little symbolic significance for the Jewish community. Moreover, not all Jewish supporters across the country were liberal, still less supporters of Fortas's nomination. Regional and ideological loyalties were sometimes more important. Goldstein told Johnson in early July that in his judgement the propects of arousing Jewish support for Fortas in Texas were poor: 'No Texas Jewish leaders with influence on Tower are available. All are Birchers and anti-Abe.'[87] In California, Sprague attempted to arouse Jewish support, and was initially optimistic about the prospects:[88]

Joseph Roos, Executive Secretary of the Jewish Community Relations Council, has called Senator Murphy and sent him a strong letter. . .

[86] Interview with Harry McPherson, 9/5/79.
[87] Goldstein to Johnson, 8/7/68, Fortas, Box 5, 'WHCF Ex FG 535/A: 3/7/68–30/7/68'.
[88] 28/6/68, Fortas, Box 4, 'WHCF Ex FG 535/A: 25/6/68–30/6/68'.

all of the big Jewish leaders are putting pressure on Murphy. Their pitch is that this appointment is analogous to the fight on the Brandeis appointment and they well remember the anti-Jewish sentiments aroused then.

But the nominations of 1968 were neither analogous to the Brandeis nomination, nor recognised as such. (Thornberry's nomination, of course, diluted the Jewish character of the case still further and weakened the significance of the nominations to the Jewish community, and hence of its impact on Senate opinion, still further.) Murphy opposed the motion to impose cloture on further Senate debate.

Sprague was equally unsuccessful in persuading Murphy of Fortas's virtues by his use of film stars and industry moguls. He told Sanders on 29 June that several figures in the industry 'are building up strong pressures on Murphy', even though Murphy had already made his opposition known.[89]

COMMITTEE CHAIRMEN AND CONSERVATIVES

In July, the lobbying for the nominations met well-organised, and passionate, opposition. The conservative response to the civil rights pressures, culminating in the violence of 1968, found ready expression in the Senate Judiciary Committee. Like the tax bill, the Fortas case starkly illustrated the great power of committee chairmen in the era before Congressional reform, and the importance of the conservative coalition. Four members of it, all southerners—Senators Eastland, McClellan, Ervin, and Thurmond—were between them responsible for delaying until 20 September the nominations in committee and hence, because of the lack of time and the erosion of support through the summer, effectively killing them. Ervin treated Justice Fortas as a symbol of a Supreme Court which defied constitutional provision. Innuendo was his stock-in-trade; delay was his, and his colleagues', trump card.

Their views were clear. Eastland told Manatos as early as 25 June that 'Abe Fortas cannot be confirmed as Chief

---

[89] Sprague to Sanders, 29/6/68, Sprague, Box 7 (1568), 'Sanders, Barefoot: Memos For'.

Justice'.[90] At the same meeting, Eastland also said that
Fortas's nomination would be filibustered on the Senate floor.
Such a threat to delay the reporting of Fortas's nomination
was menacing, and Eastland executed it effectively, frustrating
White House attempts to have the nominations reported out
by the end of July so that the Senate could consider them
after the August recess.[91] The presence of Republicans at
their party's Miami convention in late July made assembling
a quorum difficult. When White House lobbyists persuaded
Dirksen and his colleagues to return from Miami, Eastland
responded by informing Manatos that certain Democratic
colleagues of his would not attend.[92] Dirksen's agreement to
return was finally scotched when, according to Manatos,
Thurmond told Eastland that 'he will not permit a vote on
Wednesday even if there is a quorum'.[93] Eastland promised
Mike Mansfield, the Majority Leader, merely that he would
schedule a meeting for 4 September, with the possibility that
a vote would be taken 'if we all cooperate'.[94] But the issue of
the $15,000 seminar fees which arose during the August recess
encouraged Eastland to try to question Fortas once again,
with the difference that on this issue, Fortas's behaviour found
little senatorial support.

Other opponents were more disingenuous. Having talked
with McClellan on the morning of 25 July, by which time it
was clear that delay would again be the southern conservatives'
tactic, Manatos told the president: 'He [McClellan] knows of
no southern plan to have anything to do with organising or
participating in a filibuster. He has not heard this discussed
by any Southerner.'[95]

This was not a reason for presidential celebration. McClellan's opposition to Fortas, which later focused to telling effect
on the question of the Supreme Court's liberal decisions on
pornography, was evident from the end of June.[96] Shortly

[90] Manatos to Johnson, 25/6/68, Fortas, Box 1, 'Chron File: 13/6/68–29/6/68'.
[91] Manatos to Johnson, 29/7/68, Fortas, Box 2, 'Chron File: 14/7/68–29/7/68'.
[92] Manatos to Johnson, 29/7/68.
[93] Manatos to Johnson, 29/7/68, Fortas, Box 1, 'Chron File: 14/7/68–31/7/68'.
[94] Manatos to Johnson, 29/7/68, Fortas, Box 2, 'Chron File: 14/7/68–29/7/68'.
[95] Fortas, Box 2, 'Chron File: 14/7/68–31/7/68'.
[96] Temple to Johnson, 24/7/68, Fortas, Box 7, 'Additional Material: 3/7/68–
31/8/68'.

before his conversation with Manatos, Eastland had spoken to McClellan while riding on the subway shuttle to the Capitol building from his Senate office. Eastland reported him as having said, with some vehemence, that he hoped no block would be raised against the reporting of Fortas's nomination from committee. He was looking forward to having 'that son-of-a-bitch formally submitted to the Senate' so that he could fight the nomination.[97]

The opposition of key members of the Judiciary Committee was therefore evident from the beginning; there was a serious prospect of their prolonging hearings, and then filibustering on the Senate floor. To make matters worse, committee hearings revealed Fortas's advisory role to Johnson, and resulted in him being stigmatised as 'soft on crime and pornography' by those anxious to draw a connection in the public mind between the decisions of the Supreme Court and unwelcome social trends. Coupled with widespread dismay at the implications of Fortas's seminar fee, opponents now had several telling points to make. The early reliance on arguments of 'cronyism' and lame-duck presidential nominations later assumed relative insignificance. The pivotal position of chairmen in the pre-reform Congress (even of second-rate politicians such as Eastland) and the delaying power of a committee's conservative minority required only a few substantive issues to emerge for Fortas's nomination to be blocked, however skilled the lobbying staff in the White House. For those not unalterably opposed to it on political grounds, there were several sound and politically safe reasons for doubt about the wisdom of Fortas's nomination. Tactical ploys had served their purpose in delaying the nomination until the autumn pre-election session and by allowing time for damaging evidence to emerge. By September, unease was sufficiently widespread for senators to prefer a procedural burial rather than a floor vote.

SENATE WHALES

Prior Congressional consultation is as essential to successful presidential lobbying as constant attention to Congressmen's and senators' needs through active liaison. In a press

[97] Temple to Johnson, 24/7/68.

conference on 26 June when he announced the nominations, Johnson claimed that he had discussed them with several senior senators: 'I have discussed it with the Leadership, with several members of the Senate, the Democratic Leadership and Republican Leadership, and the Leadership of the Committee.'[98]

But Johnson's discussions had been neither extensive nor intensive. At most, six senators were told about the nominations before their announcement on the twenty-sixth: Mansfield, Dirksen, Eastland, and Russell, and possibly Robert Byrd and Russell Long. As Majority Leader, Mansfield clearly had to be informed. None the less, Mansfield was asked for his support for Fortas, not for his advice on the nomination. It is unclear whether Mansfield was informed on 25 June at the Congressional leadership breakfast, or on the twenty-sixth when Johnson telephoned him early in the morning. Since the president did not tell the Attorney-General of his choice until lunch-time on the twenty-fifth, he may not have discussed it with Mansfield until the following day. If so, then Byrd and Long were not consulted at all, for there were no conversations between either of them and the president between the conclusion of the breakfast on the twenty-fifth, and the announcement of the nominations the next morning.

The president was also obliged to inform the chairman of the Judiciary Committee of his choice before sending the nominations to the Senate, although the question of discussing nominees with him did not arise for Eastland was certain to oppose a nominee of Johnson's. Johnson knew this perfectly well. In any event, the president disliked Eastland, and despised his cynical use of questions of race and Communism: 'Jim Eastland could be standing right in the middle of the worst Mississippi flood ever known, and he'd say the niggers caused it, helped out some by the Communists—but he'd say we gotta have help from Washington.'[99]

Thus the 'discussion' with the 'leadership of the committee' was limited to a brief meeting with Eastland in the Fish Room (later named the Roosevelt Room) an hour before the nominations were announced to the press. With the exception

[98] Transcript of Press Conference no. 128, 26/6/68, Fortas, Box 1.
[99] Mooney, B., *LBJ: An Irreverent Chronicle*, New York, 1976, p. 50.

of Dirksen, other members of the committee, including McClellan, were not consulted. Sam Ervin's opposition was easily predicted. Johnson took a dim view of Ervin too, and relations between them were distant; there was no good reason to tell a certain opponent of his plans.

Johnson took the view that the prospects of confirmation hinged on Senators Dirksen and Russell. Here the president misjudged. He knew Dirksen was subject to growing party political pressures (and privately doubted his capacity to resist them), and over-estimated the importance of Russell's support (which was in any case fragile) for the fate of the nominations. Private persuasion being Johnson's forte, he took it upon himself to initiate consultations with these two whales and certain of their colleagues; contacts by his Congressional liaison staff would not have sufficed. Both Richard Russell and Everett Dirksen had been of immense political assistance to Johnson. Russell had helped make his Senate career a quick success, and Dirksen had given President Johnson's party advantage in Congress legislative effect by supporting him on civil rights measures. As Temple recalled, Johnson believed that their assistance would be vital on this matter as it had been in the past:[100]

The President thought that at the time the two keys in the Senate to the confirmation of these two individuals were Senator Russell and Senator Dirksen, for fairly obvious reasons. . . So the President contacted both Senator Russell and Senator Dirksen and talked to them about the nominations prior to the time that he made them. He obtained from both of them what he took to be a commitment that they would support the nomination of Fortas to be Chief Justice, and Judge Thornberry to be Associate Judge of the Supreme Court. . . Senator Dirksen made several speeches endorsing the nominations on the floor of the Senate.

Johnson was in touch with Dirksen on six occasions between the nineteenth and twenty-sixth of June. White House records show that the president made a local telephone call to him early in the morning of 22 June to discuss 'the resignation of Chief Justice Warren and possible replacements'.[101] Two days later, Johnson spoke with Dirksen for nearly an hour in the

100 Temple, Oral History, Tape no. 6, p. 23.
101 Daily Diary, 22/6/68.

evening and then, on the afternoon of the twenty-fifth, Dirksen met the president at the White House. In view both of the Congressional leadership breakfast that morning, and the press conference the following day for the public announcement, it is likely that the nominations were the subject of conversation.[102] Johnson calculated that if Dirksen backed Fortas and Thornberry, undecided Republican colleagues would fall in line. This was a plausible enough prospect. Earlier in the year, Dirksen had supported a cloture vote on the Civil Rights Act with the important open-housing clause, as he had previously done with the 1964 Civil Rights Act.[103] Although by 1968 Richard Russell was no longer the most important of the southern Democrats, he was still a significant force. More importantly, from Johnson's point of view, he had been, and to some extent remained, a confidant: he had been crucial to Johnson's success in winning the Minority Leadership after the 1952 elections, and was an intimate colleague thereafter.[104] From the beginning of Johnson's presidency, Russell was a frequent visitor to the White House for private breakfasts; discussion ranged over a number of subjects from fiscal policy to the Vietnam War.[105]

It was therefore to be expected that the two would discuss the nominations; Johnson felt in need of Russell's assurance of support. He made a long-distance telephone call to Russell's home in Winder, Georgia, on 21 June.[106] Four days later, Russell spent an evening at the White House. During dinner, the president asked his secretary, Juanita Roberts, to tell Russell all she knew about Thornberry's childhood and college days. Later, conversation moved on to reminiscences of the early 1950s when Russell was a frequent dinner guest of the Johnsons, and to the president's children and grandchildren whom, the White House diary records, the senator found more interesting than 'business': Russell was not anxious to discuss the Court succession, and avoided over-committing himself. After dinner, the president accompanied his guest to

[102] Daily Diary, 4.53 p.m., 25/6/68.
[103] Miller, M., *Lyndon*, New York, 1980, p. 177.
[104] Evans, R., and Novak, R., *Lyndon B. Johnson: The Exercise of Power*, New York, 1968, p. 63.
[105] Few of these visits are recorded in the Daily Diary.
[106] Daily Diary, 21/6/68.

the Diplomatic Entrance and talked to him for five or ten minutes before the senator finally left.[107]

It is not clear from this whether Johnson consulted Russell about the choice, or merely informed him of the decision. But the latter is much more likely since the president had decided on the nominations by lunch on 25 June, and had had only two prior conversations with Russell that month.[108] One was the telephone call to Winder on the twenty-first, and the other was on the eighth, before Warren submitted his letter of contingent resignation.[109] It is reasonably certain that Johnson succeeded in winning Russell's acquiescence, though not his enthusiastic support. Temple's recollection was that, although Russell was not a public protagonist on behalf of Fortas and Thornberry, 'it was fairly common knowledge that he was supporting the nominations'.[110]

Russell and Dirksen's agreement must be interpreted in the context of mounting conservative hostility to the Court's decisions. Russell was the third most consistent Democratic supporter of the conservative coalition in the Senate in 1968, and voted against the president on every significant proposed amendment to the Crime Control Bill; Russell's backing for Fortas is therefore all the more eloquent a testimony to the closeness of his ties to Johnson.[111] Indeed, he told both Harry McPherson and Larry Temple that he was displeased with the Fortas nomination and would have preferred to have seen Thornberry nominated for the Chief Justiceship. He added that he hoped that the nomination of his old friend Alexander Lawrence, to a Federal District Judgeship in Georgia, would not be much longer delayed by the administration.[112]

[107] Daily Dairy, 25/6/68.
[108] Christopher to Temple, 20/12/68.
[109] Daily Diary, 8 and 21 June 1968.
[110] Temple, Oral History, Tape no. 6, p. 18.
[111] His conservative coalition support score in 1968, as measured by *Congressional Quarterly*, was 83 per cent (*Congressional Quarterly Almanac, 1968*, p. 823). The Crime Control votes are CQ Senate votes 96–124, which correspond to Congressional Record Roll Senate votes nos. 129–60, omitting nos. 133 and 139 (*Congressional Quarterly Almanac, 1968*, pp. 23-S–28-S).
[112] Interviews with Harry McPherson, 9/5/68, and Larry Temple, 9/4/79. (This would have been an exceedingly difficult nomination to confirm. Thornberry was as vulnerable to the charge of cronyism as Fortas, and intellectually much inferior.)

Within days, Russell withdrew his support for the nominees.[113] In a bitter letter, he concluded that Lawrence's nomination was being withheld until Russell made a public statement backing Fortas's nomination. He was unwilling to be thought to bow to pressure of this kind, and disliked 'being thought of as a child or a patronage-seeking ward heeler'.[114] Accordingly, he considered himself released from the offer of support for Fortas and Thornberry's nominations, and added:
[115]

. . . you are at liberty to deal with the recommendations as to Mr. Lawrence in any way you see fit. I shall undertake to deal objectively with the nominations you have made to the Supreme Court, but however I may vote, I want you to understand that it is not done with any expectation that I am buying or insuring the nomination of Mr. Lawrence to either the District or the Circuit Court and that I do not propose to make any future endorsements to you for judicial appointments even in my own state.

Russell was incorrect in supposing that the president deliberately delayed submitting Lawrence's nomination: Attorney-General Ramsey Clark had done so (against Johnson's wishes) because he believed Lawrence (wrongly) to be a racist.[116] In due course, the nomination was made, and Lawrence established a distinguished reputation on the bench. But Johnson lost Russell's support for his Supreme Court nominees and his relationship with him suffered terribly as a result of Clark's mishandling of what should have been an uncomplicated case of judicial patronage.[117]

CONCLUSION

The outcome of the Supreme Court nominations is less important for the purposes of this book than for what the case reveals of the political process of Congressional relations.

[113] Richard B. Russell to Johnson, 1/7/68, Temple, Box 1, 'Russell Letter'.

[114] Richard B. Russell to Johnson, 1/7/68.

[115] Richard B. Russell to Johnson, 1/7/68. Professor Massaro is mistaken, as are certain members of Johnson's staff, in believing that no copy of this letter exists. At least one copy was made, and retained in Larry Temple's White House files (Massaro, J., 'LBJ and the Fortas Nomination', *Political Science Quarterly*, winter 1982–3, vol. 97, no. 4, p. 617).

[116] Clark to Johnson, 13/5/68, WHCF Ex and Gen FG 530, Box 255, 'FG 530/ST10'.

[117] Interviews with Larry Temple, 9/4/79; George Christian, Bob Hardesty, and Harry Middleton, 24/4/79.

Although the normal OCR team were supplanted by a special *ad hoc* unit, the techniques which they employed were similar to those used by the OCR on other occasions.

Even by his own standards, the president kept a close watch over this campaign; his judgement and tactics were none the less wanting. His encyclopaedic knowledge of Senate personalities and politics had always strengthened his hand on previous occasions, but it was out of date, and to some extent irrelevant by the last year of his presidency. In support of a trusted adviser and confidant to Chief Justice, it proved insufficient. Johnson was too weak to see off the opposition, and relied on old whales who did not, and could not, deliver. He was a lame-duck president *de facto*, though not *de jure*; his constitutional writ ran as far in the summer of 1968 as before, but his powers of leverage, pleading, and persuasion were less, as Barefoot Sanders emphasised: 'The thing that made the Fortas thing so difficult and, as it turned out in the event, impossible. . . was the accelerating erosion of presidential power on the Hill after 31st March . . . I'd go up there, and you could just feel it. There was a difference.'[118]

Even had Johnson been a candidate for re-election, and the OCR as strong and resourceful as it had been under O'Brien four years earlier, the nominations would not have been assured of confirmation, although Dirksen and Russell might then have behaved differently. In many respects, the battle to confirm was a continuation of the crime and gun-control debates of a horribly violent year. The ease with which powerful senators were able to blame Fortas's record on the Supreme Court for the weakening of 'law and order' was a major factor in delaying consideration of his nomination, and in the consequent shelving of Thornberry's. The senators capitalised on a subject of deep and genuine public concern, and time was on their side: the fragmentation of American government makes obfuscation relatively easy to organise. Progress with legislation, the confirmation of nominations, or the ratification of treaties is, by the same token, difficult. Fortas's weaknesses—the revelations of the American University seminar fees, his ethical laxity, the charges of 'cronyism', 'softness' on crime and pornography—made the

118 Sanders, Oral History, Tape no. 3, p. 23.

defeat of the nominations probable. By the beginning of September, they were in grave difficulty, and beyond the rescue of the shrewdest lobbying staff.

Mansfield recognised the hopelessness of prolonging the attempt to confirm when he rejected the option of keeping the Senate in round-the-clock session during floor debate. The final vote of 45 : 43 in favour of cloture indicated the substantial strength of the opposition forces and the impossibility of confirming the nominees in the few days left on the Senate calendar before the November elections.[119]

The circumstances of the time, and the institutional power-bases of their opponents in the Senate Judiciary Committee, outweighed the lobbying pressures which the White House were able to apply. It is certain that the hasty cobbling together of a lobbying unit did the administration's chances no good at all. More important, the president's poor choice of nominees made the task of confirming them difficult; Johnson's own mistakes, especially the identification of Dirksen and Russell as two 'keys', and the related failures on the one hand fully to appreciate the political pressures acting upon Dirksen and on the other to set Russell's mind at rest in the matter of Alexander Lawrence's nomination, did not help. The campaign's failure signalled the effective close to Johnson's tired presidency, broken by an unpopular war he could neither win nor end, and by turbulence at home. It was especially ironic that Johnson's manoeuvering with Fortas and Warren to arrange for a conditional resignation should have paved the way not for a liberal Chief Justice but for a conservative who could not be relied upon to provide judicial support for the Great Society legislation by which he set such store. The hand from the presidential grave was that of Johnson's Republican successor, Richard Nixon.

[119] *Congressional Quarterly Weekly Reports*, 4/10/68, p. 2613.

8

THE POLITICS OF PRESIDENTIAL WEAKNESS

INTRODUCTION: PRESIDENTS NIXON AND FORD

Nixon was the first president since Zachary Taylor in 1849 to enter office facing opposition party majorities in both Houses of Congress: the Democrats enjoyed advantages of 247 : 188 in the House, and 57 : 43 in the Senate. This novel circumstance in modern American government, together with Nixon's lack of ideological majorities in Congress, structured both his first, and foreshortened second, terms in office. Having succeeded Spiro Agnew to the vice-presidency in 1973 under the provisions of the twenty-fifth amendment, Ford subsequently became the first person to hold the office of president having been elected neither to it nor to the vice-presidency.

Relations with Congress under Presidents Richard Nixon and Gerald Ford were thus distinctive in several important respects which together make presidential–congressional liaison between 1969 and 1977 a less fruitful subject of study than the eight years before or after. Johnson, Carter, and Reagan all had major legislative programmes for which they required Congressional backing. They pressed them on Congresses where they enjoyed majorities of party, ideology, or both, for at least part of their incumbencies. To set condensed analyses of the politics and organization of Carter's and Reagan's relations with Congress beside the more substantial exam- ination of Johnson's, provides for their comparison in broadly similar circumstances. Nixon's and Ford's presidencies were of an entirely different kind from these three: politically confined context reduced the scope for legislative initiative, while the two presidents' primary political purposes did not require liaison organisations of comparable importance or prominence to those in the Johnson, Carter, or Reagan White House Offices.

Like his disgraced predecessor, Ford faced a Congress in the hands of the Democratic opposition. Indeed, for the greater part of his short term (from January 1975 until his departure from Washington in 1977) he laboured under especially severe Congressional disadvantage: the Congressional elections in the year of Nixon's second presidential poll victory resulted in Democratic majorities of 57 : 43 in the Senate and 240 : 192 in the House.[1] The 1974 mid-term elections, occurring in the aftermath of Ford's unpopular pardon of his predecessor increased those substantial Democratic advantages to 61 : 38 and 289 : 144 respectively.[2]

Unable to depend upon Congressional party colleagues for majority support for his legislative and spending proposals, Nixon adopted an explicitly ideological approach, seeking the backing of conservative Democrats as well as Republican allies in disputes over appropriations for defence and space programmes (where his requests were cut), education and environmental programmes (where they were increased), and in his proposed weakening amendments to the 1965 Voting Rights Act (where he was defeated). His nomination to the Supreme Court of Clement Haynsworth in November 1969 and of G. Harrold Carswell five months later also won cross-party conservative support, but insufficient to prevail over substantial moderate and liberal resistance. (The defeat of Carswell's nomination marked the first occasion since 1894 on which one president had suffered the rejection of two of his nominations to the Court.)

Nixon's main priorities lay abroad: the war in south-east Asia (or, as Kissinger later characterised it, the 'liquidation' of that protracted engagement); the development of a distinctively new set of relations with the Soviet Union, in recognition of the fact of nuclear parity; and the establishment of a radically altered political relationship with China. *Detente*, of course, was the object of liberal approval. It won general conservative acceptance not least because it was the policy of

[1] Three House seats were vacant in January 1973.
[2] Two House seats, and one Senate seat, were vacant in March 1975. *Congressional Quarterly Almanac, 1975*, pp. 24–5.

a politician whose career had been built on a platform of vigorous anti-Communism, sustained even at *detente's* birth by the prosecution of an expanded air war in Vietnam and Cambodia.

Nixon's presidency decisively affected the general balance of power between the executive and legislature during a crucial period in American government: the resurgence of Congress in foreign and budgetary policy was symbolised and exemplified in the War Powers Resolution of 1973 and the Budget and Impoundment Control Act of 1974. Relations between the president and his Congressional opposition increasingly comprised bitterly embattled confrontation, rooted in disputes of a fundamental kind about constitutional government. It was not the customary institutional and personal conflicts (bounded by constitutional law, yet the inevitable outgrowth of constitutionally ordained separations of powers) which stained Nixon's presidency, but his systematic abuse of constitutional provision, casual violation of statute, and disregard of political norm. Congress, belatedly but vigorously, exposed both, and effectively forced his resignation.

Beneath the level of presidential deceit, impoundment of appropriated funds, and the secret prosecution of a foreign war, the routine business of domestic legislation was handled by the president's Congressional staff with little leadership or demonstration of interest from the chief executive himself. He was remote, both physically and by temperament, from the judgements and calculations of his Congressional advisers. Bryce Harlow, who had led Eisenhower's Office of Congressional Liaison, took the comparable post under Nixon for the first year of the presidency, when he became counsellor to the president. His successor, William Timmons, lacked comparable influence and access. Indeed, Timmons was unable to have a meeting with the president without first securing the agreement of the White House Chief of Staff—reflecting Nixon's disdain of Congress (particularly after the 1970 elections), the consequential minor importance of Congressional liaison staff within Nixon's White House, and especially their exclusion from policy discussion. The president's remoteness from them was matched by his dislike of seeking the votes of those (very many) Congressmen and senators whom he did not regard as personal friends. Awkward and uneasy in the role of suppliant, Nixon preferred the distance of occasional telephone calls and the anonymity of prepared letters to the intimacy of private meetings; he even arranged formal receiving lines at White House prayer breakfasts.[3]

Despite the enormous Congressional majorities enjoyed by the Democratic Party in the 94th Congress, Gerald Ford publicly hoped that he might have a 'good marriage' rather than a 'honeymoon' with Congress. The social and political atmosphere was quite different to that which prevailed under Nixon, and the president's relationships with individual members were altogether warmer, lacking the suspicion and instinctive distrust which were the corrosive norm from 1969 to 1974. In deposing Charles Halleck as House Republican leader in 1965, Ford had demonstrated courage and tactical skill; as Minority Leader, he then displayed considerable charm and determination in consolidating his position within the Republican Party. These qualities served him well in the presidency: William Timmons (who continued in the post he had occupied under Nixon) and his colleagues on the Congressional liaison staff enjoyed easy access to the president who in turn supported their work, not least by keeping them fully informed of his many conversations with Congressmen and senators.[4]

Whilst Congressional relief at Ford's sheer friendliness and decency was both palpable and understandable, relations with Congress were singularly unproductive, made worse by the president's apparent weakness in understanding some of the issues before him, and his lack of grip in dealing with dissension within his administration. Already lacking an electoral mandate, Ford's freedom of manœuvre was further limited by the outcome of the mid-term elections of 1974. They confirmed him in his decision to opt for government by veto (the sustaining of which became a preoccupation for him and his liaison staff as the most promising response to Congressional Democrats' seizure of the political agenda). His first veto came just four days after he entered office. He vetoed a further twenty-four bills that year (just four of which

[3] Wayne, S., *The Legislative Presidency*, New York, 1978, pp. 156–8.
[4] Wayne, *The Legislative Presidency*, p. 163.

were overridden), and pocket-vetoed another eleven after the
93rd Congress adjourned on 20 December.[5] In 1975, the
president vetoed seventeen bills (many of them on energy and
economic policy) of which Congress overrode four; Congress
again overrode four vetoes in the election year of 1976, but
out of a total of fifteen.[6]

Ford's calculation that this approach would bring him
electoral reward proved unfounded: Carter ably turned
the political immobility of Washington against him. The
Democratic candidate's electoral strategy played on widely
shared views among the voting public of the bloated
incompetence of the bureaucracy, the inefficiency and distance
from the voting public of Congress and the presidency.
Whatever electoral advantage he drew from this, it did his
prospects of presidential leadership grave injury.

In January 1977, Jimmy Carter inherited an office low in
public esteem, weakened by predecessors' abuse of its powers,
and newly constrained by statute: the War Powers Act of
1973 and the Budget and Impoundment Control Act of 1974
placed new limits on presidential powers. The balance of
power between the branches of government at either end of
Pennsylvania Avenue had altered sharply to the disadvantage
of the presidency in the four years before Carter came to
Washington. Congress was indeed resurgent.[7]

But the relative increase in Congress's power had enhanced
neither its overall capacity to formulate coherent national
policy nor its inclination to follow a presidential lead.[8]
Furthermore, the influence exerted by Congressional parties
(especially the Democrats) over their members, had declined
since the mid-1960s. Members were increasingly independent
of party pressure and sanction—a trend accelerated by
the growing importance of Political Action Committees in
financing Congressional elections following the Federal Election Campaign Act of 1974 and the subsequent amendments
of 1976. Senators and representatives increasingly relied upon

[5] *Congressional Quarterly Almanac, 1974*, pp. 32 and 906.

[6] *Congressional Quarterly Almanac, 1975*, p. 20; *Congressional Quarterly Almanac, 1976*,
p. 3.

[7] See: Sundquist, J. L., *The Decline and Resurgence of Congress*, Washington, DC,
1981.

[8] Jacobson, G. C., *The Politics of Congressional Elections*, Boston, 1983.

their own resources rather than those of party organisations for political survival and advance. The politics of their districts rather than of their parties were usually the decisive factor in determining political behaviour, especially on roll-call votes.[9]

As parties had been weakened, so Congress had changed. The power of House committee chairmen had been much reduced by the Hansen Committee reforms of 1973 and 1975. Committee chairs, previously selected on the basis of seniority, were now subject to the approval of the Democratic caucus which also won the power to select subcommittee chairmen. Each committee member was granted a major subcommittee assignment. Subcommittee meetings proliferated, accounting for approximately 80 per cent of all workgroup meetings (in both houses) in the 95th Congress from 1977–78.[10] To characterise the political process as 'subcommittee government' was unwarranted, but full committee chairmen had certainly lost power to the subcommittees, which were further strengthened by acquiring professional staff to the extent that some had staffs as numerous as those which full committees had enjoyed in the late 1960s.[11] Power in the Congresses which Lyndon Johnson knew was concentrated in few hands but that in the Congress which Jimmy Carter met for the first time in January 1977 was dispersed among many. Bills voted out by committees were increasingly subject to floor amendment. Rotating membership of the House Budget Committee, established at the same time, meant that it was much less able than the Appropriations Committee had been to ensure floor support for bills it reported out.[12] The OCR's task of pressing the president's legislative proposals upon Congress was immeasurably complicated as a result.

The Congress which President Carter faced in January 1977 was therefore more powerful but less responsible than the Congresses with which Johnson had been familiar as president.

[9] See: Mann, T., and Ornstein, N., (eds.), *The New Congress*, Washington, DC, 1981.
[10] Davidson, R. H., 'Subcommittee Government', in Mann and Ornstein,(eds.), *The New Congress*, p. 117.
[11] Malbin, M., *Unelected Representatives*, New York, 1980, pp. 13–14.
[12] See: Davis, E. L., 'Legislative Reform and the Decline of Presidential Influence on Capitol Hill', *British Journal of Political Sciences*, vol. 9, no. 4, Oct. 1979.

Its role in the formation and oversight of policy had grown, but individual members took pains to distance themselves from the political costs of policy failure. By contrast, chief executives had a mandate, but not the means, to govern. Worse, despite their limited grant of power, presidents were held accountable for national policy.

THE ELECTIONS OF 1976

Although Carter's lack of experience in Washington proved a handicap in office, it was a distinct advantage (even necessary) in the elections for it. Party reforms enabled and required candidates for the Democratic nomination to appeal to primary electorates over the heads of party bosses: building coalitions within the party was no longer necessary to win. The changed rules fitted the temper of the times: to be associated with Washington in the circumstances of 1976, with memories of Vietnam and Watergate still fresh, was to be tainted. With great skill, Carter capitalised upon the national mood, turning the quality of being an 'outsider', of inexperience itself, to political advantage. Running against the style and substance of the nation's government was a common tactic among contenders for the presidency in 1976. Even Gerald Ford, with twenty-six years of service as a Congressman, and two as vice-president, attempted it as the incumbent president. But the hustings were one thing, government quite another. A shrewd electoral strategy provided a weak political base for legislative leadership from the White House, especially with a forbiddingly complex agenda of the sort he proposed.

Carter's leverage over members of Congress was reduced by the circumstances of his election in November 1976. He defeated President Ford by a margin of less than two million votes out of eighty million cast, winning 50.1 per cent of the total popular vote. The outcome in the electoral college was also close: 297 : 240.[13] Not surprisingly, most House Democratic candidates running at the same time won a larger share of the popular vote than their nominal party leader.

[13] Wayne, S., *The Road to the White House*, New York, 1984, p. 304.

They averaged 56.2 per cent of the total poll, and led their president (by between 4 and 9 percentage points) in every region of the country.[14] Carter ran ahead of just twenty-two victorious House Democrats (coincidentally, the same number as President Kennedy had managed in 1960).[15] In the Senate, too, Democrats ran more strongly than Carter: victorious Democratic candidates averaged 54.4 per cent of the total vote.[16]

The contrast with 1964 could scarcely be more sharply drawn. That was the last occasion on which a presidential candidate brought large numbers of his own party into Congress on his coat-tails: then, Johnson ran ahead of 134 Democratic House candidates, and level with two others.[17] Many of these were the liberal first-term Democrats who won in normally safe Republican districts and provided the margin of safety on House votes in the 89th Congress. The president assiduously exploited the widespread (and justified) feeling among them that they owed their presence in Congress to Lyndon Johnson. In November 1976, victorious Congressional Democrats knew full well that the man at the head of the ticket had not been an electoral asset to them. They had won without him, and remembered it.

THE APPROACH TO GOVERNMENT

Carter's experience of government offered almost as complete a contrast with Johnson's as did the circumstances of their respective elections. Jimmy Carter was a novice but failed to recognise it. His political experience was confined to a one-party state: two terms as a Georgia state senator and Governor of Georgia from 1970 to 1974, dealing with a relatively weak, poorly paid and staffed legislature limited by the state's constitution to forty meeting days per year. In the

---

[14] Bibby, J. F., Mann, T., and Ornstein, N. J., *Vital Statistics on Congress, 1980*, Washington, DC, 1980, Table 1:2, p. 6; Jones, C. O., 'Congress and the Presidency', in Mann and Ornstein,(eds.), *The New Congress*, p. 241.

[15] Bibby, Mann, and Ornstein, *Vital Statistics on Congress*, Table 1:14, p. 20; Jones, 'Congress and the Presidency', p. 241.

[16] Jones, 'Congress and the Presidency', p. 241.

[17] Bibby, Mann, and Ornstein, *Vital Statistics on Congress*, Table 1:14, p. 20.

tradition of Georgia governors, Carter was able to assert
executive authority, supervising the enactment of his bills
by appointing administration floor leaders in the General
Assembly with the responsibility for securing their passage.
In his gubernatorial policies, he exhibited a southern populist
enthusiasm for educational and welfare improvement, coupled
with a zealous insistence upon managerial efficiency and
budgetary discipline. The nature of his relations with the
one-party state legislature, and the substance and style of his
policy-making there, informed his approach to government
and politics in Washington. It was an unhelpful preparation
for dealing with the United States Congress.[18]

As Carter laid stress upon administrative dispatch when in
the Governor's mansion in Atlanta, so he viewed the problems
of presidential government largely in terms of procedure.
Johnson's indifference to administration cost him dear as
organisational structures and approaches established before
his accession to the presidency fell into disarray by 1966-7.
But the Johnson presidency had in any event been buoyed
until that time by fortuitous circumstance and mostly sound
political judgement, so that procedure was of secondary
import. By contrast, in the Carter presidency, the primary
difficulty arose from the president's conception of the problems
of government as capable of solution by earnest application,
rectitude, and administrative reform (though despite this, he
still failed to develop appropriately effective administrative
arrangements). However many the flaws in Lyndon Johnson's
understanding of the purposes and possibilities of politics in
America, these were not among them.

Carter's distinctive conception of presidential government
owed something to progressive and populist influence, and
much more to incoherent reactions to the aggrandisement of
the presidency in the previous two decades. It was shown to
good effect firstly in his organisation of his presidency and
secondly in the legislative initiatives which he took.

In the first of these, Jimmy Carter, like many previous
presidential candidates anxious to curry favour with sceptical
electorates, declared his intention to preside over a 'cabinet

[18] Hepburn, Lawrence R., 'Georgia', in Rosenthal, A., and Moakley, M., *The Political Life of the American States*, New York, 1984, pp. 192-3.

government'. Unlike most of them, he made a serious attempt to implement the promise. He indicated a wish to reduce the number of staff in the White House and in the offices of departmental secretaries. Questions of jurisdiction, organisation, and procedure within the White House were in future to be settled by a management committee rather than a Chief of Staff. That role was declared by no less a person than Hamilton Jordan, (later to hold the very position himself) to be 'a concept. . . alien to Governor Carter'.[19] The Domestic Council (a unit of doubtful utility and, worse, an unwelcome reminder of the organisational reforms of its creator, Richard Nixon) was abolished and its several functions disseminated among a domestic policy staff in the White House, a cabinet secretariat, and the Office of Management and Budget (OMB). The ghosts of Haldeman and Ehrlichman stalked the White House corridors still.

The purpose was to reduce the concentration of power at the centre, to move influence from the White House staff to the cabinet secretaries and the Cabinet Room. Apparently unaware of the implications which such a view of American government had for a president's reach, Carter confidently declared: 'I believe in Cabinet administration of our government. There will never be an instance while I am President where the members of the White House staff dominate or act in a superior position to the members of the Cabinet.'[20]

The experiment lasted less than two years: a meeting called by the president and attended by senior staff and cabinet officals at Camp David in April 1978 effectively marked its end. The president's exhortations there to his staff to work in greater harmony to a more co-ordinated (a euphemism for presidential) purpose translated into a gradual tightening of White House control over cabinet secretaries and departments. The incoherent rhetoric which proclaimed an era of 'cabinet government' in a presidential system was abandoned, cabinet meetings were reduced in frequency from weekly to fortnightly, and the White House staff assumed a less egalitarian organisational character. Finally, in the summer of 1979, four members of the cabinet whose virtues the president had so

[19] *National Journal*, 12/2/77.
[20] *National Journal*, 12/2/77.

often extolled were dismissed, and the resignation of a fifth, the Attorney-General, accepted. This marked Carter's final recasting of his administration, the end of the 'cabinet government' pretence—though it was, paradoxically, another attempt to seek procedural solutions for political problems. Within the White House, Jordan assumed the title 'Chief of Staff'; he also supervised the work of Frank Moore as OCR director—a task for which Jordan had neither aptitude nor experience.[21]

The president's major legislative initiatives were distinctive in two senses. Firstly, they sprang not from an unfinished liberal democratic agenda (as had some of John Kennedy's and most of Lyndon Johnson's), but from Carter's own conception of good government. His concern for administrative reform was a much more important influence on his presidency than the jumbled assemblage of Democratic platform positions. Carter earnestly pressed the necessity of civil service reform, the creation of a separate Department of Education, hospital cost containment, and energy reform. Many of the most important initiatives, including the energy programme, were left unmentioned by the president in his inaugural address; few clear objectives which sustained his campaign were carried into office. This was not the stuff of a great crusade, still less that of a Great Society. The political rationale of the legislative programme was often unclear. Many of its elements cut across traditional Democratic support and hence made coalition building in Congress a more exacting and complicated task than it had been in the more propitious circumstances of the mid-1960s. The president made matters worse by sending major legislative proposals to Congress with little regard to the scheduling requirements and difficulties of major committees; the practice did both his legislative prospects, and his relations with committee chairmen, considerable harm.

PARTY STRENGTH AND WEAKNESS

Carter's lack of experience, his ignorance of Washington, coupled with the politically unappetising nature of most items on his legislative menu (in part a result of the way they were

[21] *Congressional Quarterly Weekly Report*, 28/7/79, p. 1502.

promoted) increased the importance of party as a bridge
between the Oval Office and Capitol Hill. Upon entering
office, most of Carter's allies were young staff in the White
House (similarly ignorant of Congress and its members'
sensibilities), not experienced politicians on Capitol Hill. But
unless trust and political friendships with those politicians
were quickly established, the president had little prospect of
legislative or governing success.

New to his job, Carter faced a Speaker and Senate Majority
Leader also new to theirs but skilled in legislative politics.
The new Speaker, Tip O'Neill (D-MA), had the advantages
of long experience in Congress and of holding an office freshly
strengthened by the reforms of 1973-5. Given the implications
which the dispersal of power in Congress had for the president,
this was a development which should have won the approval
of an incoming Democratic president. He took the chair of
the Steering and Policy Group in which the power of selection
of committee members was vested. Under his direction, the
Group acted as a powerful forum for party policy discussion.
The Speaker had also been given powers of appointment of
Democratic members to the Rules Committee, and selection
of its chair; past scourge of liberal initiatives as the chamber's
master, it was now the Speaker's creature. Furthermore, the
Speaker now had considerable discretion over the referring
of bills, and the authority to create special *ad hoc* committees
to consider them. His formal powers apart, O'Neill was the
most skilful Speaker since Sam Rayburn; mindful of the
chamber's prerogatives, his loyalties lay first and foremost
with the Democratic Party.

The new Senate Majority Leader, Bob Byrd (D-W.VA),
had succeeded to the post by judicious trimming towards the
centre of the party, and by displaying the keen jealousies of
the chamber's prerogatives customarily required of Majority
Leaders. Byrd had acquired considerable influence over the
scheduling of legislation while Majority Whip under the
leadership of Mike Mansfield (D-MT); Byrd permitted no
such sharing of powers with his own Whip, Alan Cranston
(D-CA)—a relatively unimportant leadership figure in executive–congressional politics during Carter's presidency. He even
chose not to rely on Cranston for whip counts, preferring to

conduct his own, and made clear, as much by his actions as
by his words, that as far as the Congressional relations staff
in the White House were concerned, he alone constituted the
Senate leadership. But Byrd's concerns revolved around the
Senate rather than the wider Democratic Party; he also lacked
the formal powers that so assisted O'Neill.[22]

Ignorant of the subtleties of Congressional personalities and
politics, Carter's chances of legislative success rested to an
unusual extent on the party link, buttressed by a Congressional
leadership mindful of the legislative obstacles presented by a
newly fragmented legislature. Yet for much of the 95th
Congress, Carter and his White House staff seemed oblivious
of the fact. During the transition and at the start of his
presidency when the opportunities for legislative leadership
were greatest, and when the leadership should have been
cosseted, consulted, their advice heeded and absorbed, they
were by turns ignored and even insulted. Hamilton Jordan,
not an OCR member, was a prime offender: the Speaker's
understandable offence at his early rudeness was never fully
repaired (Jordan provided the Speaker with poor seats at an
inaugural concert at the Kennedy Center, declined to make
better ones available, and then compounded the offence by
offering O'Neill his money back). At the outset, few White
House staff showed the necessary political judgement in
dealings with Congress. Some were careless of the importance
of protocol, prudence, and common courtesy in dealing with
senior politicians. Too often they failed to heed the admonitions
of experienced predecessors who urged that without careful
soliciting of the Congressional party leadership's active support
for the president's programme, Jimmy Carter's legislative
prospects were poor.

Slighted (though invariably by non-OCR staff), O'Neill
still used his powers and authority to create a special *ad
hoc* committee to review the work of the several legislative
committees on the energy bill, both to ensure that those committees met the demanding schedules which he set and
that a favourable rule was granted by the Rules Committee.[23]

[22] Malbin, M., 'Rhetoric and Leadership', in King, A., *Both Ends of the Avenue*,
Washington, DC, 1983, p. 233.
[23] Malbin, M., 'Rhetoric and Leadership', p. 232.

As a result, it was hurried through the House under the Speaker's expert parliamentary guidance (mostly unrecognised by the administration) only to run into trouble later in the Senate. There, Byrd lacked formal powers comparable to the Speaker's in the House and did not in any case did not share his sense of loyalty to the Democratic Party. On the Public Works veto override, where the president's political judgement was found wanting, O'Neill declined to embarrass the administration as he had the votes to do. Byrd, sensitive to the more powerful feelings in the Senate, (especially among the now endangered species of whales such as Russell Long (D-LA)) and anxious as ever to assert his authority and status by winning votes, was only too willing to do so.[24] But on other matters such as the Panama Canal Treaties, the shelving of the B1 bomber, and the compromise natural gas pricing bill—to cite a few examples—the White House had the vital (and often generous) support of the Majority Leadership in the House and sometimes in the Senate.

In foreign policy, Carter won important Republican support. The backing of Howard Baker (R-TN), the Senate Minority Leader, was crucial in the successful lobby to ratify the Panama Canal Treaties. Aware of the Minority Leader's ambition, and of his willingness to negotiate, the two OCR Senate liaison staff consulted him regularly as they came to grips with their task. A number of Baker's Republican colleagues often supported Carter's initiatives in areas which they claimed called into question the authority of the presidency. Since Nixon's tenure, Republicans had tended to support presidents in such matters—for they thought the presidency their only route to power in Washington. Arms sales to Saudi Arabia, the Panama Canal Treaty, and the Camp David agreement all benefited from substantial Republican backing.

Baker's House counterpart, John Rhodes (R-AZ), was more partisan (he preferred the unofficial title of 'Republican Leader' to that of 'Minority Leader'), averse to bargaining, and so ignored by OCR staff.[25] In any event, fewer of Carter's domestic reforms attracted Republican support, and the OCR

[24] *The Washington Post*, 28/10/78.
[25] Confidential interviews with two members of Carter's OCR staff.

staff did not normally trouble to seek it. Those few measures that did generally divided Democrats and attracted Republicans for similar reasons. Civil service reform, for example, was viewed by a number of Democrats with strong records of support for organised labour as an issue dividing management from unions. Most Republicans took a similar view. Both in committee and on the floor, Republican Congressmen voted to preserve the main thrust of the president's proposals against the wishes of those Democrats with close union links. Without their backing, the bill would have been gravely weakened.

THE VICE-PRESIDENCY

Walter Mondale proved as useful to Carter's presidency as to his candidacy: he balanced the ticket in the polls and then provided Congressional experience in an administration which lacked it. Carter, appreciating his worth, permitted the vice-president a prominent role. The relationship between the two was historically unusual, and reflected Carter's peculiar need for political support on Capitol Hill. Symbolically, Mondale had an office in the west wing of the White House, near to the president. His assistant for Congressional affairs worked closely with the president's OCR team. The head of Carter's liaison staff, Frank Moore, generally discussed legislative matters with the vice-president twice a day, and often sought his advice and guidance.[26] In the early part of the presidency, Mondale spent much of his time attending to crises and mollifying senators offended by White House misjudgements and errors.

Later, Mondale played a major role in lobbying senators on the Panama Canal Treaties, using his Senate office for meetings with them. On other subjects, where the White House needed to prevent liberal defections rather than win moderate and conservative support, Mondale's politics made him a useful ally. Congressional liberals were a variegated breed by the late 1970s, lacking the clarity and unity which their predecessors of fifteen years before had usually proclaimed

[26] *The Washington Post*, 3/12/78.

and often demonstrated. As a sign of their growing disarray, the DSG acted increasingly as a research unit funded by all sections of the party and from which all drew benefits—and less as the liberal campaigning group, with its own whipping system, of recent memory.[27]

The vice-president none the less had to pay careful attention to constitutional proprieties. His authority, if not his political influence, derived from his formal position as president of the Senate. This made too prominent a liaison and lobbying role on the executive's behalf (as it had Hubert Humphrey's under Johnson, and Johnson's under Kennedy) a potential danger. Lobbying members of the House, with whom vice-presidents lack the fig-leaf of an institutional link, was an awkward matter, best done with discretion if at all. Pressing presidential wishes upon reluctant minorities in the Senate raised hackles too: even with Byrd's support, Mondale's breaking of the liberal filibuster by Senators Aboureszk (D-SD) and Metzenbaum (D-OH) against natural gas deregulation left him in poor standing with erstwhile allies.[28]

The efforts of the vice-president apart, Congressional party bonds were an asset too often taken for granted, and too little cultivated by the White House. Outside Congress, Carter and his staff courted liberal and other potential supporters unsystematically, infrequently, and with little panache until Anne Wexler succeeded Midge Costanza as White House Director for Public Liaison in the summer of 1978.

The appointment resulted, like Jerry Rafshoon's as White House Director of Communications, from decisions taken at the Camp David meeting in April to enhance the co-ordination and direction roles of White House staff. Wexler's previous appointment had been in the Commerce Department, and so had left her with many active contacts with business groups. Her links with influential Democrats, especially liberals and labour unions, were strong. Such qualifications earned her criticism from some staff in the Carter White House, suspicious of one so well placed in Washington's dense networks of influence.[29] Some contended that her success in wooing

[27] *National Journal*, 27/1/79.
[28] Kellerman, B., *The Political Presidency*, New York, 1984, p. 199.
[29] Confidential interviews with three members of Carter's OCR.

traditional Democratic groups and business leaders owed more
to her courting of the press corps than to her lobbying; others
took the view that she was merely doing the job that her
predecessor was paid for but failed to do.[30] Whatever the
truth of the matter, Wexler showed a striking ability to
galvanise interest groups in support of complicated legislative
initiatives requiring comparably elaborate coalitions, both
within and without Congress, to ensure passage in a form
acceptable to the president. Lobbyists from unions and oil
companies alike claimed that her contribution to the enactment
of the energy bill in 1978 was decisively important. She was
a belated but valuable addition to the staff, and her work a
necessary complement to that of the specialist liaison staff in
the OCR.[31]

MR CARTER AND HIS EMISSARIES: THE LEARNING CURVE

The tone for relations with Congress is set by the president.
This was as true of Carter as of Kennedy, Johnson, and
Reagan. Carter's apprenticeship in the Governor's mansion
had led him to suppose that the presidency would present
political possibilities and obstacles of a similar kind. This was
an astonishing view for any politician, doubly so for one who
had read widely about the office before coming to Washington.
Worse, the president-elect observed during the transition that
working with Congress would be akin to dealing with the
General Assembly in Atlanta. Both were errors. The first
weakened Carter at a time when the prestige of the office
was one of his few potential assets; the second went down
badly with a large, powerful, well-staffed Congress which had
it in its power to grant or deny the legislative victories upon
which the success of his presidency would in large part
depend. At the close of the 95th Congress, the president gave
an interview to James Reston of *The New York Times* in which
he revealed something of his ignorance of the politics of
presidential–congressional relations at the beginning of 1977:[32]

[30] Interviews with one member of Carter's White House staff and one OCR
member.
[31] *National Journal*, 30/9/78.
[32] *The New York Times*, 12/10/78.

'We had an overly optimistic impression that I could present a bill to the Congress which to me seemed patently in the best interests of our country and that the Congress would take it and pretty well pass it. I have been disabused of that expectation.

This was a remarkable admission: Congressional approval of a president's legislation is far from being a formality. Presidential success is, as Barbara Kellerman has shown so well, dependent in large measure upon the political skill and judgement of the office-holder.[33] But such skill is contingent upon a prior appreciation of the need which presidents have to elicit support from legislators whom they cannot command. Carter lacked it. He had shown consummate ability in welding together an electoral coalition effectively without the aid of party. But for the first year of his presidency, when the tone and legislative agenda of his administration was mostly set, he failed to appreciate that the creation of a governing coalition would be based on party ties and thus require different skills and other incentives. Those who had propelled him to victory could do little to enable him to govern. The reformed party system had further separated a Democratic president's electoral and governing support, and prised apart the presidential from the Congressional party.[34] By the time he began to understand the implications this had for his political success, it was too late. His presidency could not be built anew on weak foundations in mid-term. Nor were the chances good of a successful governing coalition then being assembled which might in turn ensure his re-election.

In its style, too, Carter's presidency was often curiously apolitical. Although he eventually accepted the urgent need to build coalitions of support on Capitol Hill, and generate public support to promote them, President Carter was not one to whom politicking in government came easily. Unlike Harry Truman, who concealed his dislike for occasional Congressional weekends on the Maryland coast, Carter could not hide his distaste for the politics of private flattery. Long after he had come intellectually to appreciate the importance

[33] Kellerman, *The Political Presidency.*
[34] Polsby, N. W., *Consequences of Party Reform*, Oxford, 1983.

of the Speaker's role, and after entertaining him at the White House, the president rejected the advice of senior OCR staff to address the Speaker by his nickname, 'Tip', when writing to him. Instead, the president's letters to his party colleague were invariably addressed to 'The Honorable Thomas P. O'Neill'—something O'Neill (and Carter's more sensible OCR staff) thought odd.[35]

James Fallows was not the first to realise that the president had little flair for the politics of courtship, but he captures better than most Carter's aversion to the grubby politics of persuasion:[36]

Nowhere was he surer to need help than in his dealings with the congress. His experience there was minimal, his campaign tone had been hostile, his skin crawled at the thought of the time-consuming consultations and persuasion that might be required to bring a legislator around. He did not know how Congressmen talked, worked, and thought, how to pressure them without being a bully or flatter them without seeming a fool.

Senators and Congressmen did not much care for this. Anticipating a number of relaxed, informal drinks parties with the president after eight years of being held at arms' length by Republican presidents, Democrats were puzzled by social contacts being restricted to stiffly formal and semi-formal gatherings.[37] Those who had served under Presidents Kennedy and Johnson were struck by the contrast: the earlier two positively enjoyed social contact and casual conversation about politics with Congressmen and colleagues. Their exchanges of animated political recollections, often much embellished, with Congressional visitors (mostly former colleagues) were pleasurably recalled by Congressmen and senators alike twenty years later. But Jimmy Carter did not serve his political apprenticeship in the corridors of Capitol Hill; had he done so, social contacts with legislators might have been less awkward.

---

[35] Confidential interviews with two members of Carter's OCR.

[36] Fallows, James, 'The Passionless Presidency', *Atlantic Monthly*, May 1979, vol. 243, no. 5, p. 41.

[37] Interview with Congressman John Brademas,(D-IN), House Majority Whip, Oct. 1978.

Yet it remains curious: Carter made much of his casual ✓ style, of his closeness to the people, and, in the early stages, of fireside chats conducted in open-neck shirts and pullovers. However, when the president most needed to relax, with members of Congress in the White House, he was unable to do so. Thus in persisting with informality in front of the television cameras and formality with politicians in infrequent private discussions, he struck the wrong note in both settings. Congressional reform had made the president's maintenance of informal social contact an especially demanding and time-consuming task: he had more people to court. It was by the same token no less urgent.

The Office of Congressional Relations was established by ✓ Eisenhower to help bridge the gap between the separated institutions of White House and Capitol Hill. Kennedy and Johnson retained and refined it for the same reason: it helped them in attempting to govern, to weave around obstacles, and to clear the legislative path. For Carter, lacking a strong ideological or party base in Congress, with a legislative agenda of forbidding complexity, the OCR was therefore still more important. It was one of the few resources at his disposal. ✓ But, as he squandered his resources, and failed to make the most of such party advantage as existed in Congress, so his approach to liaison revealed again the apolitical character of his presidency. For the director of the OCR, he chose Frank Moore, a man, in Fallows's words, 'whose general aptitude was difficult for anyone outside the first circle to detect, and who had barely laid eyes upon the Capitol before Inauguration Day'.[38]

But Carter knew and trusted Moore who in turn was thoroughly loyal. This was Moore's chief advantage, as it had been for other aides to other presidents—the qualities by which Carter properly set such store were not peculiar to him. To that extent, Carter's limited political experience had implications for his approach to the task of filling staff posts: he turned to those whom he knew, not to expert strangers. Those who serve chief executives must inspire trust; strangers, however expert, rarely can.[39] Yet, justly or not, Moore's

---

[38] Fallows, 'The Passionless Presidency', p. 41.
[39] Carter, J., *Keeping Faith*, New York, 1982, pp. 40-1.

inexperience was interpreted on Capitol Hill as a sign of Carter's indifference to building bridges with Congress. None the less, he had a daily meeting with the president (Zbiginew Brzezinski, the National Security Adviser, was the only other staff member to enjoy this privilege) and an office in the west wing of the White House (an institution peculiarly sensitive to the implications of location), close to the Oval Office. However, most OCR staff were consigned to the outer darkness of the east wing. Worse still, as a result of a managerial review in 1979, they were moved to the Old Executive Office Building of which Vice-President Mondale once said, 'If you are there, you might as well be in Baltimore'.[40]

None the less, a daily scheduled meeting was no substitute for effective influence. Even in the early part of Carter's term, when there was no clear staff hierarchy, and competition among aides was correspondingly intense, Hamilton Jordan was closer to the president than Moore; some Congressmen and senators were disinclined to deal with a staff member who did not have the president's ear. Nor did Carter follow Kennedy's practice of marking out his OCR director from other staff by paying him more. White House colleagues often circumvented him, to his embarrassment and the president's disadvantage: as late as July 1978, Jordan and others did not seek Moore's advice on the dismissal of Robert Griffin, a senior official in the General Services Administration and a close friend of the Speaker's. In his anger at not having been consulted, the Speaker understandably, but incorrectly, blamed Moore for the error.

During the transition, Moore sought the advice of former White House liaison aides on OCR organisation. Some Kennedy and Johnson staff made files and notes available to Moore and his assistants; some Republican figures such as Bryce Harlow, liaison director under both Eisenhower and Nixon, were also consulted. All stressed the importance of efficiency and courtesy in contacts with Congress, and of allocating separate staff to the House and Senate. Most urged that the allocation of House staff along geographic lines be

[40] Nickel, H., 'Can a White House Maestro End the White House Cacophony?', *Fortune*, 22/10/79.

continued. A common theme was the importance of catering ✓ to the needs of members, and thereby of establishing long-term relationships with each of them.[41]

Their advice was mostly ignored. Whilst staff dealing with the House and the Senate were separately organised, Moore chose to arrange House staff on a departmental basis. Instead of staff members taking responsibility for groups of members with a number of broadly similar concerns deriving from membership of a state delegation or regional group, Moore followed the president's theme of 'cabinet government' and approved an arrangement devised by the head of House liaison, Richard Merrill, whereby individual members of staff (there were just three in the early months) dealt with the legislative business of groups of departments. Thus Congressmen developed no continuing links with presidential staff; they had no single White House aide upon whom they could depend. The development of individual relationships, vital to effective liaison and lobbying, was eschewed; the inappropriate tone which the president lent to relations with Congress was made worse by unwise administrative arrangements. Switching the focus from Congressmen to departments confirmed the general impression on Capitol Hill, so damaging to the president's prospects of legislative success, that the White House cared little for the perspectives and problems of legislators.

Merrill's appointment incurred the displeasure of the House leadership and other senior Congressmen on the Hill. He was in any case a sadly inappropriate choice for the post; an eccentric organisation of House liaison reflected his poor political judgement.[42] The Speaker did not take him seriously and declined to co-operate. Merrill left the White House just three months after arriving, but the reputation for discourtesy to members of Congress which the OCR had so speedily acquired stuck—to the detriment of White House relations with Congress for a long while afterwards. Senators, Congressmen, and their staff exchanged tales of the OCR's political

[41] Interviews with Claude Desautels, Oct. 1978, Larry O'Brien, Nov. 1978, and Henry Wilson, Dec. 1978.

[42] Merrill's understanding of presidential–congressional relations was strange, as his article 'How Carter Stopped Playing Politics', *Washington Monthly*, July–Aug. 1977, shows well.

incompetence, and spread them (often in maliciously elaborated forms) to eager journalists. The significant improvements in staffing and administrative arrangements made after Merrill's departure did not fully compensate for damaging early impressions. Having failed to seize the initiative from the first week, the president never fully regained it; Congressional appraisals of the OCR's worth fluctuated with the more general rise and fall in public approval of his performance.

Congressional perceptions aside, the administrative efficiency and political judgement of the OCR sharpened considerably by the middle of 1978, and stemmed in large measure from Carter's belated appreciation of the importance of Congressional liaison to the passage of the administration's bills. In his interview with Reston quoted above, the president employed the first person plural in recalling the impression he had of the likely course of his relations with Congress. It was appropriate, for the president's view was matched by that of some senior White House staff. Similarly, as Carter's understanding grew, so the OCR was strengthened. Several studies of Congressional liaison within the White House and the departments were conducted by the vice-president, private consultants, and analysts from the Office of Management and Budget (OMB). OMB's report resulted in the adoption of more tightly organised lobbying procedures in the White House through the establishment of a co-ordination unit in the west wing. Led by the able Leslie Francis, it co-ordinated the work of OCR members with that of other White House staff, bringing much-needed organisational coherence and crispness to liaison and lobbying.

Procedure cannot, however, substitute for the ability of staff. The single most important factor behind the improvement in liaison efficiency and organisation lay in the higher quality of new staff recruited. Merrill's successor was Bill Cable, previously a senior staff member of the House Administration committee, and well regarded by the House leadership. Others he brought to the White House, such as Terry Straub from OMB and Bob Beckel from the State Department, greatly improved matters. The OCR expanded in size, too. It had begun as a four-person unit, and grew to seven. Of these, two staff were assigned to the Senate, and one, Bob Beckel, to foreign policy matters—especially SALT II ratification. The department-based organisation of the Office having been dispensed with, each House liaison staff member was assigned about ninety Congressmen, mostly from whole, but not necessarily contiguous, states. Cable judged that it would be unwise for OCR staff members to be regarded as spokesmen for regional Congressional groupings. No such formal organisation operated with the two Senate specialists—the looser rules and politics of that chamber made it inappropriate.

By the end of the 95th Congress, as the quality of liaison improved, House liaison staff worked closely with the leadership, and when on the Hill were generally encamped in the Speaker's and Majority Leader's offices. There they squeezed into the overcrowded accommodation, constantly telephoning members' offices, in frantic attempts to retain a degree of control over the scheduling of bills, to resist amendments to the president's legislation, and generally to soothe the easily wounded pride of Congressmen. No comparable arrangements were made with the Senate leadership; the dignity and independence on which Byrd and his senior colleagues prided themselves did not allow it. But much was done there, albeit less easily. Although early adverse Congressional impressions continued to hamper OCR staff, there was a general recognition, at least among Democrats and those usually well-disposed to the president, that the ratification of the Panama Canal Treaties was due in large part to efficiently directed White House lobbying.

To that extent, the campaign modified the early assumptions of the OCR's political worth and made subsequent lobbying easier. For OCR aides, tactics and methods which had proved successful in this campaign could be adopted and adapted for the future. The most important was the organisation of outside groups as part of a co-ordinated lobbying strategy by the OCR—an approach later much refined by Anne Wexler and her public liaison staff. Until the end of the administration, Carter's liaison staff continued to be blamed for wider political failures of the executive outside their control—that is partly the function (and invariably the lot) of presidential staff. Notwithstanding this, the OCR's procedures, staff, and organisation were superior, and more appropriate to the task before it, at the end of the 95th Congress than at its beginning. But political infelicity at an early stage, and a number of defeats on key legislation, fostered an impression of incompetence which subsequent improvements did not entirely dispel.[43]

DEPARTMENTAL LIAISON OFFICES: THE DILEMMA OF WHITE
HOUSE CONTROL

President Carter's early insistence that his administration would be decentralised, one of 'cabinet government', meant that the White House exercised little control over the choice of liaison officers in departments and agencies. The customary resistance to presidential wishes of notionally subordinate but practically independent executive agencies was thereby paradoxically underwritten by the White House in the first instance. The president's belated decision to tighten his reins on the departments, confirmed by the Camp David meeting in the spring of 1978, could do little to mitigate the difficulties caused by unco-operative agency liaison officers. To have attempted to replace them would have risked the intensification of bureaucratic resistance and created yet greater problems. But from 1978, new appointments were examined by a presidential counsel and an OCR staff member (together with the customary vetting provided by the FBI).[44]

In the organisation of lobbying itself, the White House increased its control over the departments during 1978 by modifying the weekly meetings between OCR staff and the departmental liaison officers. During the phase of 'cabinet government', the meetings were conducted in a spirit of equality. Political gossip was exchanged and the departments' lobbying activities discussed. The arrangement worked poorly: departmental officers soon became irritated with detailed reports of bills they deemed obscure from other departments about which they knew little, and OCR staff were reluctant

[43] Davis, E. L., 'Legislative Liaison in the Carter Administration', *Political Science Quarterly*, vol. 94, no. 2, summer 1979, p. 301.
[44] Interview with Bob Thompson, Dec. 1978.

to impress White House authority upon departmental sub-ordinates. But with the success of the lobby in the House to halt the construction of the B1 bomber, White House staff discovered that a firmer directing role by the OCR could win dividends. By the autumn of 1978, in the wake of the president's decision to dispense with the rhetoric and flimsy practice of 'cabinet government', most OCR staff regarded departmental liaison officers as responsible to the president and his immediate staff, not to the variegated interests of the departments. The Friday meetings reflected the OCR's changed view and were now employed by Frank Moore to give a sense of unified purpose to administration lobbying. By the beginning of the 96th Congress, OCR staff considered them purely in terms of the contribution they made to the interests of the president and his legislative initiatives.

If the president's early disposition to permit a free rein to departments in general, and to their own Congressional liaison offices in particular, was misguided, his tightened control over them brought difficulties of its own. Computerisation of the White House's Congressional correspondence section at the end of 1978 enabled the OCR to keep a more effective check upon the flow of mail along Pennsylvania Avenue. But computers did not provide a substitute for efficient staff work, as Democratic Congressmen re-elected in November 1978 discovered when they received letters of commiseration from the White House; the messages of congratulation intended for them were sent to defeated Democrats instead, thereby angering everyone.[45] Nor did they overcome the difficulty they experienced in ensuring quick departmental responses to enquiries on behalf of a Congressional client. This was scarcely surprising, for the administrative burden on departments was great: in 1977, the Defense Department's liaison offices alone received more than a quarter of a million telephone enquiries from Congress, and almost half that number of letters.[46] Random checks by OCR staff in 1979 revealed that answers from departments were often seriously delayed.[47]

[45] Interview with Les Francis, Dec. 1978.

[46] *Congressional Quarterly Weekly Report*, 4/3/78, p. 504.

[47] *Congressional Quarterly Weekly Report*, 4/3/78, p. 504, and confidential interviews with OMB and OCR staff.

Administrative failings of this kind damaged the reputation of an overburdened president and his staff, and partly hid the substantive improvements elsewhere in the orchestration of the president's relations with Capitol Hill.

LIAISON AND LOBBYING: AN APOLITICAL PRESIDENCY

Shrewdly used, patronage, projects, and small favours can ease the task of building bridges from the White House to the Hill. They represent the tangible resources of the presidency, the coin in which the president can bargain and exchange with Congressmen and senators anxious to promote their political interests. The use of patronage is most apparent at the beginning of an administration when a president needs to fill senior positions in the Executive Office and the bureaucracy; it is then that expectations run highest among office-seekers and among their patrons in Congress.[48] That many aspirants are bound to be disappointed in their ambition is inevitable; incoming presidents and their staff must choose, accepting the few and discarding many more. As John Kennedy's patronage adviser Larry O'Brien had discovered sixteen years before, there is little credit to be gained, and few Congressional friends to be made, in dispensing patronage: the two main requirements in 1961 and 1977 were to staff the administration with well-qualified, loyal appointees, and in doing so to pay as many debts to important Congressional supporters as possible. Whilst there was little advantage to the president in paying such debts, to default on them was to invite difficulty. In that respect, Carter's task was greater than Kennedy's; the decentralisation of Congressional power in the early 1970s had increased the number of those in Congress who demanded and expected satisfaction.

As chapter two showed, by naming O'Brien as OCR director and placing him in charge of the administration's patronage policies, President Kennedy had implicitly recognised the link between patronage appointments and liaison with Congress. Carter did not follow Kennedy's example, preferring instead to vest patronage duties in Hamilton Jordan

[48] See: MacKenzie, C., *The Politics of Presidential Appointments*, New York, 1981.

who had neither responsibility nor penchant for liaison with Congress. It is scarcely surprising that mistakes resulted, the most remarkable of which were two appointments to the State Department: two Republicans, Elliott Richardson and Evan Dobelle, were named as Ambassador-at-Large and, amusingly, Chief of Protocol, respectively. Whilst it was not necessarily imprudent to make appointments from the opposing party, it was certainly foolish to nominate two Republicans from Massachusetts, the home state of the thoroughly partisan Democratic Speaker, who had no interest whatever in promoting the careers of able opponents. Many other less prominent Democrats, such as Walter Flowers of Alabama, who had worked assiduously on Carter's behalf during the election and anticipated with pleasure the prospect of their associates replacing Nixon and Ford appointees, received no patronage reward for those constituents and friends whom they wished to help.[49]

Such frustration among Congressional Democrats resulted in a meeting during the summer of 1977 between three senior White House staff, fifty Democratic Congressmen, and the Speaker himself. There, Congressmen objected to the discourteous and cavalier way in which the White House treated requests for patronage appointments, and to the president's claim that it was impossible to fuse his policy of making appointments on the basis of merit with the need to strengthen the party's resources in departments. But Carter's oft-repeated determination to make 'merit' appointments and his dislike of party patronage was in any event viewed sceptically in the light of the customary staffing of the White House with campaign workers, and the appointments of such Georgian luminaries as Bert Lance to OMB, and Griffin Bell to the Attorney-Generalship.

The president's policy for federal project awards represented another missed opportunity. The president eschewed politicking from the start, and in the name of good government and budgetary discipline vetoed a large number of water projects including dams and irrigation systems—the original pork barrel. In the eyes of many mid-west and far-western Democratic Senators, this offence was compounded by the

[49] Tolchin, M., *The New York Times*, 24/7/77.

uncertain handling of veto announcements. In several cases, Senate and House staff were assured that their projects were not on the president's 'hit-list', only to discover from *The Washington Post* that they were. Such inconsideration unsettled the foundations for the bridge-building essential to the president's success; the damage done was never fully repaired although OCR members became more adept at using projects to strengthen relations with legislators rather than weaken them. In the early part of the administration, some among the president's staff viewed the bargaining process crudely, and foolishly threatened retaliation against legislators who could not be persuaded to follow a presidential lead. These quickly found their way into the Washington rumour-mill and further tarnished the president's reputation, as Martin Schram pithily described: '. . . they think Carter's way of playing the game is to first wave a stick enticingly in front of Members of Congress, then hit them over the head with a carrot'.[50]

Carter and his Congressional liaison staff adopted a similarly narrow view of small presidential favours, failing to exploit the single most powerful resource at the president's command— the cachet of being Head of State. Whereas the direction of Congressional relations by OCR staff was for the most part more proficient at the administration's end than at its beginning, Carter failed to master the use of small favours. The use which individual presidents make of them reflects more accurately than projects or patronage, more clearly than procedure and personnel, their understanding of the political process of Congressional relations. They are a matter for presidents themselves, in their personal gift—and the more valuable for being so.

The comparison with Johnson and Reagan is exemplified in their different approaches to the granting of favours, and the giving of presents. Johnson gave both to those whom he wished to cultivate or acknowledge. Carter hoarded most, and disposed of others: continuing his campaign attack on lavishness and waste in government, he sold the presidential yacht 'Sequoia'. Whilst the excesses of presidential power (which were in any case a thing of the Nixonian past in 1977)

[50] Schram, M., *The Washington Post*, 21/5/79.

were scarcely purged by its sale, a forum for presidential influence was lost. Other social occasions for Congress were marked more often by formality of style and frugality of substance than under Carter's post-war Democratic predecessors—to his political disadvantage. Even the Congressional leadership were caught in the net: their first few breakfasts at the White House were parsimonious. Tip O'Neill protested, whereupon the president agreed that full breakfasts should be served. He did not endear himself to his party colleagues by attempting to charge them for the cooked meal.

Even the smallest coin of Congressional relations such as the donation of presidential mementoes, and the handing of pens used in bill-signing ceremonies to senators and Congressmen who had supported bills of his, was hoarded rather than spent. Carter did not enjoy the first of these, and failed to exploit the second. At the end of the 95th Congress, Carter still declined to use more than two pens for the signing of bills. Bill Cable's arrival improved matters in some respects; he brought to the White House a ready appreciation of Congressional interests which not all his OCR colleagues, still less his president, shared. He was particularly sensitive to the charge, commonly made on Capitol Hill, that the president spoke to legislators only when he needed their votes. There was much to this: preparatory work of Congressional liaison was often not done, and too little political capital was invested for the return to be large. Lacking Congressional friendships, Carter sometimes made more last-minute telephone calls to senators and Congressmen for their votes on specific bills than was either useful or prudent. For the deregulation of natural gas prices in 1978, he called twenty-six wavering senators in just three days.[51] Failing to distinguish between the vital and the unimportant, he telephoned three senators from *Air Force One* on S. 790, a bill imposing certain waterway user-charges.[52] Whilst he won both votes, late interventions without appropriate preparation were rarely helpful, and when made on behalf of relatively unimportant legislation spent valuable political capital.

[51] *Congressional Quarterly Weekly Report*, 16/9/78, p. 2452.
[52] Reid, T. R., *Congressional Odyssey*, San Francisco, 1980, p. 104.

CONCLUSION

On arriving in Washington, Jimmy Carter found a presidency weakened by grave confrontations with Congress and the courts over matters of constitutional principle, and newly hemmed in by statute. Furthermore, although a reformed Congress was no more able than in 1961 to set the national agenda and speedily enact the items on it, it presented more numerous obstacles to a president who wished to do both, albeit in the absence of a clearly promulgated policy. The dispersal of Congressional power had in several respects made the president's task more difficult, and the art of building coalitions more demanding. Carter was an outsider, not a man of Washington—hence his electoral opportunity (which he exploited with such brilliance) and his problem in governing (which he failed to solve).

The president's White House staff confirmed rather than modified his political style. Most (including several OCR members) lacked experience of Congress, and showed little appreciation of the subtleties of Congressional courtship in the president's cause. Carter had won a narrow victory in the 1976 presidential election and had few allies on Capitol Hill or elsewhere in Washington. But such advantages as newly elected presidents and their staffs have were not exploited. The House leadership were well disposed towards the new administration, yet were often ignored. Carter presented no strategic agenda at the outset; few clear policy objectives enunciated in the campaign were sustained in government. The president's resources of patronage, federal projects, and small favours were mostly squandered—especially in the first two years of the administration when it was essential to capitalise upon such advantages as he had.

As Carter inherited a tethered presidency, he bequeathed it to Ronald Reagan in what many considered an unworkable condition.[53] From the experience of the Carter administration, grand inferences were quickly drawn. There was much despondent speculation about whether presidents were doomed to fail, whether too much was expected of them, and whether,

[53] See: Hodgson, G., *All Things To All Men*, London, 1980.

in the wake of Congressional reform and party decay, presidents and their staff could any longer give a decisive legislative lead. The politics of the year following Jimmy Carter's defeat showed that, in favourable circumstances, they could.

9

RONALD REAGAN: THE POLITICS OF PRESIDENTIAL OPPORTUNITY

INTRODUCTION

Jimmy Carter's last year in office was beset by profound international difficulty, and the president's own widely-publicised doubts about the capacity of America's political system and culture to meet distinctive foreign and domestic challenges. As his administration crumbled away, the weakness of the presidency seemed to be symbolized by the final stages of the Iranian hostage crisis. Even in his last minutes as chief executive, driving with the president-elect to the Capitol for the inauguration, Carter helplessly telephoned for the latest information on the hostages, held at the end of a Teheran runway until his successor assumed office.[1]

Popular, and frequently academic, appraisals of politics and politicians rest heavily on dramatic events such as this. In the folk lore of American government, Jimmy Carter's 'weakness' was as convincing a characterisation of his presidency as 'strength' was of his successor's. The qualities of the presidents and the contingent contexts which constrain or aid them are too glibly turned into profound observations on the changing nature of the presidency, and cyclical variations mistaken for secular trends. The popular contrast is much overdrawn and was, naturally enough, thoroughly exploited by Reagan and his supporters for political advantage. Yet symbol and myth contained their own truth; more importantly, their exploitation was a testimony to Reagan's skill and a source of his political strength.

Carter was widely regarded as having failed politically and, indeed, was the first Democratic president to be denied re-election since Grover Cleveland in 1888. By contrast,

[1] Jordan, H., *Crisis*, London, 1982, p. 16; Carter, J., *Keeping Faith*, New York, 1982, p. 13.

Reagan successfully sought a second term, achieving a more complete electoral college victory than Eisenhower or Nixon. Reagan's approach to government was equally different from Carter's. His appeals to Congress and public for quick policy change were clear; the legislative requirements for his decisively important budgetary policies were carefully prepared, loudly trumpeted, and assiduously lobbied. In defence policy, the break with the broad bipartisanship of the past, foreshadowed in the domestic budget cuts and the increased defence spending of Carter's last year, came quickly to full flower. This chapter seeks to explain how the resources of the executive branch were mobilised to achieve these legislative changes. It is on the politics of 1981, when the administration's course was set, that the analysis concentrates. My concern is not with the merits of the policies themselves, although I share many of David Stockman's injudiciously expressed doubts about the coherence of the administration's budgetary and taxation policies.[2] The major consequence of Reagan's economic strategy enacted in his first year was the creation of historically large and damaging budget deficits, perhaps to forge a sword of Damocles to hang over the Democrats in the House of Representatives. This grave problem quite irresponsibly went unaddressed until (and arguably despite) the passage of the Gramm–Rudman–Hollings Act in December 1985.[3]

Reagan successfully fused policy prescription with politics.[4] His first few months in Washington marked a sudden surge of presidential leadership of Congress and country which two years earlier had seemed an impossibility. The new Congressional and interest-group politics which had immobilised Jimmy Carter were exploited by Reagan with aplomb. Within six months, his domestic spending cuts, defence spending increases, and tax cuts had been lobbied through Congress. Such a burst of policy change and political success, carefully planned and executed, has few parallels in the history of the modern presidency.

[2] Greider, W., 'The Education of David Stockman', *Atlantic Monthly*, Dec. 1981; Stockman, D., *The Triumph of Politics*, London, 1986.
[3] Mills, G. B., 'The Budget', in Palmer, J. L., and Sawhill, I. V.,(eds.), *The Reagan Record*, Cambridge, 1984, p. 139.
[4] See: Greenstein, F., 'The Need for an Early Appraisal of the Reagan Presidency', in his *The Reagan Presidency*, Baltimore, 1983.

The president himself supplied the energy and public rhetorical urgency which made this possible.[5] He is, with Margaret Thatcher, one of the few modern western leaders to have lent his/her name to a creed. But although Reagan is the most obvious governing symbol of 'New Right' policies, his politics had changed little in the preceding twenty years. He had long lamented what he deemed the inescapable consequences of an eleemosynary state and had appealed to receptive audiences by damning federal bureaucracies for stifling the creative spirit of the American entrepreneur. The 'grave moral hazards' posed by dependence on welfare subsidies of which George Gilder wrote in 1981 had long been the stuff of Reagan's public performances.[6] He had been a dominant figure in Republican politics since at least 1964 when he delivered an outstanding nominating speech on behalf of Barry Goldwater; in 1967, President Johnson's advisers thought him the likeliest Republican nominee for the presidency the following year; four years later, Nixon's incumbency kept him out of contention, but in 1976, he nearly defeated Ford in the primaries, before easily winning nomination in 1980, and retaining it in 1984. On fiscal, defence, and social policy, he had anticipated much that New Right publicists and politicians later espoused—but, as his prospects of electoral success grew from 1964 to 1980, so a disparate collection of supply-siders, libertarians, conservatives, monetarists, and cold-war liberal defectors from the Democratic Party gathered around him.

The Republican Party found a temporary coherence around four propositions: that the federal government's role in the economy and the level of domestic welfare spending should be reduced; that the tax burden on citizens and corporations should be cut so as to stimulate entrepreneurship; that the defence and foreign policies characterised by the period of *detente* and the two SALT Treaties of the 1970s had weakened the United States; and finally that a series of social reform measures, including limits on abortion and permitting prayer in public schools, should be introduced.

⁵ Cannon, L., *Reagan*, New York, 1982, p. 371; Kellerman, B., *The Political Presidency*, New York, 1984, pp. 235-7; Hargrove, E. C., and Nelson, M., *Presidents, Politics and Policy*, Baltimore, 1984, p. 122.
⁶ Gilder, G., *Wealth and Poverty*, New York, 1981, p. 111.

The extent of the agreement within the Congressional party on these four objectives varied but Reagan's personal commitment to the first three was clear, and his conversion to the fourth widely advertised. He promoted his governing prospects by tying together presidential and Congressional fortunes with party and ideological ribbons, symbolising the union by appearing with 285 Republican Congressional candidates on the Capitol steps before the election. There, he proclaimed the 'Capitol Compact', a broad statement of party political intent. The first three of the four propositions above were included; the fourth was not.[7]

THE ELECTORAL MANDATE

Reagan's comfortable popular vote margin of more than eight million over Carter translated into an overwhelming victory of 489 : 49 in the electoral college. The 'Watergate Majority' which the Democrats had enjoyed in the House since 1974 was eliminated: the Republicans gained 33 seats (a record in the post-war period for an 'out' party entering the White House) and reduced the Democratic majority to 51. More remarkable still, the Republicans won control of the Senate for the first time in twenty-six years: their net gain of 12 seats gave a new party balance of 54 : 46; almost half of the incumbent Senate Democrats facing re-election were defeated. The shift in party control occurred everywhere but was most apparent in the south. That once 'solid' Democratic region was now highly competitive: Democrats held just 12 of its 22 seats.

Close analysis of the Senate results provides little support for the view that liberals did especially badly. The poor showings of several senior liberal Democrats obscured the equally weak performances of two senior conservative colleagues; length of service was a greater handicap for candidates of either party than liberalism. The influence of the 'New Right' within the Republican Party was reinforced by the election results, although Democratic defeats could not

[7] *The New Republic*, 27/9/80; Cohen, R. E., 'GOP Controlled Senate has Altered Policy far less than many had Expected', *National Journal*, 21/1/84.

reasonably be attributed to their prodigious efforts.[8] More convincing as an explanation of Republican candidates' success, and as important a pointer to Reagan's leadership of relations with Congress in his first term, was the Republican Party's highly efficient fund-raising and spending. The party's campaign committees raised eleven times the Democrats' total and directed the spending of it with considerable care and effect. Thus Reagan had from the start a store of political capital with his party colleagues in Congress which both Richard Nixon and Jimmy Carter lacked.[9] (Nixon had, especially in 1972, run virtually independently of his party; Carter had run against most of his to secure its nomination through the primaries.)

Reagan's coat-tails were actually little longer than those of most of his predecessors. To that extent, the general view of Reagan's strong showing at the polls was mistaken. But it was the perceptions of a presidential landslide and ideological sea change, and the feeling of release from the inertia of Carter's presidency, which shaped reactions. The phenomenon of a Republican majority in the Senate, unknown since 1954, did much to sharpen this sense of impending changes in American politics and policy. Added to the enhanced measure of Republican Party coherence in both House and Senate, the implications for Reagan's suasion over Congress in the early stages of his administration were clear.[10]

REAGAN'S APPROACH TO GOVERNMENT

To these favourable electoral circumstances, political capital, party configurations and composition, Reagan added a crucial element which Carter had lacked: an overarching strategic purpose. He appreciated that the opportunities for a radical

---

[8] Williams, P. M., and Reilly, S. J., 'The American Elections of 1980', *Political Studies*, vol. 30, no. 3, Sept. 1982, p. 378.

[9] Alter, J., 'With Friends like These', *Washington Monthly*, Jan. 1982.

[10] On increased Republican cohesion, see Wilson, G., and King, G., 'How New a Congress?', Essex Papers in Politics and Government, no. 13. Republican unity declined in the second session of the 97th Congress while Democratic unity rose in that and the subsequent year. See: 'Democrats Overtake GOP In Party-Line Vote Loyalty', *Congressional Quarterly Weekly Report*, 15/1/83; 'Conservative Strength Falters in Wake of United Democrats', *Congressional Quarterly Weekly Report*, 31/12/83.

reordering of spending priorities (the elimination of some, the reduction of many more, and the increase of expenditure on defence), together with the cutting of taxes, were greatest at the outset. He had to move quickly, making his influence felt decisively in the first months.[11] Then he had the clearest political opportunity, when his forces were most united and confident, and those of the opposition most divided and demoralised.

Reagan's strategic conception of his presidential purpose was, in economic and taxation policy, seemingly married to an organisational clarity within the White House and executive branch which contrasted sharply with the impression so quickly given by Jimmy Carter. In foreign policy, divisions between the White House and Alexander Haig, the Secretary of State, were soon apparent. But in domestic policy, broad policy agreement within the White House and between it and Capitol Hill was matched with a smoothly functioning executive. Additionally, the president's sense of urgency was shared by his staff both in the transition and in the administration itself.[12] Where Carter had often appeared to regard administrative reform as intrinsically worthy, Reagan used organisational forms only as a means to the political end of quick and fundamental policy change. In this respect, his work during the transition (much of which he spent in California) was characteristically detached from detail but strategically engaged; aided by the detailed preparation of his large staff, he prepared Congress and country for an intense burst of focused legislative activity in 1981.

THE ORGANISATION OF CONGRESSIONAL LIAISON

The transition organisation included a separate Congressional liaison office consisting of eleven professional staff (all of whom had at least some experience working on Capitol Hill) directed by Tom Korologos, a former White House Congressional aide to Richard Nixon and more recently an accomplished senior member of Timmons & Company, a

[11] Light, P., *Artful Work*, New York, 1985, p. 27.
[12] Barrett, L., *Gambling with History*, New York, 1983.

major Washington lobbying firm. He declined the offer to direct the Office of Legislative Affairs (OLA), the OCR in a new guise, in the White House after the inauguration. That post went to a former colleague from the Nixon White House and later the director of President Ford's liaison team, Max Friedersdorf, who joined the president-elect's office in December 1980.

The transition staff worked together during the lame-duck session of the 96th Congress, and then continued until the middle of February 1981. They provided continuing liaison for Reagan, arranged meetings for him with members of Congress and, in the first weeks of the 97th Congress, lobbied for the confirmation of the president's cabinet nominees. They also dealt with as many as they could manage of the 25,000 letters and telegrams (mostly from office-seekers) which arrived in the office during the transition.[13] Senator Paul Laxalt, a close friend of Reagan's, also kept contact between him, the Republican Congressional leaders, and Korologos's office during the transition.[14] (In 1983, Laxalt became General Chairman of the Republican National Committee in an attempt to co-ordinate its work with that of the White House and the Republicans on Capitol Hill.)

Friedersdorf directed the OLA until January 1982; he returned in Reagan's second term as director of legislative strategy under the new Chief of Staff Donald Regan.[15] The Office was divided, as in all administrations since Eisenhower's, into separate sections for the House and Senate. Each was staffed by four aides with a senior director. The director of the House staff, Kenneth Duberstein, succeeded Friedersdorf for the second session of the 97th Congress. Upon resigning a year later, Duberstein joined Korologos at Timmons & Company. The exchange of professional lobbyists between the corporate and White House teams was scarcely accidental: the success of Reagan's White House liaison staff in pressing for adoption of important economic legislation in 1981, and

[13] Wayne, S. J., 'Congressional Liaison in the Reagan White House', in Ornstein, N. J.,(ed.), *President and Congress*, Washington, DC, 1982, p. 50.

[14] Rae, N. C., 'Moderate Republicans in Congress During the Reagan Presidency', paper presented to conference of the American Politics Group, Exeter, 1985, p. 9.

[15] Kirschten, R., 'Regan Models Operations on Baker Plan', *National Journal*, 9/3/85.

often after that, depended in large measure on their ability to draw on the lobbying strength and expertise of private industry. They were the administration's most important external allies, and co-ordinated their work with the OLA through the White House Office of Public Liaison (OPL).

Max Friedersdorf eschewed both the geographic division of responsibility among his staff favoured by Kennedy and Johnson among theirs, and the functional arrangement initially adopted in the Carter administration. This was less important a decision in matters of domestic policy than it had been for Carter since the president's concentration upon a few key votes on budgetary and tax policy enabled lobbying resources to be directed to where they were most needed without compromising other parts of the presidential programme.

The director's staff spent most of their working day on Capitol Hill, rather than at the other end of the Avenue, so that they were thoroughly acquainted with Congressional opinion and developments. They took care at an early stage to introduce themselves to Congressmen and their staff, a task made easier by their prior Congressional experience.[16] Rapid turnover of Congressmen and senators made this initial phase important—as the Reagan liaison staff began work in January 1981, nearly half the members of the Senate and the House had been there for less than four years.[17] By late March, Friedersdorf and Duberstein had arranged nearly seventy meetings in the Oval Office between the president and important Congressmen. They organised similar meetings with sixty Democrats alone as the lobbying on the first budget resolution intensified, and personally lobbied many others on the same issue—often during concerts and opera at the Kennedy Center.[18]

After this initial period, Friedersdorf met daily with Duberstein and his counterpart on the Senate liaison staff, Powell Moore, to agree upon tactics. These three met at least twice in the morning before their assistants left to pursue assignments in the halls, corridors, and committee rooms of

[16] Wayne, 'Congressional Liaison in the Reagan White House', p. 52.
[17] 'Numerous Factors Favoring Good Relationship between Reagan and New Congress', *Congressional Quarterly Weekly Report*, 24/1/81.
[18] Kellerman, *The Political Presidency*, p. 246.

Congress, to meet Congressmen, senators, and their staff, and attend key committee sessions. Between these two meetings with Duberstein and Moore, Friedersdorf attended a meeting of the senior White House staff, and later discussed legislative progress with the president.[19] Junior staff could be contacted in Congress by an electronic paging system, but did not usually return to the White House until the early evening.[20] Only then could telephone calls from Congressional offices be returned, and casework done.[21] (As their predecessors discovered, the demands of liaison work were great: physical stamina was as necessary to political success as shrewd judgement.) Friedersdorf normally worked in his office in the west wing of the White House; the OLA was moved there from the Old Executive Office Building where most of its staff had languished in the latter part of Carter's presidency.[22]

The restoration of the liaison offices to the west wing was intended to symbolise the desire of the president and his staff for close relations with Congress, and for co-operation from its members in the president's designs. It also provided a physical hint of the integration of the liaison staff into the White House staff organisation. For while Friedersdorf and his successors retained specialist control as heads of the OLA, they were but part of an intensely political White House staff whose aim was early legislative success. Reagan's political victories, together with the transformation of the Republican Party from a divided minority into a coherent governing majority (if only for a time) was dependent upon the skill and speed with which bridges to Congress could be built on the foundations provided by passing political circumstance. Three members of staff, Wirthlin, Gergen, and Beal, drafted the 'Final Report of the Initial Actions Project'. Dated 29 January, it began: 'The direction of the country remains unsatisfactory to a majority of Americans. . . The momentum of presidential activity—a brisk but not frantic pace in the beginning—emphasizes the sense of urgency and provides the basis for the president's leadership opportunity.'[23]

[19] *Congressional Quarterly Weekly Report*, 2/5/81, p. 749.
[20] Wayne, 'Congressional Liaison in the Reagan White House', p. 53.
[21] *Congressional Quarterly Weekly Report*, 2/5/81, p. 749.
[22] Clines, F. X., 'Who Sits Where', *The New York Times*, 1/8/85.
[23] Barrett, *Gambling with History*, p. 84.

This was quickly appreciated by Edward Meese and James Baker III, the White House Chief of Staff. On 17 February 1981, they stressed to colleagues the need for efficient White House co-ordination of the administration's activities. Two members of staff were nominated as the contacts for other staff and cabinet members to 'pull together the various plans and activities related to the economic recovery program'. Four days later, Richard Darman, one of the two staff co-ordinators, suggested to Baker that such co-ordination would be of little use without a similarly organised legislative strategy.[24] Baker agreed. Accordingly, he convened and chaired a meeting of a 'Legislative Strategy Group' (LSG) which met in his large office on the ground floor of the west wing; Darman was his lieutenant. The purpose was to add the resources of the political offices of public and party liaison to those of the OLA, and to consider how all three might best meet the president's legislative objectives. It was through the LSG that the lobbying work of friendly corporations and associations was co-ordinated with the OLA's own activities. Thus Baker, as Chief of Staff and head of the White House's political strategy (policy development *per se* fell outside his brief), took overall charge of legislative strategy. The directors of the OLA (Friedersdorf, Duberstein, and, later, M. G. Oglesby) worked as part of the political staff, with distinct functional responsibilities but White House loyalties, cemented by Baker's direction and chairing of the daily meetings of the LSG which they, as successive chief liaison officers, attended.

Thereafter, the LSG provided, as Joseph Hogan has explained so well, the institutional forum for the refinement and legislative implementation of a strategic view which the Carter presidency had conspicuously lacked.[25] Reagan's first year showed vividly how essential the integration of Congressional lobbying, public liaison, and party political organisation had become to legislative success.

Such opposition to the LSG's establishment as there might have been dissolved with the heavy defeat of Reagan's social

---

[24] Barrett, *Gambling with History*, p. 89.

[25] Hogan, J., 'Managing Reagan's Legislative Agenda: The Legislative Strategy Group', paper presented to the American Politics Group, Durham, 1984; see also, Heinemann, B. W., and Hessler, C. A., *Memorandum for the President*, New York, 1980.

security proposals, foolishly dispatched to the Hill in May
1981 without sufficient time for assessment by liaison staff of
the chances of approval, or of the ways in which they might
be amended. (LSG members had in any case been preoccupied
with tactical lobbying on a crucial budget vote.) David
Stockman's enthusiasm for radical social security reform as
the best available means of cutting the budget deficit allowed
only a hurried analysis by OLA staff.[26] Even that convinced
Baker that the measure would be defeated, but at an LSG
meeting to which he was invited the day before the
announcement was due to be made, the chairman *pro tempore*
of the Health and Human Resources Cabinet Council, Richard
Schweiker, insisted that he could guarantee Democratic
support. Like Stockman, Schweiker entirely misjudged the
response: the Senate rejected the proposals by 96 votes to 0.[27]
Baker had shrewdly distanced the White House and the
president from the measure, obliging Schweiker (a former
liberal Republican Pennsylvania senator) and Stockman (a
former Congressman) to take responsibility for the impending
defeat. The Senate's decisive vote against Schweiker's proposed
economies strengthened Baker's hand and consequently the
LSG's role as the administration's central legislative unit.

Like Carter, Reagan publicly espoused the virtues of
'cabinet government'; unlike him, he did not seek to practise
it. Despite the introduction of five 'cabinet councils' on
domestic policy with the ostensible purpose of 'reviewing
issues requiring a decision by the president', policy initiative
and political management lay firmly with the White House
in conjunction with the sub-cabinet appointees in the
departments and agencies.[28] The 'cabinet councils' were a
clever contrivance of Baker's; they gave the impression of
cabinet government without the substance. As Chief of Staff
in the White House and co-ordinator of legislative strategy,
Baker did not allow the establishment of competing centres
of power in the administration. Indeed, the councils were
used by Reagan and his senior staff as a means whereby

[26] Light, *Artful Work*, p. 121.
[27] Barrett, *Gambling With History*, pp. 154–6.
[28] *Public Papers of the President, 1981*, vol. 1, p. 166.

departments might be subject to greater central control rather than be allowed latitude over policy and politics.[29]

Korologos and Friedersdorf worked carefully during the transition on appointments to departments and agency Congressional liaison posts. Reagan's habit of delegating responsibility to his staff made this task, as it had the selection and organisation of White House staff, important—the early appreciation of the need for White House direction of a co-ordinated legislative strategy made it especially so. The nature of the programme made some appointments more important to Reagan than others: many of those to the departments and agencies most threatened by budget cuts or abolition were delayed (this was true of all appointees, not just those concerned with Congressional liaison), but unfilled liaison posts caused difficulties for Republicans in Congress bent on bureaucratic reform, since they had no sympathetic departmental legislative liaison officers with whom they could discuss tactics.[30]

Both for Congressional liaison and for other posts below cabinet level in the first year, there was an unusual degree of ideological agreement and radical fervour, revealing itself in a striking commitment to Reagan's central objectives. In Barbara Kellerman's words, Reagan instilled in his administration a 'sense of shared mission'.[31] After taking up their posts, many showed considerable hostility to programmes administered by their departments.[32] This ought not to have been surprising. The White House had sought precisely those qualities in assessing applications for posts in the administration; Friedersdorf and Korologos had insisted upon them in Congressional liaison.

Once in post, William Gribben, a member of the OLA, supervised the work of departmental and agency officials, receiving weekly reports from the head of each unit, and acting on them where necessary. Friedersdorf, like many of

[29] Salamon, L. M., and Abramson, A. J., 'Governance', in Palmer and Sawhill, *The Reagan Record*, p. 44.
[30] Polsby, N. W., 'Some Landmarks in Modern Presidential-Congressional Relations', in King, (ed.), *Both Ends of the Avenue*, Washington, DC, 1983, p. 17; *Congressional Quarterly Weekly Report*, 2/5/81.
[31] Kellerman, *The Political Presidency*, p. 246.
[32] MacKenzie, G. C., quoted in Barrett, *Gambling with History*, p. 72.

his predecessors in other administrations, emphasised that the development of 'departmental positions' would not be permitted. On the contrary, he insisted upon adherence to the White House's strategy. For the most part, however, agency liaison officials were allowed to work unhindered, but to White House purposes. Their work was varied. In the case of the Pentagon, for example, it typically involved arranging for a military escort to accompany a committee chairman on a foreign visit, or assisting the constituents of Republican Congressmen and senators in applying for Defense Department contracts.[33]

The White House intervened directly only on those matters affecting the administration's strategy. A prime example was the lobby to prevent the Congressional veto of the sale of AWACS aircraft to Saudi Arabia in 1981. It was organised not by Richard Fairbanks, the Assistant Secretary of State for Congressional Affairs, but by the chairman of a special interdepartmental committee—at first by Fred Ikle, an under-secretary at the Pentagon, and then by Richard Allen, the president's first national security adviser. James Baker finally assumed personal control as the lobbying intensified in the weeks before the Senate vote.[34]

THE LEGISLATIVE PROGRAMME

Although most of the more extreme conservative groups had little choice but to support Reagan's presidential candidacy after the party convention, the Republican president had the advantage of not being indebted to them. Their support had been late in coming, and was marginal to his victory. Richard Viguerie, head of the National Conservative Political Action Committee (NICPAC), had supported Connally for the Republican nomination, a decision which did not enhance his reputation for perspicacity; Paul Weyrich, head of the Committee for the Survival of a Free Congress, actually withdrew support from the Reagan-Bush ticket, which did still less for his.

---

[33] *Congressional Quarterly Weekly Report*, 5/12/81, p. 2387.
[34] *Congressional Quarterly Almanac, 1981*, p. 134.

Reagan's appreciation, confirmed by Congressional and non-congressional staff alike, of the importance of speedy legislative action on the most important aspects of his programme ensured that school prayer, restrictions on abortion, and the like, were kept off the agenda in the first year. Those elements were, Reagan admitted later, 'adornments', 'filigree', and not part of the core of his philosophy.[35] Economic initiatives would come first in the Congressional timetable, and not become enmeshed with other less important proposals so as to risk overloading Congress, weakening both measures, and losing public support and attention. The social agenda, beloved of some supporters but by no means clearly popular in the country, was set aside for later action (when the prospects for passage were almost sure to be less propitious, and the administration would be obliged to rely on litigation in the Federal Courts for policy change in the area). This view met with some opposition from Robert Michel, (R-IL), the House Minority Leader, but with none from Howard Baker, the Senate Majority Leader.[36] Unsympathetic to the style and substance of much of the New Right and Moral Majority's social prescription, he stressed in late March 1981 that the president's budget and taxation proposals would be his first priority too.[37] In these fields, Reagan's general campaign commitments were clear but allowed him flexibility; his specific legislative requests were so managed as to appear to flow naturally from them.

The budget timetable required the first budget resolution to be passed by the middle of May. From the time of his appointment as Director of OMB in December, David Stockman worked with this deadline in mind, as did Baker, Friedersdorf, and the OLA staff. Until its passage, the budget dominated the Congressional agenda, and hence the calculations of the LSG and OLA: the Senate took almost two hundred votes on budget matters in 1981, excluding roll-call votes on the customary appropriations bills and budget votes on authorizing legislation. More than two-thirds

[35] Barrett, *Gambling with History*, p. 62.
[36] *The Washington Post*, 20/2/81.
[37] Evans and Novak, *The Reagan Revolution*, New York, 1981, p. 224.

of the recorded votes there had to do with the budget.[38] Indeed, the sale of the AWACS aircraft was the only major legislative matter in 1981 not concerned with the budget—and that was an unwonted item, placed on the agenda by a legislative veto provision of a 1976 amendment to the Arms Control Export Act (PL-94-329).[39]

Characteristically, there was little agreement among economists, even those sympathetic to what became known as 'Reaganomics', on what the president's policy should be. Monetarists were generally intolerant of supply-side theory and fiscal conservatism; supply-siders enthused about and greatly exaggerated the policy rewards of cutting tax rates. That view worried orthodox fiscal conservatives who none the less were pleased by the constraints on federal spending which tax cuts offered.[40] There was something for each of these groups in the package presented to Congress in 1981—an indication of its intellectual incoherence and political appeal.

Reagan exempted seven basic programmes from the worst of his domestic budget cuts. These programmes were, he argued, for the 'truly needy', those who did not elect to stay out of the labour market but were forced out of it by circumstances beyond their control, or were otherwise inescapably dependent.[41] But the selection of these seven, while consistent with the president's purpose of denying welfare and government support to those whom he believed capable of self-reliance, had convenient political advantages, too: all had 'large and politically active constituencies' which he and his staff judged it advisable not to antagonise.[42]

Less than a month after receiving the president's budget request, the Senate approved a reconciliation resolution instructing fourteen authorising and appropriations committees to cut domestic spending by $36.4 billion in FY 82. Party control, a demoralised opposition, and carefully

[38] See: Schick, A., 'How the Budget was Won and Lost', in Ornstein, (ed.), *President and Congress*.

[39] *Congressional Quarterly Almanac, 1981*, p. 132.

[40] Heclo, H., and Penner, R. G., 'Fiscal and Political Strategy in the Reagan Administration', in Greenstein, (ed.), *The Reagan Presidency*.

[41] Nathan, R. P., 'The Reagan Presidency in Domestic Affairs', in Greenstein, (ed.) *The Reagan Presidency*, p. 61.

[42] Kellerman, *The Political Presidency*, p. 248.

mobilised support within and without Congress, gave the president a strikingly easy victory. The House presented greater difficulties. The House Budget Committee prepared alternative proposals for the first budget resolution which cut domestic spending by rather less than the president's request, but achieved a lower projected deficit by cutting taxes less, too. It was defeated on the floor by a substitute, Gramm–Latta I, co-sponsored by Philip Gramm, a conservative Texan Democrat (since turned Republican and elected to the US Senate) on the Budget Committee, and Delbert Latta, the committee's ranking Republican, and cobbled together with the White House and OMB. This therefore became the first budget resolution. It required committees in the House and the Senate to rewrite existing laws to cut spending by the agreed total of $136 billion over the following three years.

It was a dramatic and unwonted use of the reconciliation procedure; it obliged members to concentrate on budget totals, as the president wished, and not on the individual programmes which would bear the brunt of the cuts.[43] The framers of the 1974 Budget Act had clearly envisaged that it should be used on the second resolution, to make the individual spending decisions taken since the first fit it. But the procedure offered irresistible tactical advantages to the White House and was vigorously exploited by the LSG. Quick action on a wide range of cuts (especially in entitlement programmes) could not have been achieved had established procedures been followed.

The device was not entirely unprecedented in principle; it had been used in the FY 80 budget, but under wholly different circumstances. Never before had provisions of the Budget Act been used to amend and undo authorisation bills, radically to alter statutory provisions.[44] Throughout Reagan's presidency, the focus of legislative action turned towards the Budget, Appropriations, and tax-writing committees, and away from authorising committees whose chairmen and Democratic members found themselves obliged to concentrate

[43] Cohen, R. E., 'For Spending Cuts, only the Beginning', *National Journal*, 8/8/81.
[44] Congressman R. Bolling, quoted in LeLoup, L., 'After the Blitz: Reagan and the US Congressional Budget Process', *Legislative Studies Quarterly*, vol. 8, no. 3, Aug. 1982, p. 323.

upon preserving as many of their programmes, and as much of their political influence, as possible.[45]

Later, in what Jim Jones, the Budget Committee chairman, described as a 'tobacco auction', the House passed the Economic Recovery Tax Act, cutting federal revenues by $749 billion over five fiscal years. Individual legislators found sound political reasons to give the president even more generous tax cuts than he had proposed. Compared with lobbying a bill through Congress to contain the inflation of the costs of medical care (as Jimmy Carter attempted), this was simplicity itself. For the president, the difficulty in lobbying for tax cuts was to stop Congressional bidding for yet more, as Heclo and Penner observed: '. . . supply-side theory was the equivalent of laughing-gas when compared to the monetarists' and orthodox conservatives' devotion to chemotherapy. It is not difficult to convince people that the world would be a better place if their taxes were cut.'[46]

THE POLITICS OF A DIVIDED CONGRESS

The Leadership

As Reagan was new to the Oval Office in 1981, so Howard Baker and Robert Michel were new to the Senate Majority Leader's and House Minority Leader's offices respectively. The unity of Republicans in both Houses on the main items of policy in 1981, discussed in greater detail below, was due in large part to the skill with which the Republican leadership led them. Michel's fierce loyalty to Reagan's programme, born of years in frustrated opposition, linked to his preoccupation with the political needs of his party colleagues, made him an ideal Minority Leader for the White House's purposes.[47]

In contrast to Byrd's Senate leadership under Carter, and Mansfield's under Johnson, Baker strove to maintain

[45] 'Peter Rodino Turns Judiciary into a Legislative Graveyard', *Congressional Quarterly Weekly Report*, 12/5/84; 'Twilight of the House Education and Labor Committee', *The Washington Post National Weekly Edition*, 1/10/84.

[46] Heclo and Penner, 'Fiscal and Political Strategy in the Reagan Administration', in Greenstein, (ed.), *The Reagan Presidency*, p. 27.

[47] Green, M., *Who Runs Congress?*, New York, 1984, p. 334.

consistently high support for the president's legislative programme. He had an easier task than Byrd or Mansfield in
this respect: his party formed a relatively coherent majority
on the politically attractive items of budgetary and taxation
legislation of the first session of the 97th Congress. He had
throughout his Senate career been genuinely well liked by his
colleagues (an unusual thing among senior politicians, and a
useful asset in a position whose incumbent was a broker,
where Johnson had in the 1950s been a commander) and
found doing favours easy: one of his first acts was to allow
Senator Byrd to retain his old office accommodation. In
contrast to the common practice of Democratic House
Speakers, he declined to alter party ratios on Senate
committees as much as he might have managed, and his more
enthusiastic colleagues urged. But his generosity of spirit did
not hide a striking partisanship on matters of policy; he
quickly shepherded the budget legislation through the Senate
by persuading the Appropriations and Finance Committee
chairmen to allow the Budget Committee to decide where
cuts should be made.[48]

Baker's reservations about the coherence of Reagan's
economic policies, largely justified by the large budget deficits
which followed, did not prevent him from supporting them,
and allowing the president to make the most of his brief
legislative opportunity in 1981. The Majority Leader behaved
very much more like his House counterpart than most of his
Senate predecessors: he considered himself part of President
Reagan's party, 'as one platoon in a Republican army'.[49] But
he took care not to press his colleagues too hard for their
support. For the AWACS vote in late 1981, he lobbied
intensively but prudently, stressing the need to present a
united Republican front for a Republican president, yet not
to the point of damaging future relations with those who
opposed him.[50]

By contrast, the Democrats were effectively leaderless in
the 97th Congress. In the first session, Baker's carreled

---

[48] 'Under Baker's Leadership', *Congressional Quarterly Weekly Report*, 12/9/81,
p. 1745.

[49] 'Under Baker's Leadership', p. 1745.

[50] Destler, I. M., 'Reagan, Congress and Foreign Policy in 1981', in Ornstein, (ed.)
President and Congress, p. 76.

Republican Senate majority enabled the LSG to concentrate their attention upon the House. There, they were greatly assisted by the virtual capitulation of the Speaker at the outset. Together with many of his colleagues, he responded to what he thought an implication of the 1980 election results, that the president had a mandate for his central economic purpose. O'Neill agreed to a timetable of the LSG's choosing for consideration of the budget and tax legislation, promising his support for final action on the budget by mid-July, and on the tax bill immediately thereafter. O'Neill thereby acknowledged Reagan's political momentum, and in turn increased it; he also anticipated that the president's personal warmth (which evoked O'Neill's perplexed admiration) might well improve his chances of legislative success.[51] His view was shared by Jim Wright, who, by his own admission, 'stood in awe . . . of his political skill'.[52]

Only after Reagan had achieved his central political objectives in 1981, was obliged to address their consequences in the following year with a bill to increase taxes, and saw twenty-six Republicans go down to defeat in the 1982 mid-term elections, did O'Neill begin to reassert his leadership of House Democrats through his chairmanship of the Democratic Steering and Policy Committee. He initiated a series of rule changes, advantageous to the Democrats and hence vigorously opposed by the Republicans, and set new party ratios for committees which exaggerated the Democrats' overall majority in the House.[53]

Mr Reagan's Coalition

The implications of the Republican gains in the 1980 Congressional elections were considerable. Neither Nixon nor Ford had enjoyed a party majority in the Senate, and the Republican disadvantage in the House during Ford's presidency was immense. Eisenhower had also lacked majorities on the Hill for six of his eight years in the White House. Gains of thirty-three House, and twelve Senate, seats in 1980

[51] Cannon, *Reagan*, p. 407.
[52] Kellerman, *The Political Presidency*, p. 253.
[53] Plattner, A., 'House Panel Seats Assigned', *Congressional Quarterly Weekly Report*, 8/1/83, p. 4.

offered President Reagan a rare opportunity for political change.

Republican party unity in the Senate under Baker's leadership was higher than in any Congress since at least 1949. The average Republican voted with the majority of the party 84 per cent of the time on the 101 recorded party-line votes. GOP Senators voted unanimously on 30 per cent of the recorded votes from January to August 1981.[54] Two Republican senators voted against the first FY 82 budget resolution, and none against final passage of the Reconciliation Bill; one voted against the Tax Bill.[55] Just eighteen, fifteen, and ten Democrats respectively voted 'nay', giving the White House overwhelming majorities on all three (though they were inflated by some Democratic Senators deciding to support the measures when they realised that their passage was inevitable).

In the House, the nominal Democratic majority of fifty-one meant that if Republican unity could be maintained, the president and the Minority Leadership had to persuade just twenty-six conservative Democrats to support the legislation. The sponsors' names on the Reconciliation and Economic Recovery Bills symbolised the LSG's strategy: Philip Gramm co-sponsored the first (in close co-operation with the White House and the Director of OMB David Stockman, his former House colleague), and Kent Hance the second. Both were conservative Democrats from Texas (where Republican gains in Congressional elections made ambitious Democrats anxious); each later defected to the Republican Party.[56] Democratic sponsors enabled Reagan to present both bills as bipartisan, in a broadly based national, rather than a narrow partisan, interest.

On Gramm–Latta I, II, and the Conable–Hance Economic Recovery Bills, the Congressional liaison staff had what seemed the unusual luxury of almost unanimous party support in the House: no Republican votes were cast against the first two measures, and only one against the third. But Republican

---

[54] 'Under Baker's Leadership', p. 1745.

[55] LeLoup, 'After the Blitz', Table I, p. 332.

[56] Tate, D., 'Gramm: An Unrepentant Weevil', *Congressional Quarterly Weekly Report*, 8/1/83, p. 5.

support for budget resolutions has been consistently high since the Budget and Impoundment Control Act's provisions came into force. By contrast, because of liberal and boll-weevil defections, the Democratic House leadership had always found it difficult to have their budget resolutions passed.[57] Although the White House successfully won over enough conservative Democrats to construct a winning coalition, a smaller proportion of the Democratic Party defected on Gramm–Latta II than on any final resolution vote since 1974.[58] The point is that few were needed: it was the Republican gains in the 1980 Congressional elections which made possible the legislative achievement in the first year. Net mid-term election losses to the Democrats of twenty-six House seats effectively restored the control of the House to the Democratic leadership, so fundamentally altering OLA calculations.

The inference often drawn from the first year was none the less one of presidential invincibility—despite a later legislative record which was much less the object of wonder than many experienced politicians had found the first year's. The growth of the deficit in succeeding years fractured the fragile coalition of political interests in the Republican Party. The division of opinion which had always been present, but was temporarily silenced by what Howard Baker termed the politically attractive 'riverboat gamble', now appeared in the open with debates in successive years about solutions to the structural deficit which too few participants had compelling political reasons for addressing seriously.

Despite the weakness of moderate Republicans in the House, their numbers in the Senate actually grew from 1980 onwards and some (particularly Lowell Weicker) were sufficiently resourceful to oppose the adoption of the social policies to which the president pledged his commitment.[59] Moderate and liberal Republican senators also succeeded in opposing parts of the president's policies for the production of nerve gas, the proposed basing mode for the MX missile, and elements of the president's economic policy where most were

[57] Schick, A., 'How the Budget was Won and Lost', in Ornstein, (ed.), *President and Congress*, p. 20.
[58] LeLoup, 'After the Blitz', pp. 332–3.
[59] Rae, N. 'Moderate Republicans in Congress during the Reagan Presidency', p. 19.

willing,(and some anxious) to moderate the rate of increase in defence spending as a means of cutting the budget deficit.[60]

Presidential Intervention and Political Incentive

The character of White House lobbying derives from the politics and personality of the president. This was exemplified, in sharply contrasting ways, by both Jimmy Carter and Ronald Reagan. Carter, preoccupied with the detail and rectitude of his policies, eschewed politicking; politics was separated from policy. Reagan, sure of the broad merits of his proposals but uncaring of their details, delighted in the art of selling them; in his first-year budget, politics and policy were one. As Carter's approach had handicapped his OCR staff, so Reagan's was his legislative staff's single greatest asset.

Both in public displays and in private meetings, Reagan matched a sound tactical sense to simplicity of purpose. The substance of Carter's energy bill was consistent only in its complexity whereas Reagan's themes on the hustings and in the Oval Office of less spending, less taxation, and stronger defences were easily delivered and understood. Whilst exploiting party and ideological support in Congress, he and his staff fully appreciated the need to blend it in the era of a reformed Congress with shrewdly managed public appeals. Co-ordinated through the Legislative Strategy Group, private persuasion and the building of public support were seen as two sides of the same lobbying coin.[61] It was spent with great urgency in the first half of 1981.

Reagan threw himself into private and public persuasion with every appearance of enthusiasm. In his first 100 days in office, the president held 69 meetings with Congressmen and senators in which 467 of the 535 took part. Through Senator Laxalt's mediation and his own direct contacts organised by White House legislative staff, the Republican leadership in both chambers were fully involved in tactical planning. The concentration on weaning conservatives away from the Democratic leadership in the House did not preclude

---

[60] 'GOP Moderates: Balance of Senate Power', *Congressional Quarterly Weekly Report*, 26/5/84, p. 1287.
[61] Wayne, 'Congressional Liaison in the Reagan White House', p. 63.

Reagan from negotiating directly with the Speaker when he needed (as he did with the 1982 tax increase) nor, as O'Neill recalled, from wooing him on others: 'He's always got a disarming story. . . I don't know where he gets them but he's always got them, stories about the World Series, football games, everything. "Tip, you and I are political enemies only until 6 o'clock. It's 4 o'clock now. Can we pretend it's 6 o'clock?" '[62]

For those to whom they were directed, Reagan's personal efforts at persuasion appeared warmly unhurried. The president's ease in the role matched his determination to make his mark early; he told OLA staff that he would call whomever they asked him to. The offer was accepted. In the final stages of lobbying for the adoption of Gramm–Latta II, the liaison staff sent telegrams to each of the 253 Congressmen who had voted for Gramm–Latta seeking their support. During a speaking engagement in Los Angeles, Reagan asked sixteen Democrats and a number of Republicans to support the procedural measure for a single vote on the budget; eleven of the Democrats did so. After his success, the president telephoned another seven Democrats, seeking their backing for the decisively important vote on the budget itself.[63]

Reagan's public performances were equally carefully timed and staged. In his first speech to a Joint Session of Congress, he listed the seven government programmes which would be protected from the heaviest cuts, but appealed for Congressional and public support for his broad objectives of cutting government spending and stimulating the economy through tax cuts.[64] Later, on 28 April (less than a month after the attempt on his life), Reagan made a further speech to a Joint Session in which he publicly embraced the 'bipartisan' Gramm–Latta bill as his own.[65] These were supplemented by television broadcasts, timed to precede important Congressional votes, and by vigorous lobbying campaigns in the districts of Congressmen who were undecided.[66] Pressure from corporations, organisations, and

[62] Cannon, *Reagan*, p. 406.
[63] Kellerman, *The Political Presidency*, pp. 243–4.
[64] Barrett, *Gambling with History*, p. 152.
[65] Kellerman, *The Political Presidency*, p. 236.
[66] Wayne, 'Congressional Liaison in the Reagan White House', p. 95.

campaign contributors, prompted by the Office of Public Liaison in co-ordination with OLA staff and managed by the LSG, duly stimulated floods of correspondence and telephone calls to Congressional offices. Rep. Bo Ginn (D-GA), reflecting ruefully on the effectiveness of the president's television broadcast in late July to promote his tax legislation, commented that 'The constituents broke our doors down. It wasn't very subtle.'[67]

After a personal meeting with the president, Rep. Jack Brooks, a moderate Texan Democrat, suggested to Friedersdorf's deputy, Kenneth Duberstein, that the White House should repurchase the *Sequoia*, the presidential yacht which Carter had sold. Neither this nor the offer of some Republican businessmen to loan it to the president was accepted.[68] None the less, small favours, some of which were paid for by the Republican National Committee, were widely dispensed — perhaps too much so, for the president's pleasure in giving them away became well known. Reagan none the less managed to turn this to humorous advantage. At a reception for Congressmen in May 1981, the president began by observing, to loud laughter, that guests who had not yet received a pair of cuff-links or tickets to the Kennedy Center, should complain to Max Friedersdorf about it, and have the matter put right. After the legislation's successful passage in the summer of that year, Reagan similarly made light of the practice of presenting to supporters pens used in the bill-signing, wishing publicly that his name were longer so that he might have more of them to use, and so to give away.[69]

As discussed above, the administration approached the matter of patronage appointments with great care, placing special emphasis upon ideological affinity. Later, OLA staff did not hesitate to assist Congressional allies, and those whom they wished to encourage or reward, with patronage appointments, provided that the terms of the agreement were private. The AWACS sale produced several examples of this kind, notably the acceleration of a US attorney appointment

[67] Barrett, *Gambling with History*, p. 170.
[68] Barrett, *Gambling with History*, p. 150.
[69] 'Remarks on Signing the Economic Recovery Tax Act of 1981 and the Omnibus Reconciliation Act of 1981', 13 Aug. 1981, *Public Papers of the President*, 1981.

for a candidate promoted by Senator Charles Grassley (R-IO). But the mutual interest of each side in discretion was matched by the usual absence of a simple exchange. This enabled Reagan's staff (as it had his predecessors') to deny that deals were struck; for the most part, Reagan did not join in patronage bargaining, whether direct or implied.[70]

With federal projects, there was less opportunity to conceal bargaining. The administration's primary objective of reducing domestic spending meant that there were fewer opportunities for initiating projects in the hope of winning a senator's or Congressman's support; the announcement of those that were begun or extended was devolved to the department and agency concerned. Equally, the pressure to cut spending meant that the White House was in principle able to exempt certain projects if they thought it necessary. This they often did: the AWACS campaign resulted in the administration's approval for a Public Health Service hospital for Senator Gorton (R-WA) and of a coal-fired power station in Montana for Senator John Melcher (D-MT). Reagan showed his appreciation of Senator Baker's efforts on his behalf in the Senate by proposing an increase in funding for the Clinch River Fast Breeder Reactor, a project whose virtues Baker had long espoused, and which President Carter thought a waste of public money.[71] Reagan also induced John Breaux, a Louisiana Democrat, to support Gramm–Latta II by promising to reinstate federal price supports for sugar, a programme which David Stockman reckoned scandalously expensive. Breaux, reflecting the mores of his Congressional district, observed that he had secured the best deal he could, whereupon a journalist enquired whether such an attitude implied that his vote was for sale. 'No', he replied memorably, 'but it's available for rent'.[72]

CONCLUSION

Reagan's leadership of the executive branch in the early part of his presidency was directed towards the achievement of quick and profound policy change. In pursuit of it, he and

[70] *Congressional Quarterly Almanac, 1981*, p. 135.
[71] Kellerman, *The Political Presidency*, p. 251.
[72] *The Almanac of American Politics, 1984*, Washington, DC, p. 493.

his advisers drastically narrowed the policy agenda by focusing on the budget and, in particular, upon the reconciliation clauses of the 1974 Act to secure large cuts in domestic spending.[73] Thanks to the skilful manipulation of a favourable political climate, Reagan thereby effected quicker and sharper policy change than either of his Republican presidential predecessors had achieved. Later, with mid-term Congressional losses, White House staff changes, and early intense competition among senior politicians (many of them in Congress) for the right to the presidential succession, Reagan's victories were far fewer. But the early part of his presidency was the more important; it was then that the major changes were made.

More importantly for the purposes of this argument, the means by which the changes were legislated in 1981 were strikingly effective. The use of the reconciliation clause was the single clearest example of a general disposition to concentrate executive energies in the early months, (whatever the long-term institutional consequences). Reagan's legislative accomplishments prompted a new optimism about the presidency: White House leadership was still possible. The fragmentation of institutional power, the central feature of American government, could be overcome—even allowing for the recent decline of party, the dispersal of power within Congress, and the influence of sophisticated private lobbies on policy-making. Indeed, Reagan and his supporters did much to restore the strength of party, promoting a degree of unity with party and ideological allies in Congress and outside, as Johnson had done in 1964-6. The president enlisted in his cause such sources of coherence and leadership within Congress as there were, and turned the strength of the lobbies to his legislative advantage.

Overall, the experience of the Carter and Reagan presidencies does not so much reveal new truths as confirm old ones. A president with a clear programme, partisan and ideological backing in Congress, public opinion and interest-group support, and a well-organised White House legislative staff possessed of fine judgement, organised to meet his needs

[73] Salamon, L. M., and Abramson, A. J., 'Governance', in Palmer and Sawhill, *The Reagan Record*, p. 43.

and to help him mobilise and consolidate his support in Congress and the country, stands greater chance of legislative success than he who lacks one or more of them. Some of these factors are beyond his control, others within the scope only of his influence. Those which he controls more directly, such as the shape, composition, and quality of his staff, and which are crucially important for marshalling such inherent advantages as the office-holder has, must therefore be adeptly arranged and deployed if the passing opportunities for presidential government are to be exploited and sustained.

10

CONCLUSION

INTRODUCTION

Presidential government is rare in American politics: after the triumphs of his first year, Ronald Reagan's rate of success both in formulating his own policies and then in lobbying them through Congress fell sharply. He was markedly less successful even than Jimmy Carter in developing a coherent foreign policy towards the Soviet Union, the Middle East, or Africa. He lacked the intellectual command and political will to overcome the intense clash of personal ambitions and world-views within his own administration, yet where Carter had been so grievously damaged by hesitancy and indecision, so Reagan's extraordinary skills of presentation and rhetoric enabled him to avoid the full political consequences of failure in policy creation, legislation, and implementation.

The overarching structural deficit, the ineluctable result of the combination of huge tax reductions provided for by the 1981 Economic Recovery Act and the large defence expenditure increases of his first term, provided a focus for conflict within the executive branch, with Congressional Democrats, and with the several factions within the Republican Party on Capitol Hill. The substantive issue of a large and growing deficit was left unresolved, with no party to its creation willing to accept the political costs involved in reducing it. He made only indirect administrative and litigious advances with the social agenda which his more fervent New Right supporters enthusiastically backed. As his second term approached its mid-point, relations between the executive and Congressional branches were therefore closer to their customary political condition. They were made still less productive by Republican trimming in advance of the mid-term elections, and the early signs of waxing presidential ambition among several senior legislators.

The less propitious circumstances in his second term made the imperative of Congressional liaison no less important: the role of bridge-builder is inescapable for modern chief executives who preside over big government, even for those who would reduce its size. Irrespective of circumstance, policies, or ideological preferences, contemporary presidents are obliged to engage with Congress, to join the separated institutions of government, by organised liaison with Congressmen and senators. Reagan's 'conservative' purposes (if his radical rhetorical rejection of incrementalism can be so characterised) required such liaison just as much as Johnson's and Carter's. In the absence of sustained Congressional engagement, his objective of reducing the size of the federal government and the importance of its role could not be realised; to make smaller government possible, a large, active, and highly organised presidency was (paradoxically) required.[1]

In post-war years, Republicans have depended upon a strong presidency to spur policy change precisely because they have had little prospect of forming party majorities in Congress. Even after Reagan's crushing defeat of Walter Mondale in the 1984 presidential election, he lacked such majorities; ticket-splitting continued apace and effectively denied him the means to govern. The majorities which he and his legislative staff so ably crafted for his economic policies in 1981 were a temporary phenomenon, built on intensive and highly organised appeals to loyalty, party cohesion, and ideological clarity. It is unlikely that a partisan realignment of the kind which some scholars discern at the presidential level will show itself in comparable strength in voting for Congress; the faint prospect of ideologically coherent Republican Congressional majorities in the House of Representatives ensures that Republican presidents will generally face opposition to their legislative proposals from an entrenched Democratic majority in the House. Democratic presidents will also face doubts and hostility from their nominal party colleagues on Capitol Hill; party aside, the behaviour of Congressmen will continue to be grounded in shifting combinations of principled opposition and shrewd assessments of rational self-interest.

[1] Lowi, T., *The Personal President*, Ithaca, 1985.

PRESIDENTIAL GOVERNMENT

Johnson's political experience between Kennedy's death and the close of the 89th Congress, and Reagan's in the first year of his first term, were unusual periods in the history of executive–congressional relations. This book has shown that party or ideological majorities (in the case of the 89th and 97th Congresses, both) combined with a clear and widely supported presidential purpose, political judgement of high quality, and a well-organised unit of legislative liaison staff in the White House who have the confidence and backing of the president, form a rare, distinctive, and productive mixture. Controlled conflict is the more common condition of relations between presidents and legislators; the interests of a single chief executive and a majority coalition of the 535 Congressmen and senators are rarely congruent. The president's constant need is to make them so.

The fragmentation of the political system usually denies presidents legislative majorities and makes mandates difficult for them to demonstrate, or for observers to locate. Presidents can therefore govern only by winning Congressional co-operation and support which in turn has to be elicited through processes of constant exchange, political support, and courtship; it cannot be demanded or assumed by presidents or Congressional party leaders for they have few sanctions at their disposal to enforce compliance. The powers granted the president by the constitution are few in number and limited in extent. Moreover, the power of presidents to affect Congressional decisions is usually limited by partisan or ideological opposition, or a combination of both. Presidential claims to primacy in foreign policy generally rest on arguments based on speed of decision-making and secrecy; the resurgence of Congress since Vietnam has neither eliminated the force of these arguments, nor reduced by much the effective role of the presidency in foreign policy-making. But these claims have little relevance to domestic policy. It is in this sphere that the power of the presidency is most obviously constrained by the actions (and inaction) of Congress, and where presidents are in the greatest need of continuing skilled staff support to organise and supplement their own political efforts.

In a system of government where the constitution legitimates conflict between the executive and legislative branches, an active legislator-president therefore needs a specialised channel for his dealings with Congress, messengers for their views and his, brokers to act on his behalf. John Kennedy and his successors have organised their relations with Congress through just such a channel, an Office of Congressional Relations, acting as the White House's instrument for the bridging of the gap between separated institutions sharing power over policy-making. A president's political skill and judgement is by no means confined to the techniques of such engagement with Congress; it is present also in the timing of policy, in its presentation to Congress and, increasingly, to voters through the electronic media. This study has examined the means by which presidents and their specialist OCR staffs deploy the resources of the Head of State to influence Congressmen and senators. It has in turn considered the nature of presidents' resources, and the means by which they are organised, invested, and spent in the cause of bolstering their political strength and enacting their legislative proposals. The book thus has broader implications: presidential power consists in large degree of the skill with which presidents bring their political influence to bear on individual legislators over whom they lack the formal sanctions available to party leaders in most other democracies.

THE DEPLOYMENT OF PRESIDENTIAL RESOURCES

Presidential suggestions of future help, hints of understanding, appreciation, and reward are invariably made in private, not public, settings. Private understandings, privately concluded, are the essence of political exchange for presidents in need of legislators' assistance. The terms of trade are usually implicit, thus enabling the parties concerned to deny their existence with greater conviction and plausibility. The bargaining process is made more subtle and complicated by the necessity for politicians to deal in futures: political capital is acquired and invested, debts are incurred, and called in. Again, however, the process is usually private, and favours are rarely exchanged in the public gaze. It is better for politicians to be able to deny that simple trading in projects and patronage takes place at all than to have to assert the insignificance of particular bargains which become the subject of public scrutiny. Any exchanges made in public between a president and individual members of Congress transform the nature of the bargaining process by raising other actors' expectations; they also allow political opponents to claim that decisions which result from such a process are sullied. In any event, it is usually unnecessary for bargains to become known: Washington, as liaison staff and their Congressional charges have all known, is not a city where politicians have to ask for favours to be returned.[2] From the presidential perspective, the process of exchange and bargaining in the pursuit of influence is, ideally, implicit and seamless.

The difference which the skilful use of presidential resources by chief executives and their liaison staff may have on the judgements of Congressmen and senators, and hence on Congressional outcomes, can be neither simply characterised, nor precisely determined. As chapter one showed, simple aggregate measures are of little assistance. They are by themselves incapable of determining the effectiveness of presidential influence over legislators on Congressional outcomes. They do not discriminate between great and small measures, and fail to allow for presidents claiming credit for legislation which in final form bears little resemblance to that which they submitted—something which Johnson's majorities and skill usually made unnecessary, which Carter unconvincingly attempted, but at which Reagan was immensely successful even after his first year. But this book has shown that the skill with which presidential resources are deployed can make a difference to Congressional outcomes. The skill with which presidents orchestrate their relations with Congress through the OCR, and cause their staff to supplement effectively their own liaison and lobbying efforts, materially affects the fate of their legislative proposals, and so contributes to their effective political power.

[2] Interviews with G. Christian, Mar. 1984; M. Manatos, Oct. 1978; H. McPherson, May 1979 and Apr. 1981.

THE POLITICS OF PRESIDENTIAL PERSUASION

Lyndon Johnson's administration provides the setting for the burden of this study. His presidency encompasses periods of great power, buttressed by ideological majorities on Capitol Hill, and a final phase of comparative weakness. The combination of advantages he enjoyed in the earlier part was due partly to luck, partly to historical circumstance, and partly to his and his staff's sound political judgement; he recognised at the outset that these unusual conditions were bound to be short-lived. Many loyal liberal Democratic freshmen Congressmen were likely to lose in 1966; the ideological edge in the House would go with them. Johnson's own popularity would decline; his leverage over Congress would diminish. These he could do little about. Yet, as chapters three, six, and seven illustrate, Johnson had little interest in administrative matters. The OCR's procedures and staff, and the place of both within the White House Office, were inherited from his predecessor. As staff departed, procedures lapsed, and the OCR's authority within the White House and over departments became weaker. When, in the 90th Congress, crisp liaison work was urgently needed, OCR staff had less authority within the White House, were less well organised, generally less able, and carried less political weight than their predecessors. Chapter three shows how presidential inattention to these matters contributed to the Office's later weakness and to a reduction in Johnson's own influence over Congress; chapters six and seven consider the implications of this weakness for the lobbying campaigns to secure the passage of the income tax surcharge and the two Supreme Court nominations.

Presidential weakness in the last phase of his presidency apart, these two case-studies illustrate how Lyndon Johnson's OCR staff employed interest groups in their support and, as in the case of labour unions and the tax surcharge of 1968, how they persuaded them to moderate their opposition. Both show, as do chapters four and five, something of the nature and effect of presidential resources employed to strengthen the president's hand in his dealings with Congressmen and senators. Throughout, the contribution which presidential tokens of favour and esteem, whether small favours or the better-known inducements of projects and patronage, make to the preparation of the political and psychological conditions within which Congressional figures responded to White House wishes has been stressed. The constitutional separation of the presidency from Congress could not be bridged without constant courting by president and staff alike. More generally, as part of a presidency grown large since being thrust to the centre of American government by economic depression and global war, legislative staff in the OCR under Kennedy, Johnson, and Carter, and the OLA and LSG under Reagan, have had the responsibility of bolstering the president's political prospects while organising such courting.

In the first two phases of Johnson's presidency, and in Reagan's first year, such staff assisted the two presidents' purposes by arranging and deploying their limited resources to the best effect, capitalising upon opportunities to their advantage. The members of the OCR were for Johnson, and are for Reagan, extensions of presidential skill and expressions of their orchestration of relations with Congress—the assembly of 535 politicians with interests of their own whose support they need but cannot command. To that extent, persuading them that their interests can be merged with the president's own is a task demanding political skills of a high order from chief executive and aides alike. This is so whether the ostensible objectives are liberal or conservative—for presidents of both persuasions are obliged to be energetic in their dealings with Congress. Thus the programmes of John Kennedy and Lyndon Johnson, and the economic policies of Reagan, required specialist legislative White House staff support if the inherent weaknesses of the presidency were to be overcome, and temporary strengths exploited. Placed at the hinge of American government, at Pennsylvania Avenue's metaphorical mid-point, the Office of Congressional Relations is an appropriate place from which to examine the approaches of different presidents in varying circumstances to the task of bridging the constitutional divide separating the White House from Capitol Hill.

INDEX

Carter, President Jimmy (*cont.*):
  foreign policy 197, 207
  formality 201–3, 212–13
  Georgia governorship 191–2, 200
  'good government' 194
  ignorance of Congressional politics
    194–6
  lack of government experience 190–2
  legislative programme 194, 196–7
  lobbying 212–13
  narrowness of election victory (1976)
    190–1
  patronage and projects 210–12
  political judgment 194–7, 210–13
  relations with Speaker O'Neill 195–6,
    201–2
  small favours 212–13
Celebrezze, Anthony
  federal grant announcements 90
Christopher, Warren
  considered as nominee to Supreme
    Court 156
  Supreme Court nominations (1968) 170
Clark, Attorney-General Ramsey
  income tax surcharge (1968) 134
  Judiciary Committee 163
  Lawrence, Judge 181
  lobbying for Thornberry 169
  nominees to Supreme Court (1968) 156
Clifford, Clark
  closures of military bases 87–8
Cohen, Wilbur
  Appropriations Committee cuts 121
Committee Chairmen
  OCR scheduling assistance 57–8
  power of 146, 151, 189 (*see also under
    individual chairmen*)
Congress
  reform in 1970s 189–90, 195
Congress, 89th
  disappearance of liberal majority 30, 147
  distinctiveness 245
Congress, 90th 30–3
Congress, 94th (Watergate) 187–9
Congress, 97th
  distinctiveness 245
Congress, committees
  OCR influence over membership 58–62
  reform 189
  see also under individual committees
Congressional breakfasts 55–7
Congressional correspondence 41–2
Congressional elections

OCR assistance 106–7
Congressional leadership
  liaison with the OCR 53–7, 59–62
  support for President Eisenhower 17–18
Congressional receptions 98–102
conservative coalition
  support for President Nixon 185
  support for President Reagan 234–7
  Supreme Court nominations (1968)
    161–2
Conyers, Congressman John
  Judiciary Committee membership 60
Council of Economic Advisers
  'New Economics' 115
  income tax surcharge (1968) 138
Cranston, Senator Alan
  Majority Whip 195–6
Culver, Congressman John
  Johnson's attitude to Congress 102

Daly, Chuck
  committee membership changes 61
Darman, Richard
  Legislative Strategy Group 225
Davis, Eric 6
Defense Appropriations Subcommittees
  Pentagon lobbying 111
Democratic Party
  elections
    (1960) 19
    (1964) 28–9
    (1966) 30
    (1968) 33, 184
    (1974) 185
    (1976) 190–1
    (1980) 219–20, 278
  party disciplinary measures 61
  projects and patronage 67–77, 81
  see also Carter, President Jimmy;
    Kennedy, President John;
    Johnson, President Lyndon
Democratic Study Group
  changing character in late 1970s 199
  income tax surcharge (1968) 122–3, 128
  liaison role with Johnson and White
    House 69–70
  Supreme Court nominations (1968) 171
Departmental Legislative Liaison Offices
  46–50
  Agency for International Development
    37
  bargaining process 85–91
  head-counting 63–4

INDEX

259

Congressional leadership 53–5
federal projects 66–7, 79–81, 85, 240
head-counting 62–5
interest groups 110–11, 138–41, 168–74
patronage 73–8, 146–7, 166–7
relation to liaison 52, 70–3, 91, 92–3,
    95–6, 102, 104–5
results of 24, 108–9, 213, 237–8
small favours 92–102, 114, 201–2, 212–
    13, 239
statutory restrictions upon 46–7
presidential political skill 6–8, 21–2, 34–
    5, 63, 217–18, 237–40, 246–7, 249
presidential power
fragmentation of government 2–4, 12–
    15, 114, 214, 243–9 (see also under
    presidential–Congressional rela-
    tions)
presidents, see individual presidents
projects see federal projects
Pryor, Congressman David
Appropriations Committee member-
    ship 62
Public Works Committee, House
OCR lobbying 109

Rayburn, Speaker Sam
agreement on Kennedy's legislative
    priorities 19
death 53
relationship with OCR 53
Rules Committee expansion (1961)
    23–4
support for President Eisenhower 17–18
Reagan, President Ronald
decline in Congressional success 241,
    243
economic policy 217–18, 229–32, 235–6
Economic Recovery Act (1981) 232
elections
    (1960) 19
    (1964) 28–9
    (1966) 30
    (1968) 33, 184
    (1974) 185
    (1976) 190–1
    (1980) 219–20, 278
federal projects 81, 87, 91
foreign policy 218, 221, 228, 236–7,
    239–40
fund raising in 1980: 220
ideological coherence in 1981: 218–19,
    235

influence of New Right 219–20, 228–9
moderate dissent 236–7
New Right 228–9
patronage 75–6
perceived mandate 220, 234
political judgment 14–15, 234, 237–40
political purpose 1–2, 227–30
public interventions 237–9
Republican Party 14, 218–20, 222, 228,
    232–7, 243–4
small favours 237–9
social issues 229, 243
strength of the presidency 217, 236,
    241–3
voting unity in 1981: 235
'Record-Write'
organisation 111–13, 132, 167–8
Regan, Donald 222
Republican Party see Ford, Gerald;
    Nixon, Richard Milhous
Reuther, Walter
and Supreme Court nominations
    (1968) 172
Revenue and Expenditure Control Act
    (1968) 115–49
corporate support for 138–9
enrolling and signing 132–3
the Excise Tax Bill 119
illustration of OCR techniques 147
liberal and labour distaste 122–3, 139–
    41
signing statement 133
Roberts, Juanita
recollections of Homer Thornberry 179
Roche, Chuck
contribution to liaison 45–6
income tax surcharge (1968) 129, 131
Rostenkowski, Congressman Dan 123, 127
Roybal, Congressman Edward
Johnson's attention to 97–8
Rules Committee, House
expansion under Kennedy 23–4
income tax surcharge votes 140–1
Russell, Senator Richard
conservatism 180
consultations about Fortas 177, 179–80
Lawrence, Judge 180–1
relations with Lyndon Johnson 178–9
withdrawal of support from Fortas 181

Sanders, Harold Barefoot
Albert, Carl 132
background 44

DATE DUE

DEMCO